**Thai Peasant
Social
Structure**

Jack M.
Potter

# Thai Peasant Social Structure

The University
of Chicago Press

Chicago
and London

The University of Chicago Press,
Chicago 60637

The University of Chicago Press, Ltd.,
London

80  79  78  77  76    987654321

JACK M. POTTER is professor of
anthropology at the University of
California, Berkeley. He is the
coeditor of **Peasant Society: A Reader**
and the author of **Capitalism and the
Chinese Peasant** and numerous articles.

Library of Congress Cataloging in Publication Data

Potter, Jack M.
    Thai peasant social structure.

    Bibliography: p.
    Includes index.
    1.  Ethnology—Thailand—Chiang Mai (Province)
2.  Villages—Thailand—Chiang Mai (Province)
3.  Chiang Mai, Thailand (Province)—Social life
and customs.  I.  Title.
GN635.T4P67        301.35′2′09593        75-43237
ISBN 0-226-67635-8

To S. and E.

# Contents

# Preface

This study was carried out by me and my wife, Sulamith Heins Potter,[1] from October 1971 through November 1972, while we were resident in the village of Chiangmai and in nearby Chiengmai city. Altogether we spent nine and one-half months living in the village. We spent the first three months living with a family in one part of the village, moved into the city for the birth of our daughter, Elizabeth, and then returned with the baby to the village to spend the final six and one-half months living in our own village-style house, which we built in a family compound in another part of Chiangmai. We managed to continue learning about the village even during our stay in the city because we employed a daughter of one of its headmen, and two daughters of one of the families with whom we lived, in our household throughout the study.

My wife, whose special field in anthropology is Thai studies (my previous work had been on China), learned the Northern Thai dialect spoken in the village very rapidly and in the last ten months of the study worked in the native language without an interpreter. I had little previous background in the Thai language when I arrived in the village, and although I studied Northern Thai diligently throughout my stay I never achieved fluency. Consequently, I employed locally born research assistants who spoke Northern Thai, Central Thai, and English to assist me.

Although my understanding of village life was inevitably influenced by the two families with whom we stayed and their immediate neighbors, whom we came to know very well, my findings were buttressed by acquaintance with people throughout the village; by a comprehensive questionnaire which was designed to elicit basic social and economic information and which after careful testing and checking was given to every village family; and by several other surveys given to random samples of the village population to gather systematic information on topics such as group affiliation and age at marriage. I have summarized the results of these questionnaires in tables and charts scattered throughout the book.

I am grateful to the Senior Fulbright-Hays Program and Chiengmai University's Faculty of Social Sciences for sponsoring my stay in Thailand and for giving me time for research. Professor Narujohn Iddhichiracharas of the Department of Sociology and Anthropology at Chiengmai University (now completing his Ph.D. in anthropology at Berkeley) helped make arrangements for the study. He also assisted us in innumerable ways throughout our stay in Chiengmai, for which we are grateful.

Herbert P. Phillips, my colleague at Berkeley, encouraged me in my work on Thailand and helped secure research funds for me from the Center for South and Southeast Asia Studies at the University of California, Berkeley, while I was in Chiengmai. I appreciate his support, his friendship, and his willingness to encourage the expression of views which differ from his own. Professor Charles F. Keyes of the University of Washington made valuable bibliographic suggestions and generously gave me access to manuscripts which he was preparing for publication. I owe a special debt to Professor Manning Nash of the University of Chicago, one of my former teachers, who read an early draft of this book and made invaluable suggestions for its improvement. Only I, however, am responsible for the views expressed here.

Grace Buzaljko did the initial editing of this book and improved it greatly. Adrienne Morgan drew the maps and figures. Toni Cord typed the manuscript. I am indebted to these talented women for their excellent work.

I thank the people of Chiangmai for allowing us to live in their village, for putting up with us with much good humor, and for furnishing the data for this study. To protect them, I have used pseudonyms throughout for the people; and Chiangmai village is not the village's real name.

I am grateful to Professor Charles F. Keyes for permission to quote from his unpublished manuscript "Baan Noong Tyyn: A Central Isan Village"; to Professor Koishi Mizuno for permission to quote from his mimeographed work *Social System of Don Daeng Village: A Community Study in Northeast Thailand*; and to Professor Lauriston Sharp for permission to quote from *Siamese Rice Village: A Preliminary Study of Bang Chan, 1948–1949*.

# Note on the
# Transliteration of Thai

The Northern Thai ("Kammyaŋ") terms used in this book in my analysis of Chiangmai village (except for common place names) have been transcribed according to the Haas phonetic system (see Mary Haas, *Thai-English Student's Dictionary*, Stanford: Stanford University Press, 1964). The five tonal markers, however, have been omitted. The system is as follows.

> Voiced unaspirated stops are b, d, and g
> Voiceless unaspirated stops are p, t, c, k, and ʔ
> Voiceless aspirated stops are ph, th, ch, and kh
> Voiceless unaspirated spirants are f, s, and h
> Voiced semivowel sonorants are w and j
> Voiced nasal sonorants are m, n, and ŋ
> Voiced lateral sonorant is l
> Voiced trill sonorant is r

**Vowels**
> Front unrounded: i, ii, ia, e, ee, ɛ, ɛɛ
> Central unrounded: y, yy, ya, ə, əə, a, aa
> Back rounded: u, uu, ua, o, oo, ɔ, ɔɔ

The Northern Thai nasal sound which replaces the Central Thai j in initial position in many words is transcribed as nj.

The Thai terms used by other authors (those quoted in Chapter 8) are transcribed following their usage. Since authors use different systems, and because the words are from different Thai dialects, I have made no effort to transcribe them in my system.

# 1    Introduction

## The Loose-Structure Controversy

Thomas S. Kuhn, in his book *The Structure of Scientific Revolutions*, discusses scientific paradigms, or models, which shape scientists' ways of seeing the world and supply the foundations for coherent traditions of research. Science normally operates within the frameworks of such established paradigms. But the nature of scientific activity sooner or later leads to the discovery of anomalies which do not fit the prevailing set of fundamental assumptions and which must be taken into account. Then what Kuhn calls "scientific revolutions" occur: paradigms are shattered and new ones created (1970, p. 6).[1]

Ethnography also has its paradigms.[2] The anthropological model for Thailand was established by John Embree in 1950, when he characterized Thailand as a culture with a "loosely structured" social system. This paradigm has dominated the interpretation of the social life of the Thai peasant for over twenty-five years. It has, in Dewey's words, become "familiar furniture of the mind" for anthropologists and other scholars studying rural Thailand. By "loosely structured" Embree meant that, in contrast to the people of Vietnam, China, and Japan (and the United States in some respects), the Thai allow considerable variation in individual behavior; place less importance upon observing reciprocal rights and duties; have a "determined lack of regularity, discipline, and regimentation"; and are without a strong sense of duty and obligation in family relations. According to Embree, Thai villagers, in contrast to those of Japan, have rights and duties that are less clearly defined and labor exchange systems that are "less closely woven." Village relationships do not emphasize long-term obligations.[3]

1

The loose-structure paradigm (as Kuhn suggests is the case with other paradigms, too) was created from arbitrary elements which happened to coalesce at a given point in the intellectual history of anthropological studies in Thailand. In addition to Embree's impressions of Thai society set forth in his 1950 article, there was the historical accident that the first place studied intensively by anthropologists in rural Thailand happened to be Bang Chan, a community of an unusual kind located in the outskirts of Bangkok near the town of Minburi (see map 1).

Bang Chan exhibited several features which caused difficulties for Lauriston Sharp (the first anthropologist to work in rural Thailand and the initiator of the Cornell Thailand Project) and for his colleagues: Robert Textor, Kamol Janlekha, and Hazel Hauck. One problem was that, unlike the nucleated villages characteristic of many peasant societies and of much of the rest of Thailand, Bang Chan was strung out along several canals in a spiderweb pattern with no clearly defined boundaries. Sharp and his associates defined the Bang Chan people as those who lived in administrative villages in which most of the inhabitants patronized the Bang Chan temple and school.

Another difficulty was that the Bang Chan community is crosscut by arbitrary government rural administrative divisions in a way extreme even for Thailand, where it is not uncommon. The rural community of Bang Chan, centered on the temple and school, is composed politically of seven administrative hamlets, is divided into two communes, and belongs to two administrative districts, all of which create an administrative tangle of nightmarish proportions (Hanks 1972, pp. 73–79).

Finally, Bang Chan has had a short history and is ethnically diverse. It was settled only after the year 1850, literally carved out of a swampy, bamboo-forested, and malaria-ridden wilderness in the lower delta by an odd assortment of proletarians from in and around Bangkok, Muslim prisoners of war from the south, Laotian prisoners from the northeast, and freed Bangkok slaves. From Hanks's account (1972, p. 14) of the three brothers, their wives, and their widowed mother who were the first settlers of Bang Chan, it seems likely that they were part Chinese. This deduction is based not only upon their family form (which resembles an extended Chinese patrilineal family) and their sister's marriage to a wealthy merchant (most merchants in Thailand are Chinese), but also their former residence in a town called Samsen, north of the palace in Bangkok, which was a boat port settled, according to Hanks (1972, pp. 74–75), "mainly by Chinese from Canton and Hainan who married Thai women." G. William Skinner (1957, p. 84) observes that Samsen contained the oldest Hainanese temple in Bangkok, and that the Hainanese residents "were hand sawyers, market gardeners, fishermen, domestic servants, waiters, tea-shop operators, and, not infrequently, "coolies," miners, and peddlers. They were the poorest of all the [Chinese] speech groups, and their general low social standing was undisputed" (Skinner 1957, p. 136).

Skinner (1957, pp. 83–84) also mentions that as early as the first decade of the nineteenth century some Chinese had settled as agriculturalists in the lower delta region around Bangkok and the gulf coast. The same author informs us that "early in the [nineteenth] century Chinese had *settled* in considerable numbers in certain rural areas of the Southeast, Lower, and Southwest Siam; they married Thai women and to a large extent recreated peasant life in South China" (1957, p. 111). These first Chinese settlers, whose wives were probably Thai, must have complicated the social and cultural patterns of Bang Chan from the very beginning.[4]

The variegated social practices of the people who settled in Bang Chan such a short time ago (the Muslims were Malay and, like the Chinese, had a variant culture), the early participation of Bang Chan farmers in commercialized rice agriculture, the nonnucleated settlement pattern, the administrative complexity, and the rapid changes that must have been occurring at the time of the Cornell study because of the proximity of the village to Bangkok obscured the underlying social structure of Bang Chan.

Sharp, Textor, Janlekha, and Hauck were working in an unfamiliar and unexplored social terrain which initially was just as featureless for them as the great rice plain that surrounded them. With no previous ethnographic landmarks to guide them, and with a primitive theoretical apparatus inherited from the time of Radcliffe-Brown and designed for the study of discrete and bounded societies, it is understandable that they grasped at the theoretical guideline offered by Embree. Nevertheless, this was a mistake because the very notion of loose structure, as several scholars have subsequently pointed out, is defeatist and makes any kind of structural analysis difficult (see, for example, Stanley Tambiah's remarks [1966, p. 424]). If they had probed a bit deeper (as it is now easier to see with hindsight), Sharp et al. would have discovered that Bang Chan society is constructed according to the same basic structural plan as are all other villages in Thailand. Sharp et al.'s interpretation of Bang Chan, as I shall show in Chapter 8, was due more to the blinders effect of Embree's loose-structure theory than (as has often been thought) to the regional peculiarities of the lower delta region in which Bang Chan is located.

The major characterization of rural Thai society that emerged from the initial Bang Chan study, *Siamese Rice Village* (1953), was Sharp's statement that "the exceptionally amorphous, relatively unstructured character of all Thai society is clearly reflected in the undifferentiated social organization of Bang Chan" (Sharp et al. 1953, p. 26). Although Sharp modified his position slightly in a later paper (1963), this conclusion gave added credence to Embree's description of Thai society and put the finishing touches on the loose-structure model. This paradigm greatly influenced subsequent work on rural Thailand, most of which was carried out by Sharp's colleagues and students at Cornell. Of special significance in the perpetuation of the loose-structure paradigm is the work of David A. Wilson (1962), Herbert P. Phillips (1965, 1969), Steven Piker (1968b, 1969), and Lucien Hanks (1972).[5]

Wilson, in his book *Politics in Thailand* (1962), writes that loose-structure, Embree's "felicitous bit of jargon, . . . etches one of the most striking qualities of Thai society." Wilson describes the Thai as "determinedly autonomous" and as carrying "the burden of social responsibility lightly" (1962, p. 46). One cause of Thai individualism is, according to Wilson, the Buddhist emphasis on salvation by individual accumulation of merit. He characterizes Thai rural communities as having weak patterns of village allegiance and community solidarity, lacking any corporate identity or legal status, and owning no community property. One reason why the villages are loosely organized, he believes, is that there is surplus land and a very low population density in Thailand (pp. 47–48). The Thai "individualist personality" goes together with geographical and social mobility to "contribute to the weakness of group and community institutions" (p. 48). This "fluid system" makes "any analysis of Thai society in terms of class structure . . . most problematical" (p. 50). Wilson concludes his remarks on loose structure by saying that "social mobility and fluidity of social groups are, if anything, a greater reality than formerly" (p. 52).

Phillips, in his book *Thai Peasant Personality* (1965), portrays the Bang Chan villagers as "1,771 individualists—polite, gentle, nonaggressive, but nevertheless individualists—pursuing their own purposes." The community is "placid" and contains no factions or power struggles like other peasant communities (1965, p. 30). There are only five social units to which villagers are psychologically committed: "the nuclear family, a loosely defined, laterally oriented kindred," the village monastery and school, and the nation-state. "There are in Bang Chan no castes, age-grade societies, occupational groups, . . . neighborhood groups, or groups expressive of village solidarity (such as councils or governing boards) which might impose a sense of obligation on the villagers, or to whose norms or functions the villagers might have to conform. Bang Chaners do not have to contribute their labor to their community, serve as village guards, contend with the dictates of village elders, or even actively cooperate with fellow villagers" (pp. 21–22). The Bang Chan nuclear family is loosely structured, variable in form and tends to be unstable (pp. 23–26). Village kinship institutions tend to be amorphous, and kinship relations are unpredictable and inconsistent (p. 29).

Piker, in his article " 'Loose Structure' and the Analysis of Thai Social Organization" (1969), notes several characteristics of rural Thai society in the Central Plain which he feels support Embree's characterization. Villages exist only as administrative units demarcated by the central government and not as natural, bounded social units that are clearly distinguishable. Villages do not operate as separate social units; all they do jointly is to elect a headman. There are no extended kinship groups. Those kinship ties that do exist crosscut village boundaries. Neither the temple nor the school defines integral rural communities because each draws patrons from more than one village. Absent is any strong loyalty to or identification with the village by its inhabitants. Furthermore, there is a paucity of enduring rural social groups. Cooperative labor exchange groups are based upon ad hoc dyadic ties that do not last. The villagers carry out little concerted social activity related to the school or temple. Piker concludes by saying that, other than the nuclear family, the kindred, and the monkhood, there are almost no lasting, functionally important groups in the countryside (1969, pp. 62–63). Moreover, even participation in the monkhood, the family, and the kindred is voluntary. One goes in and out of monastic life at will. The kindred is a nebulous group that resembles a voluntary association; members are recruited according to individual choice, and relations are not lasting. Even the family is nebulous; children may be given to other families; a person remains with his family voluntarily and sometimes makes an impromptu decision to leave; and parents are afraid that their children will not take care of them in their old age (1969, pp. 64–65; also see Piker [1968b] for a similar argument).

Lucien Hanks, in his book *Rice and Man* (1972), completes the characterization of the loosely structured rural community of Bang Chan: "As the Thai build their simple bamboo houses so that they can be readily modified and quickly dismantled," says Hanks, "so too they build their groups." He translates the Thai term *khraub khrua* as "household rather than family to avoid suggesting a limited and fairly stable group of people" (1972, pp. 80–81). Family and kinship relationships are contractual rather than ascriptive: "the parent-child relationship, rather than an inescapable obligation, becomes a matter of choice. Siblingship is also voluntarily contracted" (p. 83). Moreover, family and kinship ties are but a set of personal experiences shared in the same household or womb. Such ties are brittle and can be ended whenever they become inconvenient for either party. For Hanks, the kinship system is a "set of voluntary reciprocities" (p. 86). Hanks believes that, unlike in what he calls the "rigid occidental family," the "looseness" of the organization of Bang Chan households gives them strength (p. 152).

Lucien Hanks (1975) and Edward Van Roy and James V. Cornehls (1969), in the only other major attempt since Embree's to characterize Thai society, seize upon one social structure—the entourage (a patron-client group)—and try to use this as the key to understanding Thai social structure as a whole. In his most recent exposition of this view, Hanks (1975) portrays Thai society as one based upon what Durkheim called mechanical solidarity (a society made up of like units, such as clans, which are not functionally differentiated). Hanks sees

> the Thai social order as repeating a standard arrangement, the
> entourage and the circle [linked entourages], as if it were a geodesic
> dome. The American social order . . . is built from many
> differentiated specialized parts, implied in such terms as the "organs"
> of government, the economic "system," the residential "zone." In
> contrast the Thai have no specialized governing, economic, or
> residential institutions. The same institution governs, feeds, and
> shelters, as if it were a protozoan carrying out in one cell all functions
> needed for living. In sum the Thai social order comprises a collection
> of self-sufficient units rather than specialized and differentiated ones
> like ours; it is like a coral reef rather than a leviathan. [Lucien Hanks
> 1975, p. 197]

Hanks goes on to say that in the Thai social order "no universals order all the people, and no special economic apparatus supplies the consuming public. Indeed, there are no publics, no masses, nor even a proletariat" (1975, p. 207). Even the Thai government has "no precise territorial jurisdiction and vague sovereignty" (p. 210), and "concepts of class, elite, and specialized institutions becloud our vision" (p. 218).

Then, applying his model to rural Thailand, he says:

In Bāng Chan . . . no organization oversaw the common interest of all villagers or acted for the public good. Even the temple under the head priest consisted in little more than his entourage of resident monks and a dozen or so elderly laymen whose concern over their next existence led them to merit-making before they died. [Hanks 1975, p. 215]

Edward Van Roy and James V. Cornehls (1969) give essentially the same analysis of Thai society as that given by Lucien Hanks. They add that Western notions of stratification are only superficially applicable to Thailand: "Considerations of class do not take precedence, nor is the economic element considered a distinct fact of differentiation or stratification." Furthermore, underscoring points made previously by Hanks, Van Roy and Cornehls say that the entourage is so dominant a principle in Thai society that "in this environment social relationships cannot be generated contractually, nor can undertakings of a lasting order be viable on a peer group or purely cooperative basis" (Van Roy and Cornehls 1969, p. 24).

Van Roy and Cornehls see their analysis of Thai society, based upon Hanks's ideas, as an advance over the loose-structure theory of Embree, Phillips, and Piker, a theory which they say "has been unreservedly adopted by economists in their analyses of Thailand's development options" and has, together with the biased notions of orthodox economics, prevented an accurate analysis of Thailand's development (Van Roy and Cornehls 1969, pp. 28–30).

Although they are to be congratulated for isolating one important principle of Thai social structure (see Chapter 8), Lucien Hanks's and Van Roy's attempts to explain the highly differentiated society of modern Thailand are over-simplified and not convincing; in their hands the entourage becomes a Procrustean bed. Furthermore, they retain the picture of Thailand as a society with a vague, shifting, unstable structure. The entourage itself is, according to Hanks and Van Roy (although they do not use the term), loosely structured. Hanks says that "because of the special characteristics of these circles [by which he means linked entourages], the Thai social order faces unique problems. Circles, because they are *ephemeral* [emphasis mine], provide few stable functions in the social order" (1975, pp. 207–8). Van Roy and Cornehls describe the strength of the bonds between patrons and clients as "varying markedly from one entourage to the next and within each over time"; and they describe these bonds as "always ephemeral" (1969, p. 25), "permanently amorphous," and frequently "fleeting" and "unstable" (1969, p. 26).

The total model of Thai society as being composed of entourages and their combinations, developed by Lucien Hanks and Van Roy, is loose structure in a new guise, closely related to Embree's and Sharp's view of Thailand (this is especially apparent in Lucien Hanks's work). Not only is the basic notion of loose-structure retained, there is also a retention of the image of Thailand as a society unlike any other in the world, which cannot be studied by the usual concepts and methods of the social sciences. Lucien Hanks's and Van Roy's view of Thai society is well within the loose-structure paradigm and does not differ greatly from the view of Embree, Sharp, Wilson, Piker, and Phillips.

This characterization, based upon the work of Embree, Sharp, Wilson, Phillips, Piker, Lucien Hanks, Van Roy, and also Textor, Janlekha, and Hauck (Sharp's coauthors), has become known widely in the scholarly world as the loose-structure model of Thai society—especially of rural Thai society. And Thailand has gained the reputation of being something of an oddity—a strange, exotic society in Southeast Asia that is so lacking in social structure as to always be on the verge of dissolving.

This characterization was controversial from the start. John E. de Young 1955, p. vi) noted two decades ago, and Jacques Amyot (1965, pp. 163–64) and Charles F. Keyes (1966, p. 794) have noted more recently, that the loose-structure model of Bang Chan formulated by Sharp and those who followed him does not accurately portray all of rural Thailand. Michael Moerman (1966b) concluded that the term "loose structure" does not have much heuristic value in helping him characterize the society of his northern Thai village, Ban Ping. In spite of the fact that some of the loose-structure theorists have modified their positions somewhat,[6] the issue remains the most important theoretical controversy in the study of rural Thailand to this day, and permeates anthropological thinking about Thailand in subtle ways. Thus one reads statements like the following: "In situations such as one finds in Thailand where there is an absence of clear-cut rules defining kinship ties and obligations, domestic structure can adequately be treated only through the use of statistical data" (Wijeyewardene 1967, p. 65).

The controversy reached a high pitch in 1969 with the publication of *Loosely Structured Social Systems: Thailand in Comparative Perspective*, a book in which Thai scholars like Phillips, Piker, Moerman, J. A. Niels Mulder, A. Thomas Kirsch, Boosanong Punyodyana, Clark E. Cunningham, and Hans-Dieter Evers argued the issue somewhat heatedly. There has been no resolution of the arguments over theory and facts raised in this volume. Thus S. J. Tambiah, in his book *Buddhism and the Spirit Cults in North-east Thailand* (1970, pp. 149–51), describes a collective activity organized by his villagers to build a temple structure which, he says rather politely and vaguely, "reveals two features which are worth emphasizing in the context of the doctrines of 'loose structure' and 'economic inefficiency', which some writers attribute to the kind of society I am describing." In 1971, Koichi Mizuno, in his village study, *Social System of Don Daeng Village: A Community Study in Northeast Thailand*, devotes his concluding chapter to a discussion of the loose-structure issue (1971, pp. 237–56). Although Mizuno presents data in his book which cannot possibly be fitted into the loose-structure paradigm, he backs off at the last moment from rejecting the paradigm entirely. In two later articles, Mizuno reflects the ambivalence and confusion of many Japanese scholars who have studied Thai and other Southeast Asian villages over the loose-structure paradigm. On the one hand they have been impressed, according to Mizuno (1973, p. 231), by the "looseness" of the village societies they have studied; but on the other hand, they do not like the concept itself because it is misleading and because it has little heuristic value (Mizuno 1975, pp. 133–34). Like many others, they seem to accept Embree's characterization of Thai society, but do not like his terminology.

In 1973, Jane Bunnag, in the last chapter of her book, *Buddhist Monk, Buddhist Layman*, says the following:

> A recurrent theme in Thai anthropological literature has been a concern with the alleged "looseness" of Thai society. Since the publication of John F. Embree's seminal article "Thailand: A Loosely Structured Social System" (in the *American Anthropologist* 52, 1950), his assertion that Thai society is loosely structured has achieved fairly general recognition and acceptance. . . .
>
> More recently a number of students of Thai society have assumed a somewhat more critical stance (see Evers, 1969), but on the whole they have chosen to refine rather than reject the concept of "loose-structuring", despite the fact that most of them recognize that Embree's knowledge of the Thai situation and his theoretical tools may have been less than adequate. [P. 180]

Although Bunnag speaks critically of the concept, she inexplicably incorporates in her own discussion some of the myths about Thai rural society which are part of the loose-structure model. Thus she says that "social roles are relatively simple and unspecialized in content"; she speaks of "the relative lack of specificity" of roles and the "ease of role-shift in Thai society" (Bunnag 1973, pp. 180–82). She continues:

> In Thailand . . . there are very few corporate groups, or permanent co-operative groupings of any kind, which at the level of individual behaviour means that actors move quite easily from role to role both within and between spheres of activity, and freely relinquish social ties which they no longer consider to be of any importance. [P. 187]

Bunnag's critique is somewhat bewildering because she ends up accepting some of the basic elements of the loose-structure model which she has set out to criticize and perpetuating some of the factual inaccuracies about rural Thailand.

Finally, there is the anthology *Southeast Asia: The Politics of National Integration*, edited by John T. McAlister, Jr., published in 1973, in which is reprinted (pp. 234–49) Embree's original loose-structure article from 1950. In addition, in an article written for that volume, A. Thomas Kirsch mentions the loose-structure model in a not disapproving manner and gives no indication that he thinks the concept out-of-date:

> Some observers, struck with the fluidity and mobility of Thai social relationships, have characterized the Thai social order as "loosely structured" (see Embree, 1950, Hanks, 1962, Evers, 1969). . . . Buddhist conceptions and values provide a symbolic framework within which such fluidity and mobility is not only made meaningful but is legitimized and encouraged." [1973, p. 197]

Old myths have a way of persisting; and even today the loose-structure paradigm, although controversial, influences anthropological thinking within the ranks of Thai specialists. Outside the field of Thai studies, the loose-structure model remains the most widely accepted characterization of rural Thailand. I agree with Moerman (1975, p. 151) that "the world's view of rural Thailand is biased by Bāng Chan." As Clifford Geertz (1973, p. 27) remarks, "old theories tend less to die than to go into second editions." One reason why the myth has persisted is that, with but few exceptions, objections to the model have been based upon theoretical grounds rather than upon an examination of the ethnographic facts. Kirsch (1969, p. 51) claims that Embree's loose-structure model persists because no subsequent investigation of Thailand (including his own) has contradicted the empirical evidence that Embree used to support his argument.

In the present study I present data from a northern Thai village and from other Thai villages (see Chapter 8) which contradict the loose-structure model of rural Thailand. Unlike previous critiques of the model (with the exception of Michael Moerman's somewhat indecisive article [1966b] "Ban Ping's Temple: The Center of a 'Loosely Structured' Society," and Hans-Dieter Ever's article [1969] "Models of Social Systems: Loosely and Tightly Structured"), I challenge it on the basis of ethnographic facts as well as mode of analysis. I am not particularly interested in continuing the unproductive, inconclusive, and confusing "theoretical" discussions in the book *Loosely Structured Social Systems* (Evers, ed. 1969). In spite of their reservations and qualifications, the fact remains that many influential writers on Thailand have portrayed rural Thai society to the outside world as one strangely devoid of structure or form. This picture is inaccurate and misleading. My purpose in this book is to present what I consider to be a more accurate and realistic portrayal of Thai peasant social structure.

I am interested in formulating cross-cultural comparisons. I see Thai society as an example of a recognized social type and not as an exotic peculiarity in Southeast Asia. It is necessary to clarify the nature of rural Thai society so that Thailand may be compared with China, India, and other peasant societies.

# 2    Village in Arcady

Chiangmai village is a rural community of eight hundred and seventy-five people located in the Chiengmai Valley of northern Thailand, about an hour's drive south of the city of Chiengmai (see map 1).[1]

## The Chiengmai Valley

The Chiengmai Valley (see map 2) is one of the loveliest places in the world. Standing in the center of the valley near the village, one sees a rim of hazy blue mountains on all sides as one's eye sweeps the horizon. Over the mountains, populated by exotic tribal peoples who slash-and-burn and grow the opium poppy, one can go north to China's Yunnan Province, once the home of the Thai peoples; westward to Burma and Mandalay; or east to Laos. The Ping River, one of Thailand's principal rivers, traverses the length of the valley, running from north to south, passing through the city of Chiengmai and just a few kilometers west of the village, on its way to Lamphun, the old Mon city, and then down through the mountains to the plain of central Thailand. Mount Doi Suteb, four thousand feet high, dominates the valley and the city, which nestles at its foot, and is an ever-present backdrop to the village scene. On top of the mountain is a palace of the king of Thailand, to which he comes every year in the warm season. Also on the mountaintop is a famous temple and monastery thought to contain a relic of the Lord Buddha. The monastery is visible from the village as a small golden toy house on the distant slopes.

**Yearly Agricultural
and Climatic Cycle**

During two of the three seasons into which the Thai divide their year, the
village, the valley, and the surrounding mountains are a region of spectacular natural beauty. At the beginning of the rice-growing season in June,

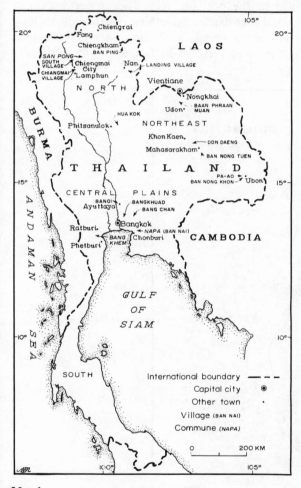

**Map 1**

the paddy fields, softened by the first monsoonal rains of the year, are
plowed by water buffalo, oxen, and, of late, by tractors and hand-guided
cultivators. The seed plots are prepared and the sprouting rice is sown on
the bed where it will be allowed to grow a foot or so in height before it is
transplanted into the larger fields. By July and early August the fields have
been plowed and harrowed, the weeds removed or pushed under the mud,
and the rice fields puddled by the peasants' feet. They tramp back and
forth with arms folded behind their backs, smoothing out the bottom mud
and pushing under any remaining weeds, as if they were performing a
strange ritual dance. As the rains increase in frequency, the irrigation

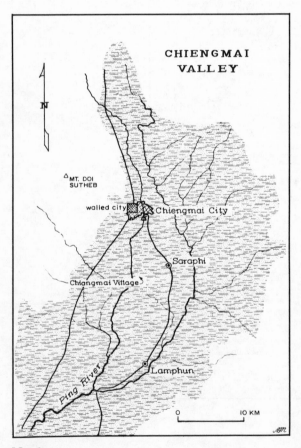

**Map 2**

canals which crisscross the valley flood the rice fields, and the peasants, as they transplant, gradually extend a fresh carpet of green across the valley floor. From the air, the newly planted rice fields, divided and subdivided over the generations into tiny plots, are like a myriad of tiny glass prisms. This is the loveliest time of year in the valley. As summer passes into fall the monsoonal rains come more often to cool the hot tropical air, if only briefly. The valley takes on the appearance of a lush parkland with a gigantic, evenly trimmed lawn of rice interspersed with wooded areas which follow the main watercourses and whose trees shelter the villages under cool and shady branches. Monsoonal rain clouds appear almost daily, and wisps of monsoonal mists float across the face of Mount Doi Sutheb.

The rainy season reaches its climax in September, when the rainfall is so heavy that the Ping River reaches flood stage. It runs swift and full and washes away the bamboo and sand weirs, which the peasants had patiently built across the river in the dry season to raise a head of water for their irrigation canals. The river swells and overflows its banks, flooding the irrigation canals and then the roads and highways. After September the monsoon rains taper off, and the rice grows waist-high. The rainy season gives way to winter. The weather begins to turn cold enough in the evening and night to force the peasants to huddle around fires built in their courtyards and to pile on extra blankets. At midday it remains hot, but at night the light and open houses, built for the tropical heat of most of the year, give little protection against the cold. One has the sensation of sleeping on an exposed platform in the middle of an open, windswept plain.

In November and December the air turns cool and dry, and the maturing rice is heavy and yellow in the plain. At harvest time the valley floor looks like a van Gogh painting, with the dark green tree line and the blues of the sky and mountains setting off the tawny yellow of the rice fields. The fields are liberally sprinkled with the colorful costumes of the villagers, who beat the sheaves of rice into giant baskets, knocking off the rice grains, and carry and cart their full baskets back to the village granaries.

By December the harvest is over, but the cold season lingers on through February. This is the time of year when the villagers plant crops that supply the money to pay their taxes and to buy the goods and services they themselves do not produce. The rice-growing season is for growing the family's yearly food supply of glutinous rice; the cold season, after harvest, is for making money. Many of the empty rice fields are planted in garlic, peanuts, and soybeans. It takes money to buy seed garlic, fertilizer to make it grow, and time to prepare the fields; sometimes the price isn't good, but in a good year garlic yields the most money. Peanuts usually have good yields, but the cost of hiring tractors to till the earth for them and the cost of seed peanuts sometimes eat up the profits; occasionally the fields are too wet and the peanuts are spoiled. Soybeans yield the least profit of all for the space they require, but they take only a small investment in seed and are easily planted underneath the rice stalks, without the necessity of plowing or hoeing. Highland fields are suitable for garlic and peanuts and soybeans. The wetter, lower-lying fields are suitable only for growing a second crop of nonglutinous rice and are thus less valuable.

The cold season gives way to the hot, dry season of March, April, and May, which shows the valley at its worst. The sun beats down mercilessly day after day on the paddy fields, which, if not planted and irrigated, dry and crack in the heat of the sun and give the farms an unkempt appearance. The deciduous forest on the lower slopes of the surrounding mountains turns an ugly brown and yellow as the leaves drop. The valley floor turns to dust as the rains end and the heat of the sun increases. Passing cars and trucks throw up clouds of dust on village roads and lanes, and the dust penetrates the village houses, leaving a gritty pink layer over everything. Villagers whose houses lie near the main roads draw water and throw it on the roads in front of their houses in an effort to prevent the dust from rising. And finally, to cap it all, the valley is filled with a dirty gray smog, hiding the mountains and the sky, caused in part by the hill tribes, who burn their swidden fields (for slash-and-burn agriculture) at this time of year, and by the valley farmers, who burn the old rice stubble on empty fields. The Ping River, which winds its way down from the highlands at the north end of the valley, is at its lowest point in May, the end of the dry season. Brush grows on exposed high points of the riverbed, and large expanses of sand, rock, and gravel lie bare like the skeleton of a giant serpent.

The first showers of April and May and the heavier rains which begin sporadically in June offer a welcome respite from the heat and dust and the smog. And then the yearly cycle turns again when the rains sweep up from the Indian Ocean and the Gulf of Thailand. The river rises, filling its bed and the myriad irrigation channels, and nourishes the fields. The thousands of tons of silt deposited on the valley bottom by the flooding river and irrigation canals enrich the valley soil and permit the villagers to grow one and, in some areas, two crops of rice yearly without using fertilizer. Add to this the industriousness of the peasantry, and you have on the Chiengmai Plain, and especially in Saraphi District, where Chiangmai village is located, one of the most fertile and densely populated rice-growing areas in the world.

## The City of Chiengmai

The valley (see map 2) is by far the most important part of the province of Chiengmai, which in 1972 had a population of a little over one million. The city of Chiengmai, only an hour's truck ride from the village, is the capital of the north and the second most important city in Thailand. It is justly famous for its climate, its spectacular scenery, and its beautiful women. The city dates from the thirteenth century, when it was founded by King Meŋraaj, a Thai prince from Chiengrai who conquered most of northern Thailand and laid the foundation for the Laannaathaj kingdom, which was based in Chiengmai and maintained its independence until the late nineteenth century. Throughout most of their history the Chiengmai kings were embroiled in wars with the other city-states of what is now northern Thailand, Laos, Burma, and central Thailand. For several centuries Chiengmai was ruled by the Burmese and was subjected to Burmese cultural influence, which is still evident in some temples and in arts and crafts. Since the late nineteenth century Chiengmai has been part of the modern Thai nation (formerly known as Siam) and subject to the political, cultural, linguistic, and economic influences of the capital city of Bangkok.

Chiengmai could once have been considered the ethnic cul-de-sac of Asia and the end of the earth by Westerners. Over the past century it has, however, been increasingly brought into the modern world. In centuries past Chiengmai was isolated from Bangkok, six hundred miles to the south, and could be reached only by a boat going up the river in certain seasons. As recently as the nineteenth century, Daniel McGilvary, an American who was the first Protestant missionary in Chiengmai, spent several months coming up the river from Bangkok (see McGilvary 1912). After the railroad from Bangkok to Chiengmai was completed, in 1921, the journey became an overnight train trip; Moerman (1968, p. 4) spoke of the distance in this way as recently as 1968. At present Chiengmai village is only a couple of hours by air from Don Muang Airport in Bangkok. If the plans to build an international airport near Chiengmai city, discussed in 1972, come to fruition, the village will be only a few hours away from most of the world's metropolitan capitals.

The city of Chiengmai has been profoundly affected by recent changes brought about through increased contact with the outside world. Today only a few fragments remain of the ancient city's gates and walls, although the lovely moats are still there, a legacy from the past, flooding every year as they must have done for the past seven hundred. The once-lovely city's soul and character is, unfortunately, now gone. The old palace of the kings of Chiengmai is now the American consulate. The spirits of the Chiengmai kings must stir restlessly in their burial tombs in the Suan Dɔɔg Temple, one of the most beautiful in Asia, disturbed by all these changes and by the Thai border police, who have built a souvenir shop selling goods from the hill tribes to tourists at the entrance to the temple.

In 1972, the city was on its way to becoming a little Bangkok. From only 38,000 in 1947, the population has grown to 87,000 by 1969, and the city had long overgrown its walls and spread an unsightly urban sprawl across the river and outward in all directions.

But the city has made progress. Its economy was stimulated by the establishment, in the early 1960s, of Chiengmai University, Thailand's first regional university, on the western outskirts of the city in the foothills of Doi Sutheb. There has been a great influx of central Thai students and professors from Bangkok, and the city has modernized to meet their tastes. Hundreds of Chinese stores and shops line the streets, with the merchants lurking to catch the unwary peasant, tribesman, or student. In 1972 the streets were beginning to look like those of Bangkok, with hundreds of pedicabs, motored pedicabs, pickup truck taxis, buses, bicycles, motorcycles, and an occasional private car choking the city and making it all but impossible to cross the main streets on foot. But the city does now have a permanent medical school and two modern hospitals, as well as radio stations, an airport with daily flights to Bangkok, a superhighway going south, and all the other trappings of modernity.

To get to the village of Chiangmai from the city, one avoids the superhighway and goes south on the old two-lane Chiengmai-Lamphun highway, lined with giant white-barked rubber trees. After ten kilometers one reaches the small town of Saraphi, the seat of Saraphi District.

### Saraphi District
### and Town

Saraphi is a famous district of Thailand, notable in many respects. In area, it is the smallest district in Chiengmai Province (128 square kilometers), but, except for one other district six times its size, it has more villages (98) than any district in the province. In 1971, its population density was 471 per square kilometer, or 1,220 persons per square mile, making it one of the most densely populated rural areas in Thailand and the world, comparable to central Java. In some important ways it can be seen as the highest development of Thai peasant society in a fertile, irrigated, multi-cropped farming region, where the population density has reached its limit and is straining against its resource base.

Saraphi is also notable as one of the oldest Thai-inhabited districts in all of Thailand. King Meŋraaj, the Thai conqueror of the valley in the thirteenth century, first established his capital near the river at Saraphi and only later moved it north to Chiengmai city. A lovely pagoda and some other ruins are still visible north of Saraphi where the old capital was supposed to have been built. The two "people's canals," as they are now called by the Thai government, which water many of Saraphi District's fields, diverge from the river near the ancient city, and they or ones just like them might even date from Meŋraaj's time.

Saraphi town, the district seat, is about twenty minutes by bicycle or jeep from Chiangmai village. It has a railway station and the inevitable Chinese noodle shops, tailoring shops, general stores, rice stores, and also a large Chinese-owned morning market, where many of the villagers buy and sell. In the town are the headquarters of the district government, where the village heads meet the Naajamphǝǝ, as the district officer is called, and other low-level representatives of the national Thai governmental bureaucracy. It is in Saraphi that the villagers pay their taxes and register property transfers and marriages, and it is here that they are taken if arrested by the district police, who also have their headquarters in Saraphi. In addition to all this, Saraphi town contains several large warehouses owned by Chinese merchants, where the garlic, soybeans, and peanuts purchased from the villagers are stored, and finally resold and shipped to Bangkok. Finally, some of the village children are sent here for their post-primary education.

### The Village Setting

To get to Chiangmai village from the town one turns right off the blacktop highway and follows the red dirt road which runs westward toward the Ping River in the center of the valley. When we first came to the village in late September, 1971, just as the rainy season was ending, the road was barely passable, a treacherous series of mud ruts, rocks, and potholes. At that time of year, the rice was a shimmering waist-high ocean of greenery in the hot tropical sun of a Chiengmai autumn. The cool green waters of the swiftly flowing irrigation canals ran along both sides of the road and occasionally under it, beneath crude bridges of rough-hewn timbers. Black tropical water-snakes darted silently across the road and back into the rice marshes. Flocks of domesticated ducks in the fields and streams quacked noisily, startled from their daily task of eating the crabs and insects that were attacking their master's rice. From the village, as we were later to learn, our vehicle looked like a boat plowing its way across a sea of rice fields to the village, rolling slowly, as with waves, from the ups and downs of the tortuous roadbed.

Approaching the village from a distance, one first sees only a khaki-green tree line punctuated with towering coconut palms, rising like a tropical island from the level floor of the valley. The canopy of trees makes the village houses invisible from the outside. Upon entering the village, one passes suddenly from the glaring heat of the fields and the dust and mud of the road into a cool and shady interior. Until recently a stranger could be right in the middle of the village without realizing it. In 1973, the village progress committee erected a new green and white sign at the main entrance saying "Welcome to Chiangmai Village," in English.

Chiangmai is a large, oval-shaped village that is elongated roughly on a north-south axis. Its shape is distinctive because it encloses a large area of fields in its center (see map 3). The main roads leading into the village converge at its northern edge and then run directly to the temple complex at the village center. The complex contains an ornately carved wooden and stucco temple, decorated with colored glass mosaics and built with the lovely multiple roofs and flowing lines of the north. A utility pavilion with space for village meetings, the temple kitchen, and storage for drums and gongs surrounds the temple, forming a square compound. At one side of the compound is a large, two-story pink stucco building which contains the living quarters, office, and study halls for the abbot and his novices. Adjacent to the temple grounds is the village's four-year primary school and its playground.

From the temple and school complex a one-lane dirt road runs around the circumference of the village and back again to the temple. Spacious lanes lead off the road and pass through the living area of the village to the edge of the surrounding fields, cutting up the village in a series of pie-shaped wedges. The shady lanes are lined with high, arching palms, giant bamboos, and green hedges. Cool irrigation ditches crisscross the village alongside and under the lanes and paths.

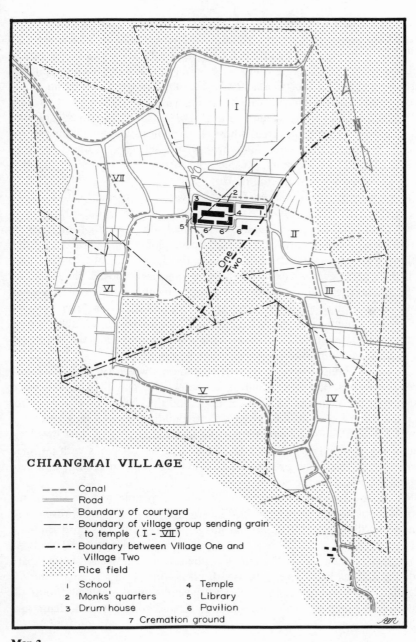

CHIANGMAI VILLAGE

————— Canal
═══════ Road
————— Boundary of courtyard
——— — Boundary of village group sending grain
          to temple ( I - VII )
—·—· Boundary between Village One and
          Village Two
::::::: Rice field

| | | |
|---|---|---|
| ı | School | 4  Temple |
| 2 | Monks' quarters | 5  Library |
| 3 | Drum house | 6  Pavilion |
| | 7  Cremation ground | |

**Map 3**

Off the village road and the lanes lie spacious courtyards, behind boundaries demarcated by bamboo, wood, or stone fences. The houses are only half-visible through the luxuriant foliage of shrubs and trees in the peaceful Japanese-style gardens, which rely on natural wood textures, pounded earth, and stone for their classical effect. Courtyard gardens contain lamjaj trees, cousins of the lychee, which are the villagers' most important cash crop, and the ubiquitous banana palms, as well as the tamarinds, jackfruit, mangoes, and other exotic trees whose Thai names are unintelligible to the foreigner. Almost every tree and shrub in the villagers' gardens has economic as well as ornamental value; the hedge, for example, supports vines which provide greens for food.

The courtyards also contain fenced-off vegetable gardens, duck coops, and enclosures for water buffalo and brown oxen, if the family owns them. Every compound has a brick and concrete well with a shadoof, or counterpoised sweep, and a galvanized water bucket for drawing water; a brick bathing enclosure, shoulder high, where the family members take turns with their baths every evening of the year; and an enclosed flat toilet, set at ground level with a water seal which separates it from the concrete-lined septic tank buried below. In addition, every house has a large wooden granary set about eight feet off the ground upon tree-trunk-thick foundation posts. There the year's precious supply of glutinous rice, the distinctive staple food of the northern Thai peasant, is stored.

Chiangmai houses vary from a few modern, two-story concrete structures to the beautiful traditional teak houses with clay-tiled roofs owned by most of the villagers, to small bamboo and thatch houses of the poorer families, which cost around U.S. $25 to build. The best indicator of a family's wealth and social standing is the size and quality of their dwelling. The lovely, distinctive wooden houses are large and spacious with polished floors of inch-thick teak or kapok wood and high vaulted ceilings that help to cool the house in the summer.

Rooms are sparsely furnished, if at all, and people usually sit on the floor without benefit of mats or cushions. One wall of the living room contains a Buddhist altar shelf with an image or picture of the Lord Buddha. It is set high on the wall in a position of honor and respect. The living room also contains a glass-fronted cupboard or two which holds spare bedding and clothes. Every house displays prized family snapshots, a calendar, and a picture of the king and queen. A wealthier household will also have a Japanese-made pendulum clock and solid wooden chairs and a table.

The bedrooms may contain European-style wooden beds if it is a wealthy household, but most bedrooms have neatly draped mosquito nets hung over a thin Japanese-style mattress, which is folded up during the day. Bedrooms have other chests for clothes and bedding.

Kitchens are simple affairs. They contain a clay brazier or two for burning kindling or charcoal, with a cupboard to hold the clay or metal rice-steaming equipment. Baskets, a few enameled dishpans, plates for the curries, and a few plastic pans will usually be found. The kitchen may be on the back porch or in a separate shed in the compound.

The houses are kept immaculately clean, neat, and polished. The best of the traditional-style houses, with their vaulted clay-tile roofs, whose tiles are visible from within the house and whose floors are polished to a mirror sheen are beautiful dwellings by any architectural standards. Shoes are left below and feet are washed before people climb up the stairs into the house. Courtyards are swept free of debris each morning by a woman or girl of the household, and the refuse is burned. The gardens are carefully tended. Shrubs are trimmed, flowers are admired, and the invaluable lamjaj tree limbs are propped up with wooden stilts so they will not break under the weight of ripened fruit.

Chiangmai houses are built on two levels. Like the rice granaries, they are raised about eight feet off the ground on cement or wooden foundation posts. This leaves a protected under-the-house area as large as the house itself. During most of the year, when they are not busy in the fields or with other business, the family spends the days sitting on wooden platforms covered with woven bamboo mats in the cool area under the house. The under-the-house area serves as a social center where the whole family or compound group (many compounds contain two or three houses) can gather during the day to chat with neighbors, fellow villagers, or the frequent peddlers.

The people of Chiangmai are open, friendly, and sunny on the surface but deep, self-contained, and unfathomable beneath. The contradictions in their personalities are like the contrasts in their religious culture between the lovely, if somewhat garish, temple, with its delightful ceremonies, and their witches, with heads of horses, mouths frothing with blood, who are believed to canter through the village at night. Superficially Chiangmai villagers are charming, colorful, and carefree people, but underneath they have dark and brooding natures, with abiding hates, jealousies, and fears that pass from one generation to another.

Chiangmai women are impressive. They have the strength of character, independence, and self-assurance of women who live in a society where they are in a strong position. Residence here is matrilocal. The daughters stay at home and their husbands come in to live with them. Inheritance is bilateral, and the women share equally with the men; daughters inherit the parental home and the matrilineal ancestors. In case of divorce, it is usually the man who leaves and the woman who stays home. Women work in the fields, rear the children, keep house; they are also the merchants who earn money for their family selling in the markets. They are the ones who keep the money, for fear that their men will waste it on gambling or drinking, or on other women. There are many strong men in Chiangmai village, but what impresses a Western outsider is the strength of the women. McGilvary was so struck by Khonmyaŋ women that he was moved to write: "the Lao [an old term for the Northern Thai] have a proud pre-eminence among non-Christian races in the position accorded to women" (1912, p. 144).

The diet of the villagers is based upon glutinous rice as a staple. "Sticky rice," as glutinous rice is known, is soaked overnight and then steamed. It forms a mound from which a person breaks off a piece with his hand, rolls it into a compact ball, dips it into his curry, and then pops the morsel into his mouth. Glutinous rice is steamed once a day and kept in covered baskets to be eaten throughout the day (see Moerman 1968, App. A, for a discussion of glutinous rice).

Fish caught from the irrigation canals are the villagers' basic source of protein. Small freshwater fish are netted, trapped, speared, caught with hook and line, and, finally, if they escape all this, are caught by the peasants damming up the ditches, dipping out the water, and simply lifting them out into a creel. Each morning at the crack of dawn village men go out singly to the fields and streams to empty their traps and nets. Just after dawn breaks the men return with the day's catch, which is cleaned and curried by a woman of the family who gets up early to make the fire, steam the rice, and prepare the family's breakfast.

The village lies downstream, at the foot of the two major irrigation canal systems, and many of the larger fish are caught by the villagers upstream before they reach Chiangmai. Any fish that swims through the gauntlet of village traps, hooks, and nets and escapes into the outlet canal and back into the river is a wise and able fish indeed.

In addition to fish, the villagers trap eels and freshwater crabs and shrimp from the streams and paddy fields. The eels and shrimp are eaten or sold in the market; the crabs are sometimes eaten, but usually they are mashed up and fed to the ducks. Along with fat pork and duck eggs, and a leafy vegetable which resembles mustard greens, these aquatic foods form the major ingredient in the curries which the villagers eat with glutinous rice.

Besides being a major source of food, fishing is a major sport. All the villagers, especially the girls and women, spend hours each day during slack times in the agricultural cycle fishing the streams and canals. In the dry season, the villagers dig out the mud bottoms of the ditches, where fish burrow to hibernate through the dry months.

"Meenaam Ping," literally "Mother-waters Ping," the Thai name for the Ping River, is appropriate. The waters of the river flood the valley each year, furnishing moisture for the rice, silt to replenish the soil, and fish and other aquatic foods for the villagers' tables. Chiangmai village culture is a riverine culture.

**Population,
Emigration, and
Birth Control**

The history of Chiangmai's population growth mirrors that of Thailand as a whole over the past century (see Caldwell 1967). The population in the Chiengmai Valley was much lower in the nineteenth century than it is now, largely because of epidemic diseases and malaria. The horrible situation is described by McGilvary in the late nineteenth century when he came to Chiengmai:

> Malarial fevers often run on season after season, creating an anemic condition such that the least exertion would bring on the fever and chills again. . . . I have often been in villages where every child, and nearly every person, young or old, had chills and fever, . . .
> The ravages of smallpox had been fearful, amounting at times to the destruction of a whole generation of children. The year before our arrival had witnessed such a scourge. Hardly a household escaped, and many had no children left. [1912, pp. 88–89]

The arrival of modern medicine in the late nineteenth century, with the introduction by missionaries of smallpox vaccination, relieved the situation somewhat. Around 1920, according to one of the villagers, there were only about 60 households in the village, compared to the 206 there now. Since the population was smaller, family landholdings were larger and the courtyards more spacious.

Since then, the number of people living in Chiangmai has grown by natural increase and by families moving in to settle the rich land. Courtyards, fields, and orchards were divided equally among sons and daughters, and as the population increased over the years the average family estate became smaller. By 1953, the population had grown to 842.

So successful was the malaria-eradication program, begun in Saraphi district in 1949 (Kingshill 1965, p. 16), that in 1953–54 a rapid and dramatic increase in the number of children in the 0–3 age group foreshadowed a period of even more rapid population growth.

By 1972, the village was bursting at the seams. Some families had no courtyard in which to build a house, and so they built on converted paddy fields beyond the village boundaries. The village is today inching along the roads and waterways toward neighboring villages. Once Chiangmai and a village to the northwest were clearly separated, but now one can barely tell where one village ends and the other begins.

In January, 1972, our census showed that Chiangmai contained 875 people, 33 more than lived there in 1953, two decades earlier (see table 1). The population pressure in Chiangmai, however, is not sufficiently indicated by these figures; there is every indication that the village's population was burgeoning over the past twenty years and that the pressure was relieved only by extensive out-migration of villagers to find jobs elsewhere or to settle new land.

The most popular place for village emigrants has been the Fang Valley, near the Burmese border, about a hundred kilometers north of Chiengmai city (see map 1) where population density is less and land is for sale at cheap prices. Chiangmai village migrants have settled mainly in two villages, one only a mile outside the small city of Fang. In 1972 I visited the large emigrant community, jokingly referred to by some of the villagers as "little Chiangmai," built one or two houses deep in a long strip along the road to Fang city (see a similar situation described by Keyes [1967b, p. 15] for the northeast). Their temple was a makeshift structure, suitable for a frontier community, built in the middle of the village. South of the temple, immigrants from Lamphun had settled; north of the temple were the people from Chiangmai village and other villages in Saraphi District.

A farmer from a village next to Chiangmai had come to Fang thirteen years before, in 1959. He said that he had been a poor man in his native village, owning only 13 tax raj (1 raj phaasii [tax raj] equals 0.395 acres), but after moving to Fang and working for a few years he owned 40 tax raj. In 1972, land in Fang near this emigrant village was selling for 1,000

Table 1                    The Population of
                           Chiangmai Village
                           (January 1972)

| Age Group | Male | Female | Total |
|---|---|---|---|
| 0–4 | 20 | 22 | 42 |
| 5–9 | 41 | 43 | 84 |
| 10–14 | 69 | 64 | 133 |
| 15–19 | 38 | 63 | 101 |
| 20–24 | 42 | 44 | 86 |
| 25–29 | 23 | 23 | 46 |
| 30–34 | 23 | 30 | 53 |
| 35–39 | 44 | 28 | 72 |
| 40–44 | 31 | 34 | 65 |
| 45–49 | 28 | 20 | 48 |
| 50–54 | 16 | 16 | 32 |
| 55–59 | 9 | 10 | 19 |
| 60–64 | 14 | 16 | 30 |
| 65–69 | 10 | 15 | 25 |
| 70–74 | 11 | 7 | 18 |
| 75–79 | 1 | 11 | 12 |
| 80–84 | 5 | 2 | 7 |
| 85–90 | 1 | 1 | 2 |
| Totals | 426 | 449 | 875 |

to 2,000 baht (about U.S. $50 to $100) per tax raj, whereas Chiangmai village land was selling for around 10,000 baht (about U.S. $500) per tax raj.

In 1972, the emigrant village in Fang still had the look of a frontier settlement. The houses were crude compared to Chiangmai's fine old houses, and most dwellings, especially those of the younger people, were made of bamboo and thatch. It is not a rosy life for the Fang emigrants. The land is undeveloped. It will take a generation or two of labor to carve terraced paddy fields from the floor of the valley and to build effective irrigation systems like those in Chiangmai. The fields of the Fang village were too wet during the rainy season; much of the land was a swampy marsh which the villagers were just beginning to drain. At harvest the fields are wet and miserable to work in, and they do not yield nearly as much as Chiangmai's. Furthermore, the Fang farmers do not have access to a good market for cash crops. In an effort to gain more land, some of the villagers practice slash-and-burn agriculture on nearby mountains.

The emigrants still have not forgotten Chiangmai. Visiting takes place at least once a year between relatives in Chiangmai and Fang. At these visits much time is spent bringing the Fang emigrants up-to-date on the happenings and the gossip of their home village. The settlers' eyes still get misty when they leave their old village in Saraphi. Fang isn't Chiangmai and never will be.

The Chiangmai villagers' adoption of birth control over the past few years has made future explosive growth of its population unlikely. Table 2 shows its effect on the population statistics. A dramatic decline in the number of children born in the village first became evident around 1969, when the birth control program in Chiangmai had gotten well under way.

**Table 2**                     Distribution of
                                Children of Various
                                Ages in Chiangmai
                                Village (1972)

| Age in Years | Number of Children |
|---|---|
| 0–1 | 4 |
| 1–2 | 4 |
| 2–3 | 12 |
| 3–4 | 9 |
| 4–5 | 13 |
| 5–6 | 13 |
| 6–7 | 13 |
| 7–8 | 15 |

Forty-seven couples in Chiangmai practice some form of birth control. Thirty-two couples rely upon birth control pills distributed mainly by the Thai government through the local village health posts at nominal fees; four depend upon male vasectomy; and eleven upon injections given by McCormick hospital in Chiengmai city, that prevent the implantation of the fetus.[2] Most of the women who take birth control pills are young, between the ages of twenty and twenty-four; and most are from the poorer families in the village. Most of the couples who practice birth control do so because they are trying to buy land and build a house, and establish financial independence from the wife's parents. There is a long tradition in the village that young couples work during the early years of their marriage—the man in the fields and the woman selling in the marketplace—to establish themselves and to get ahead. The adoption of birth control fits neatly into this village pattern.

The second group of couples practicing birth control—a much smaller group than the first—are people in their mid-thirties who already have several children. These couples adopted birth control, when it became available, to prevent any future births. Most women do not wish to have large families, but they want to have a minimum of two children. "If one dies, then you will have one to give comfort and support in your old age," they say.

The basic motivation for birth control is economic. The villagers love children, but they are well aware of the cost of raising them. "One child will keep you poor for seven years," is a village saying. The villagers are also conscious of the rising population pressure and the shortage of land. The people of Chiangmai village adopted birth control very readily. One reason is that birth control is not seen as a religious matter at all. Buddhism is much more accepting in this respect than Catholicism; in fact, according to the villagers, the government health personnel advocating birth control spoke at a meeting in the village temple. Another reason is that village women are independent enough to make the decision to limit births themselves, without paying so much attention to their husband's wishes.

In 1971 only eight children were born in Chiangmai, four of whom died within a few days after their birth. Meanwhile, during the same year, thirteen villagers died, decreasing the total population by nine persons from the previous year, not counting migrations in and out. If this short-term trend continues, and there is little in-migration, the village population may well stabilize, or at least grow at a much slower rate.

**Relations with the
Outside World**

Chiangmai has never been an isolated village; the village people always considered themselves to be part of the old Chiengmai city-state and have always had contact with the political rulers, the religious centers, and the markets of the city. In recent years the villagers' contacts with Chiengmai and the outside world have intensified. Local taxis called tug-tugs—small Japanese pickups with two parallel benches built in the truck bed, a luggage-carrier on top, and a body decorated with garish paint—carry at least a dozen villagers to the city and back three or four times daily. These taxis are miracles of transportation; there is no apparent limit to the number of villagers who can be packed into the back (some standing on the rear bumper and hanging on with one hand) and the amount of baggage that can be piled and roped onto the top. In addition to the village market women, who take fruit, coconuts, and banana leaves to sell in the city market every morning, the taxis are filled with other villagers going to town, to market, or to the hospital. Also, in addition to the bicycles which everyone owns, many of the wealthier people of Chiangmai own Japanese-made motorcycles or motor scooters, which allow them to buzz over the country roads to the city in about forty-five minutes.

Links to the outside world are also provided by the frequent trips and outings that the villagers take (usually by chartered bus and supposedly for religious purposes) to places as distant as Bangkok or the Burmese and Laotian borders. Daily newspapers are available for all the villagers to read, on a table in the temple compound, but few take advantage of this opportunity. Finally, the outer world is brought nearer by the omnipresent Japanese transistor radios which loudly blare forth the day's news, current hit songs, and special northern Thai songs, from morning until night. Even though most village houses now have electricity, the battery-run transistor radios will not be replaced because they can be taken along and listened to while the villagers are engaged in the lonely drudgery of the rice fields. Another important thing the radios do is to familiarize villagers with the standard Central Thai language and acquaint them with events of nation-wide significance.

That the villagers have access to the world outside the village does not necessarily mean that they are interested in it. Most villagers, with the exception of one or two of the teachers, have only a dim notion of the world beyond Thailand. Many villagers knew that Thai soldiers were fighting in Vietnam, but they were surprised to hear that Americans were fighting there too. The villagers' knowledge of the outside world is not increased by their compulsory four-year primary education in the village school. The village schoolteachers teach by rote learning, which gives no encouragement to originality. The result is that the children emerge from primary school semiliterate at best, not even knowing how to multiply or divide and, worst of all, with their sense of originality and creativity permanently damaged. Those who can read seldom do; village culture is largely an illiterate culture. Few students have the means or the parental encouragement to continue their education beyond the compulsory four grades, though a few of the young people go on to a teachers' college in Chiengmai city after their primary education; they attend twilight school everyday, leaving the village at two in the afternoon and returning at nine in the evening. Some families in the village are too poor to buy even primary-

school books and uniforms for their children, but the children attend anyway. In 1972 the government allotted funds for a new primary-school
building in the village, which will improve school facilities, but the curric-
ulum and the teachers will be the same.

## Ethnic Identity

Since their incorporation into the Thai nation at the end of the nineteenth century, the people of Chiangmai village and Chiengmai have been
under the authority of Thai central government officials, have been taught
Central Thai in the schools, and have been subjected to pressures, directly and indirectly, which tend to acculturate them to modern urban Thai
culture emanating from Bangkok and to assimilate them into the national
Thai society dominated by the Bangkok Central Thai. These forces have
had their effect, and the village is now definitely a part of the Thai nation.

Nevertheless, the villagers have not forgotten their separate ethnic
identity, established during six centuries of independent existence as a
nation. The villagers still speak Kammyaŋ, Northern Thai, which is in-
telligible, but with difficulty, to a Central Thai speaker. And still, when
they say "Khonthaj" ("a Thai"), they are referring to the Central Thai
and not to themselves, whom they identify as "Khonmyaŋ," "people of
northern Thailand" and, more specifically, people of the old Chiengmai
city-state.[3] Thus they distinguish themselves from the Central Thai, who
serve as officials over them and who look down upon the northerners with
ill-disguised disdain as semibarbarians having loose sexual habits and
speaking a different language.

The villagers don't like the Central Thai. They see them as exploiters—
evil people who cannot be trusted, and who seek to lure northern girls into
the brothels and massage parlors of Bangkok. This impression has been
reinforced in the few cases of village girls who have married Central Thai
men; in every case they have been deserted.

The Chiangmai villagers also distinguish themselves from the Chinese,
whom they call by the derogatory term "ceg." The Chinese own almost all
the shops and businesses in Saraphi and in Chiengmai city and are the
middlemen and brokers who collect the villagers' agricultural produce and
ship it to Bangkok. The Khonmaŋ view the Chinese with mixed emotions.
On the one hand, they admire the industriousness and the business ability
of the Chinese. Khonmyaŋ girls like to marry Chinese so that they will be
well-supported and their marriage will be permanent. On the other hand,

the villagers are envious of the wealth of the Chinese and the economic power that the Chinese have over them. The Khonmyaŋ explain the differences in life situation between themselves and the Chinese by the following story:

> The Lord Buddha, in one of his incarnations, came to a stream that was too wide for him to cross. Two men, a Chinese and a Thai, were standing on the bank. The Thai did not offer to help; but the Chinese pitched in and carried the Lord Buddha across the stream on his back. As a reward, the Lord Buddha proclaimed that from that time on the Chinese would be very rich and the Thai would have to sweat and labor in the fields.

The villagers are aware of linguistic and cultural differences between themselves and other kinds of people in or near the Chiengmai Valley. With an air of confident superiority, they often joke about how people from such-and-such places speak. Roaring with laughter, they mimic how the people of adjacent Lamphun Province pronounce certain words, like that for elephant. They are aware of the differences between themselves and the many kinds of tribal peoples who live in the mountains surrounding the Chiengmai Valley and who appear occasionally in the city market and sometimes come through the villages selling medicine. The Khonmyaŋ villagers feel free to exercise toward these tribal peoples the feeling of unbridled superiority which they cannot exercise toward the Chinese or the Central Thai. Their attitude toward the tribal peoples is not unlike the old American attitude toward the American Indians. The dances of the Meo, a local tribal people, are taught in village schools much as an Apache rain dance might be learned by a Boy Scout troop in the United States.

The Khonmyaŋ attitude toward the Central Thai is ambiguous and suffers from a real feeling of inferiority. The Central Thai represent progress, modernity, power, prestige, and wealth and hold the leading position in the Thai state; and villagers admire them as much as they resent them. Villagers who want to rise socially "take on airs" by beginning to speak Central Thai and to adopt Thai customs. Many of the Khonmyaŋ in Chiengmai city try to pass as Central Thai by feigning ignorance of their own language. And a wealthy landlord in a village near Chiangmai even changed his Khonmyaŋ name to a modern Thai name. This tendency can be seen in the names the village women give their children; the younger ones all have names of Central Thai origin.

The attraction that the Khonmyaŋ feel toward Central Thai culture is often blunted, however, by the hostility of the Central Thai themselves, who make fun of their northern cousins. It does not take a person from Chiengmai long to find that his "school Central Thai" is considered hilarious by people in Bangkok and that in any case his northern accent identifies him as a person from "up-country," little more than a foreigner. The Khonmyaŋ know that they are considered Thai rustics at best, and they are on the horns of a dilemma. If they admit the superiority of Central Thai culture and begin to adopt it, they admit their own inferiority. On the other hand, rejecting Central Thai identity and clinging to a Khonmyaŋ identity no longer has any future. There is a saying among the villagers that Khonmyaŋ who take on Central Thai airs "forget the rice paddies and the fields of the homeland." For better or for worse, more and more of the Khonmyaŋ are doing just that.

# 3    Village Social Groups

The social life of Chiangmai village is tightly and intricately structured. Over the long period of time that people have lived in Chiangmai, they have developed groups and institutions in the context of which they regulate their social intercourse and manage their affairs. In contrast to the descriptions that have been written of life in Bang Chan, the Thai peasants of Chiangmai navigate a well-charted social life. They operate in the context of a corporate village community which is divided into social strata, factions, kin groups, cooperative labor-exchange groups, and groups which rotate the responsibility for sending rice and food to the village monastery. In addition, there are clubs and associations and other cooperative activities in the village, including the all-important irrigation associations. In Chiangmai, social position is clear, family life and kinship relations are stable, role behavior is well-defined, and the people are permanently attached to their community.

## The Village Community

Chiangmai village is a distinct community, spatially separated from other villages in the countryside.[1] The people who reside in Chiangmai feel a special unity because of their common residence; they speak of "baan haw," "our village," and identify themselves as people of Chiangmai. Those who emigrate elsewhere, on a temporary or permanent basis, miss their village home, speak of it with nostalgia, and return frequently to maintain their social ties. Children who wrote essays for me on Chiangmai wrote of their village in highly emotional terms.

Village unity is enhanced by endogamous marriages. Over 79 percent of the men and 86 percent of the women marry within the village. This makes the village a special kind of kinship unit in which almost everyone is related by consanguineal and affinal ties of diverse kinds. Its people conceive of the village as a large, expanded kin unit in which all villagers, whether or not they recognize close relationship, address each other by appropriate kinship terms. The villagers are grandparents, parents, uncles, aunts, siblings, and children to one another, and appropriate behavior follows the terms of address. In addition, every villager is known by a nickname, which is used within the village community. The use of a nickname is a linguistic marker of membership in the village social group; the familiar name is rarely known or used by outsiders.

Village identity and loyalty is also expressed in relationships with people of other villages. When fights break out between young men over girls they are courting, the boys of Chiangmai village as a group often fight men of other villages. There are lasting enmities, originating in conflict over irrigation water, between Chiangmai and nearby communities which belong to the same irrigation system. Conflicts and hostilities between Chiangmai and other villages are expressed ritually once each year in a drumbeating contest. The villagers take their large drum, fashioned from a tree trunk, from its storage place in the temple pavilion, load it onto an oxcart, paint its face to look like a woman, and take it to Saraphi town, where they compete in drumbeating with other villages in Saraphi District. The loudest drum wins.

The people of Chiangmai characterize whole villages as either good or bad, and other people characterize Chiangmai village in the same way. Village identity is an important aspect of social identity in the countryside; and to say that a person is from Chiangmai is to say something important about him.

Chiangmai village is a corporate group in that it has an independent social identity and owns common property, and its people have organized themselves to make decisions for the village community as a whole.

## The Temple and
## the Monastery

"Wad Chiangmai," the village "Buddhist temple," is the symbol of village identity and the focus of village society.[2] Together with its associated pavilion, its monastery, and its library of sacred books, the temple is the center of village activity and the object of pride. The villagers want their temple to be a lovely one with a modernized pavilion that is well-maintained; they want it to be the symbol of a self-respecting village which has pride in itself. The people who live in Chiangmai form the temple congregation, and they attend the temple's important religious ceremonies. Conversely, persons who do not live in the village rarely attend the temple. Important members of the temple congregation—the members of the temple committee—are concurrently important social leaders of the community. The Chiangmai temple has reciprocal exchange relations with the temples of other villages in the surrounding countryside, as far north as the city of Fang on the Burmese border. In the ceremony that marks the end of the Buddhist period of abstinence—the period in the rainy season when the monks are confined to their monastery—people from other temples come to present robes and other goods to Chiangmai village monks and novices; at appropriate celebrations of the other temples, Chiangmai village sends a delegation to reciprocate. Exchanges with other communities are also made when they organize temple fairs to raise money to repair their temples, build roads, or perform other useful social acts.

As I interpret it, the temple (the symbol of village society) receives gifts of wealth and service from the villagers, who are rewarded by the religious merit which is thought to accrue to people who do socially useful things. Villagers who contribute food for the support of the abbot of the temple and his novices gain merit; people who contribute labor to clean or repair the temple or to rebuild it also gain merit. Religious merit is believed to determine one's fate in the next world; a couple who perform good deeds and behave in socially approved ways will accumulate the merit necessary for them and their dead parents to be born into a wealthier and higher-status family in the next life. Behavior in village society which is in accord with social ideals and which is valuable to the village advances one's status in that society. Social merit and religious merit are almost the same; a good man is a good Buddhist; high-status persons in village society are people who have lived correctly and performed socially useful acts in their previous existence. Religious merit awarded by the priests is also social prestige awarded by village society.

The temple is the social, political, and recreational center of village life. Villagers come to the temple compound to read the newspaper and to gossip. The temple is also the town hall; meetings held by the villagers to discuss or decide upon important matters take place in the temple or the pavilion. In the fall of 1971, when a political coup occurred in Bangkok, the village men called a meeting at the temple to discuss the event. Again, when the government offered to share the cost of installing electricity in the village in 1971, the men met to discuss the matter and to appoint committees to make the necessary arrangements. Meetings discussing a temple fair to raise money to rebuild the library were held at the temple. On important matters such as these, representatives of all village families who are interested come to participate in the deliberations, and the discussion is lively.

The village owns common property. Although the temple may be formally owned by the Buddhist monkhood and the school by the government, the villagers consider these buildings to be their responsibility. The temple, its pavilion and the surrounding courtyard, the library, the monastery, and the school are in fact the corporate property of the village as a group. Villagers contribute labor to the upkeep of these edifices, manage the property, and contribute sums to rebuild and refurnish them. In the same way, the irrigation canals which crisscross the village, the cremation ground at the south end of the village, and the village roads are all common property of the village community. Everyone uses them, and everyone helps maintain them. All citizens of the community must contribute labor to repair the public property when called upon to do so by the leaders of the village; this is one of the obligations of citizenship.

**The Temple
Committee and the
School Committee**

To manage the collective property and to make all other decisions on matters that concern the village, the villagers elect members to serve on various representative committees. The most important of these is the temple committee. The building of a new temple pavilion and the arrangements to hold a religious fair are examples of matters which the temple committee manages. When the new pavilion was built in 1972, the temple committee let out the construction bids, purchased the necessary building materials, and oversaw the construction itself.

In a similar way, the school is run by the school committee. The school committee is second in importance only to the temple committee because, next to the temple, the school is the most important village institution. It is also a symbol of the village and a focus for village solidarity. All village children attend school for about four years, or until they reach the age of fourteen, if they fail to graduate earlier. Within the informal age-grades of the school, friendships are established which last a lifetime. In the fall of 1972, just before I left the village, all the village men came together to clear the building site for the new school; it was a scene of great civic cooperation. The new school, built with the support of the Thai government in 1973, is a source of village pride.

## The Young
## People's Club

The unity of the village is also expressed by the Chiangmai young people's club. From about the age of fifteen until they marry, all the young people in Chiangmai village belong to a service and recreational association run by leaders elected by the young people themselves. The young people's club assists the villagers during all important ceremonial occasions. When a villager is married, the young people carry the tables and chairs kept in the temple for this purpose and set them up at the house of the bride, where the wedding is to be held. After the wedding feast, club members help the family clean up and return the furniture to the temple. At weddings, funerals, temple fairs, visits of important dignitaries, and any other occasion at which people gather, the young people's club manages a parking lot to care for the bicycles and motor scooters of the guests. During village fairs or other religious events or ceremonies, such as the formal opening of a new road, the young people's club helps prepare and serve food and refreshments to visiting dignitaries from the district office. At temple fairs, club members man the admission booth, do most of the work, and help keep order. Sometimes the Chiangmai club helps the youth of nearby villages on an exchange basis. Young people from the club go on joint pilgrimages, attend religious meetings at important temples, and send representatives to participate in special government youth programs.

In 1972, as part of the Accelerated Rural Development Program carried out in the village by the Thai government (see Moore 1974, p. 423), the youth club was given a more modern Central Thai name and divided into several subdivisions: handicrafts, homemaking, community singing, and sports. New leaders were elected under the direction of young members of the Thai "ʔAasaa Phadthanaa," the Thai "community development corps," who had been sent to the village from Bangkok to develop the community. The Thai government was attempting to utilize a traditional basis of village social organization for developmental purposes, and succeeded at least partly in doing so.

## The Village Dancers

Chiangmai village supports a dance company, made up of about a dozen young, unmarried village women. The Chiangmai temple purchased the traditional Chiengmai-style dance costumes for the girls and also furnishes the drums and gongs, played by expert village musicians who accompany the dancers. Practice sessions under the direction of older and more experienced women, who serve as choreographers, are held in the temple pavilion; in the evenings before a performance, the village throbs to the sounds of the slowly beaten gongs and drums.

The village dancers are the official hosts of the village and the temple. When another village sends a delegation to a Chiangmai village temple fair, or when visiting dignitaries come to the village for some official function, the Chiangmai dancers perform a welcoming dance at the entrance to the temple. The dancers also head the procession of Chiangmai villagers when they go to attend fairs and ceremonies at another village. The host villagers await the visitors, preceded by their own dance troupe; the visitors dance first and then the host dancers reply. Some villagers from north of Chiengmai, who came to Chiangmai village's temple celebration in 1972, performed a hill tribe dance and wore appropriate costumes. Sometimes there are intervillage dance contests in which the Chiangmai troupe participates. The villagers are genuinely pleased if their dancers win.

## The Funeral Society

Like most surrounding villages, Chiangmai has a funeral society. The Chiangmai village funeral society is a voluntary association to which almost every family in the village belongs. Its purpose is to give financial assistance to families who face the enormous expense of a funeral service and cremation. In Chiangmai the village as a whole comes together to console the bereaved family and bury their dead—another expression of village unity. Since member households receive more from the funeral society than the cost of the funeral, the association is also a kind of life insurance society.

Households join the Chiangmai funeral society by paying 20 baht each (about U.S. $1) to representatives of the Chiangmai committee which oversees the operation of the society. This initiation fee pays for the notebooks in which records are kept, and it also gives the committee members compensation. When a member of the association dies, every other household has to contribute 2 baht to the collector, who gives it to the head of the committee, who in turn gives it to the family of the deceased. The larger the funeral society, the more money the family receives in case of death.

The head of the Chiangmai funeral society is, traditionally, the head of Administrative Village One, one of the two administrative units into which Chiangmai village is divided. This officer keeps the membership books up-to-date and, together with a trustee committee, is responsible for collecting funds, for certifying deaths, and for dispensing funds to legitimate claimants. In return, he receives initiation fees, which he shares with the committee members, and he also gets his membership free of charge. The Chiangmai funeral society has members in other villages in the countryside surrounding Chiangmai. Chiangmai people who have married into these villages serve in them as the Chiangmai funeral society's representatives. They solicit new members and collect contributions from a village's members when a death occurs. These representatives do not have to pay the 2-baht contribution when a death occurs, and they are permitted to keep part of the initiation fees paid by new members they solicit.

In the same way, the funeral societies of surrounding villages operate in Chiangmai. They have a representative there who solicits members and collects dues. Village families frequently belong to several funeral societies in addition to the Chiangmai society. Thus some families receive sizable sums upon the death of one of their members.

## Divisions for Sending
## Food to the Temple

The Chiangmai village monastery houses the abbot of the temple, together with a dozen or so young village men, whom he instructs as novices in Buddhism and magic. Also housed in the monastery are the younger temple boys who serve the novices. As in all Thai communities, abbot, novices, and temple boys are supported through contributions from the laity. In most of Thailand, the monks and novices go out at dawn every day to receive offerings of food in the village or city streets. Those who give offerings to the monks and novices gain religious merit; part of this merit is transferred by the priests to deceased family members of the donors, absolving the dead of their sins and helping them to be reborn again.

Like many (but not all) surrounding villages, Chiangmai has organized its activities so that each household does not have to cook special food for the religious community every day of the year and the monks and novices do not have to go out into the village each morning to collect food. The villagers have divided the village into seven territorial units, which contain from twenty to forty households each (see map 3). People from the different sections take turns preparing and taking food to the temple each morning; on the first day women from Section I send food; on the second day those from Section II take food to the temple; and so on, in a never-ending cycle.

Every section has a leader, who is usually a woman from an established village family and who usually belongs to the dominant matrilineal kinship group inhabiting that particular part of the village. On the evening preceding the morning when it is her section's turn, the leader beats a gong loudly in her courtyard, reminding the women in her section to prepare food that evening to take to the temple the following morning.

Although some of these sections are made up mainly of the households of one matrilineal kin group, they are defined on the basis of common residence, not kinship. If new people move into the village, they join the section in which their house is located. If a family moves into another section of the village, they become members of the section where their new house is located.

## Temple Loan Fund

Still another example of how the villagers cooperate for the common good is the temple loan fund, established with the 2,500 baht that the two foreign anthropologists donated to help poor families buy schoolbooks and school uniforms for their children. The school committee lent this money out at interest to one of the village shopkeepers, who wished to purchase a television set to draw customers to her shop. The interest that she paid, part of it in advance, was used to buy books and uniforms but the capital was not touched, and the interest is used every year to help poor students.

If I had donated money to the Chinese villagers that I studied in Hong Kong (Potter 1968), I would have expected them to use it for a revolving credit fund, but I did not expect the Chiangmai villagers to do so because of previous reports about the inability of Thai villagers to cooperate. I was surprised when they organized the credit fund on their own. Apparently they are accustomed to taking funds donated to the temple and lending them out in this way.

## The Cooperative Ethic

"Cuaj kan," "cooperation," is the basic theme of social relationships within the village. It is the basic village ideology. "Everyone is alike in this village; we all help one another; we are all kinsmen," is the way village society is described to an outsider. In ideal terms, the Chiangmai people conceive of their village as a group of community-spirited citizens who are always ready to help each other for the good of the community, in a spirit completely lacking in self-interest. Like all idealized versions of social life, reality does not come very close to this; but the existence of such an ideology does affect behavior. Members of the village cooperate in feeding the monk and novices; in keeping up the temple, the pavilion, the cremation grounds, and the roads; they cooperate in cleaning and maintaining the irrigation system and sharing its precious water. And, at funerals, representatives from every village family come to help and to pay their respects. Cooperation is, in fact, the basis for the organized social life of the community. Such an ethic contrasts markedly with the picture of Thai villages as composed of free, undisciplined souls who follow their own hearts, and who are unable or unwilling to cooperate—even to put out a fire in the village temple (see Phillips 1969, p. 32). The ideological basis of Thai village social relationships is one of *cooperation*. Previous descriptions of Thai social relations within the village setting that ignore this cooperative ethic are, I believe, erroneous; at least they are not applicable to Chiangmai.

## Cooperative Labor-Exchange Groups

In Chiangmai, as in almost every other village in Thailand, many farm families carry out the most onerous tasks of rice agriculture—uprooting seedlings, transplanting, and harvesting—by exchanging labor with other farm households. These labor-exchange groups are activated for rice agriculture only, not for growing cash crops like garlic, peanuts, and soybeans. Each household has its own group of people who come to help it, and whom it goes to help. Each household participates in many different groups; the group that helps one family is slightly different in membership from the group that helps another. The various groups have overlapping memberships: household A may exchange labor with a group made up of households B, C, and D; whereas household D may exchange with another group made up of A, C, E, and F, and so on.

In the spring, at rice-planting time, the households of a neighborhood whose groups overlap a great deal stagger the sowing of their small seed plots so that the seedlings of each member household will be ready to transplant a few days apart. If all members of a labor-exchange group in a neighborhood were ready to transplant their seedlings at the same time, cooperation would be difficult because everyone would be busy on the same day in their own fields. Besides the staggering of the sowing, some additional flexibility is possible because the unit of cooperation is the household; since each household has a number of workers, it is possible for them to divide their labor and send different members to fulfill their obligations with different cooperating households on the same day. The same households cooperate with each other year after year.

When the fields have been plowed, harrowed, and weeded, word is passed on to the members of the group that the first household to transplant will do so on a certain day. Cooperating households then arrange to send the required number of helpers on the appointed day to help dig up the seedlings growing in the nursery bed, cut them to an even length, and transport them to the larger fields, where they are transplanted jointly by the group. The host household is responsible for furnishing a meal of raw chopped buffalo meat and rice wine for those who come to help them. On subsequent days the other households' fields are transplanted in turn. At harvest the same process is repeated as the labor-exchange groups go to the fields in large numbers to cut the rice, thresh it in large bamboo baskets, winnow it, and carry it back to the granary of the owners in the village.

Cooperative labor exchange allows the villagers to carry out the hardest work in rice agriculture quickly and cheerfully. It would be possible for many households to get along with just their own labor, but the work would be lonely and not nearly as much fun. In the fields, there is much camaraderie. Men tease younger men about their village sweethearts, sometimes until the younger men hit back at them in anger. Villagers tell ribald and bawdy stories about their fellows. Young, unmarried boys and girls take the opportunity to flirt with each other. Cooperative labor exchange turns a difficult task into a pleasant experience which is looked forward to with anticipation rather than dread.

The guiding principle of labor-exchange groups is reciprocity, or, as the villagers put it, "aw wan, tɔɔb wan" ("give a day and take a day"). A household must repay the number of labor days it receives from one of the households with whom it exchanges labor. The adult men who direct the work activities of their families keep careful mental records of these transactions. Male heads of village families can be heard in the early morning during the planting or harvesting season directing members of their families to go help such and such a family to whom labor is owed. One of the signs of adulthood occurs at the age of fifteen or sixteen when a young boy's or girl's labor is counted as a full adult day in the exchange system.

If a family is unable to fulfill its commitments on a certain day, its members are expected to offer to pay the rice equivalent of a day's wages or to hire someone to take their place. If a family fails to fulfill its labor-exchange obligations, other households with whom it exchanges labor will come to complain about it. If a family fails repeatedly, it will acquire a bad reputation, and no one will want to exchange with it. The ultimate sanction of village society for errant households is simply to refuse to cooperate with them. This is done but rarely. The only case I knew of in Chiangmai village is that of a man suspected of being a witch; no one cooperates with or has anything to do with him.

The size of their particular labor-exchange group is a matter of concern to village households. Villagers like to own large amounts of land and to have a large, extended matrilocal family with labor power that enables them to establish and maintain labor-exchange relations with many fellow villagers. A family is proud and its members' faces beam when forty people or more show up to help them with planting or harvesting. Such a large group of helpers establishes its status as a family which has achieved success in village society, and it gives its members a sense of well-being.

The size and nature of one's labor-exchange group is one of the most sensitive topics in the village, and villagers are loath to discuss the matter. The same households cooperate with each other year after year, but over a long period the composition and size of one's group may change if a family's fortune rises or falls. One establishes numerous ties with important families as one's status rises, and loses these ties if one's family declines in status. The ties are reaffirmed publicly each year when members of other households show up in one's fields at the start of transplanting. The fiction is maintained that no one knows exactly who will show up to help each year, so that no one loses face if some of last year's helpers fail to come. The ultimate social disaster for a villager would be if no one showed up to help his family and if fellow villagers told him that they

Village women bundle rice
seedlings for transporting
to larger fields.

A traditional village house.

A village woman washes clothes.

The village temple.

Villagers winnow rice
with fans at harvest.

Using a water buffalo,
a farmer harrows a field.

A village family.

A farmer gathers rice
straw after the harvest.

A cooperative labor-
exchange group trans-
plants rice.

An unmarried village
woman.

didn't need his help that year and turned him away from their fields. In such a situation the family would find itself with the same status as a village witch.

Only three-fourths of the village households participate in cooperative labor exchange. The poorest families, who neither own nor rent land, cannot participate. They join the work groups in the fields but as hired laborers who are paid in cash or in rice at harvest time, rather than as exchange partners. Poor village households make a living by plowing, planting, threshing, and carrying the rice of richer farmers. Each rich peasant has a number of dependent households attached to him as part of his village entourage (see Hanks 1966); he pays part of his rice to these households at harvest time, much as landowning castes give grain to lower laboring castes in India. A major difference is that in Chiangmai village dependent families can more easily switch allegiance if it suits them.

Some rich families do not participate in labor exchange because they no longer farm. Some rent out all their land and live off the rent; and some have given their farms to their children to manage. One of the wealthiest farmers in the village says that labor exchange is too much trouble and prefers instead to hire labor to help him on his farm.

Table 3 gives the distribution of cooperative labor-exchange groups in the village according to the size of groups. The 146 households in the village that participate in labor-exchange relationships reported that they cooperate with 1 to 25 other households: 64 households exchange labor with 1 to 5 other households; 50 exchange labor with 6 to 10 households; and 32 exchange with 11 or more.

Cooperative labor groups are not purely kinship groups, although they almost invariably include kin. The number of kinsmen in a villager's group and the proportion of kin to nonkin depend upon his life situation. If a man is poor, with little land to farm, his cooperative labor group will be small. If this same man's mother and father are both Chiangmai village people and if he himself married a Chiangmai village girl, his small labor-exchange group will be made up almost entirely of bilateral kinsmen, usually the families of his and his wife's sisters and brothers. Many of the smaller labor-exchange groups in Chiangmai village approximate this arrangement. If the man is poor and has married into his wife's family from another village, the relatives in his small labor-exchange group will be almost entirely the relatives of his wife. Wealthier farmers have larger reciprocal exchange groups which include neighbors, friends, and political allies in addition to close kin. Wealthier men tend to have wider-ranging ties, which include political allies of their own class as well as households who are dependent upon them.

**Table 3**                         Size of Labor-Exchange
                                    Groups in Chiangmai
                                    Village

| Size of Labor-Exchange Group, in Households | Number of Households with Labor-Exchange Groups this Size |
|:---:|:---:|
| 0* | 60 |
| 1 | 10 |
| 2 | 5 |
| 3 | 14 |
| 4 | 18 |
| 5 | 17 |
| 6 | 7 |
| 7 | 12 |
| 8 | 15 |
| 9 | 10 |
| 10 | 6 |
| 11 | 12 |
| 12 | 4 |
| 13 | 2 |
| 14 | 7 |
| 15 | 2 |
| 16 | 3 |
| 17 | 0 |
| 18 | 1 |
| 19 | 0 |
| 20 | 0 |
| 21 | 0 |
| 22 | 0 |
| 23 | 0 |
| 24 | 0 |
| 25 | 1 |
| | Total 206 |

*Families who do not participate.

No one villager's exchange partners are exactly the same as any other. However, households in the same village neighborhood tend to cooperate more with one another than they cooperate with more distant villagers. Neighborhoods also tend to correspond to important village factions and to center around a coalition of two or more powerful men and their entourages; labor-exchange groups thus tend to correspond to important political factions within the village.

The importance of reciprocal labor-exchange groups in Thai village social structure has not been recognized. Phillips (1965, p. 22) remarks that these reciprocal work groups are "transient," and Janlekha (1955, pp. 11–12) says that they are purely bilateral and involve no group responsibilities. In Chiangmai the reciprocal labor-exchange groups differ from household to household, but they are not organized at random or on a completely ego-centered basis. These groups, in Chiangmai village at least, are of a kind that is intermediate between a corporate group, like a Japanese village or a Chinese lineage segment, and a friendship group with no corporate characteristics but based upon dyadic ties alone. These are the kinds of relationships which Bott (1971) and Barnes (1972) call dense networks. On map 4, showing the reciprocal labor-exchange ties between all Chiangmai village households, clear clusterings are evident. These clusterings are not openly recognized by the villagers; they emerged only after months of tracing out the patterns of labor exchange.

In sum, Chiangmai village exchange groups are relatively permanent, and the membership changes very slowly over the generations; they are not momentary groups that are formed anew each year. They reflect other important social ties in the village. The members of the two separate administrative villages of Chiangmai (see map 4) share comparatively few labor-exchange relationships. Reciprocal labor-exchange groups, since they include one's most important connections in village society—kinsmen, friends and neighbors, and potential allies—include the same people upon whom one depends in the other important affairs of life. If a family wishes to build a new house, hold an ordination when a man enters the village monastery as a novice, stage a wrist-tying ceremony for a family member who is leaving the village, or hold a wedding, the members of his labor-exchange group will help him.

**Administrative
Divisions and Factions**

Although Chiangmai village is a social and religious unit, it is divided into Administrative Villages One and Two of a Saraphi rural commune (here-

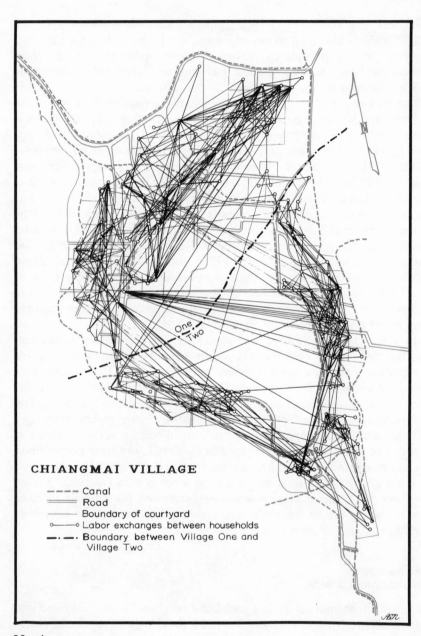

CHIANGMAI VILLAGE

----- Canal
══════ Road
────── Boundary of courtyard
o────o Labor exchanges between households
─·──·── Boundary between Village One and
        Village Two

**Map 4**

after referred to as Chiangmai One and Chiangmai Two). The dividing
line runs almost exactly through the center of the village, splitting it into
two halves almost equal in size (see map 3). Administrative Village Two
also includes a few households in an adjacent village which happen to lie
on the Chiangmai side of a major irrigation canal. These households really
belong to the natural community of the adjacent village and not to Chiangmai. Administrative Villages One and Two each have an elected headman
and assistant headman who are responsible to the Kamnan, the commune
head, and then to the district officer of Saraphi District. The headmen
transmit government policies to the villagers, oversee government activities,
maintain law and order, and help the powerful men of the temple committee and the school committee to run village affairs.

The government's administrative divisions divide the natural village of
Chiangmai in a somewhat arbitrary manner; but the divisions seem also
to correspond to a dual organization which is not uncommon in villages
in the Chiengmai Valley. Large villages reach a certain size, and then the
factionalism of village entourages and kinship groups tend to crystallize
into an opposition between the two village halves which oppose each other
on almost all issues and which channel most of the tensions and hatreds
in the village. Within the memory of living villagers, some of the neighboring villages have split into two and later established separate temples (see
Keyes 1975, p. 277, for a similar case in the northeast). Many of the villages of the Chiengmai Valley resemble amoebas in the process of division,
a process finally completed when a temple "nucleus" is established in the
new organism.

In Chiangmai the members of Administrative Villages One and Two
hate each other with a passion, gossip maliciously about the people and
leaders in the other half of the village, accuse them of stealing public funds,
and refuse to cooperate with people from the other half in village affairs
(at the same time accusing the others of refusing to cooperate). Tensions
in Chiangmai reached such intensity in 1972 that the abbot of the temple
(a man from Chiangmai One) publicly denounced over the temple loudspeaker system the headman of Chiangmai Two. We were told by members of one half of the village that people who lived in the other half had
leprosy and tuberculosis, that they were thieves, and that they stole food
from the temple and offerings from the monasteries.

One reason why tensions run so high between the two administrative
units is that the four most powerful and wealthy men of the village, the
traditional leaders, are evenly split, two in each administrative unit. Their

struggle for power and leadership in the village is often translated into conflict between Chiangmai One and Two. Also, the headman of Chiangmai Two, a modern-minded leader who sought to bring about progress in his village, in 1971–72 was ranged against the wealthier and more traditional villagers in Chiangmai One. His attempts to attract government programs to the village were opposed by the traditional leaders and were implemented in Two only, a situation that aroused even more jealousy. In 1972, the headman of Two talked the government into choosing Chiangmai Two as an Accelerated Development Village for the state of Chiengmai. The government sent Thai development workers to organize Two, a move that aroused such jealousy and opposition in One that the entire program failed and the Thai official in charge of the local commune development office had to leave his post. During 1972, the villagers from One refused to help repair the roads of Two and refused to participate in a religious ceremony held by the headman of Two to raise money to open a new road on his side of the village.

It is extraordinary that such an important dual division can be maintained within a natural village community that is bound together by the unifying sentiments and associations discussed in this chapter. Like many other human groups, the village is a unity when seen from the outside but is seriously divided internally.

# 4

# The Big People and
# the Little People

## Social Stratification

**The Importance of
Land Ownership**

In Chiangmai village a central fact of existence is land—the amount available, who owns and rents it, and what social organization and technology are used to exploit it. In Chiangmai, wealth, power, and social standing are not completely determined by the ownership of land, but it is still of major importance. All the powerful men of substance in Chiangmai village are also large landowners, with the exception of the village head of Chiangmai Two, whose money comes from small-scale entrepreneurial activities such as the buying and selling of lamjaj, garlic, and soybeans and whose power comes partly from the Thai government. I should point out, however, that the large landowners of Chiangmai are not very large landowners by any except the village standards; they are big fish in a very small pond.

The ownership of sizable amounts of land is important in many ways in village society. It gives a family power over the lives of their many fellow villagers who, lacking sufficient land of their own, depend for their livelihood on working as agricultural laborers or on renting land from those who have more than they can or need to work. If a tenant rents land from a landlord, he is dependent upon the landlord for the source of his livelihood. He will tend to support the landlord in disputes within the village and to form part of the landlord's entourage. In Chiangmai, it is possible for a landlord to take back his land if the tenant suddenly becomes "lazy" and "doesn't work the land well," so the tenant must be careful to ingratiate himself with his landlord.

The large landowners of the village also are often moneylenders because they are, with few exceptions, the only members of the village who have a surplus over and above the amount needed for their yearly expenses. Since land deeds are usually required as collateral for large loans, and since interest runs 36 percent per year, it is difficult for a debtor to pay off his loan. If the borrower defaults, the lender has the right to sell or buy the land at the going market price and recoup the amount loaned, plus the interest that has accrued. If one owns land and has money to lend to the many families in the village who live with little margin, one can acquire more. In Chiangmai village, if one owns land one can "breed" land.

The handful of men in the village who are large landowners form the pool from which most village leaders are selected. Many villagers are dependent upon these men, who are greatly admired and respected. According to Buddhist ideology, as propounded by the villagers, successful men in this life must have led meritorious lives in their previous existences to be born into such wealthy families. On a more down-to-earth level, the villagers prefer to have wealthy men as village leaders on the theory that, since they already have money, they are less likely to run off with funds entrusted to them. The members of the important and prestigious temple committee and the school committee (except for the village headmen, the abbot, and the head teacher) are the largest landowners in the village—a simple one-to-one relationship. Unlike in other Thai villages, the abbot (because of personality) and the headmaster (because he lives outside the village) are not important leaders, although they are accorded prestige. Until recently, the landowning families controlled the village completely. Now they are being challenged by the progressive head of Chiangmai Two, whose position of leadership is based upon contacts within the central government. If village politicians do not have the support of at least some of the powerful village families, however, they can accomplish little.

The ownership of land enables a family to enjoy a leisurely and comfortable life-style. Unlike most village families, who have to work from dawn to dusk every day of the year in the blazing hot sun of the fields, wealthy families do not go to the fields or, if they do, usually go only to supervise hired laborers who perform the agricultural tasks. Time can be whiled away sleeping on the bamboo-mat platforms in the shade underneath the house or sitting there talking with friends, neighbors, and fellow villagers. Wealthy families eat better, have better houses, clothes, and material goods (clocks, fans, motorcycles, and furniture), and are relieved from the constant and more immediate worries of making a living.

The life cycle of wealthy families also differs from that of poor ones. When a wealthy man gets older, he takes on the responsibilities of village leadership, if he is so inclined, and spends much of his time at the temple tending to public affairs. When a family has enough land to live off the rental of it or to farm it with hired labor, and when it has a large, comfortable, suitably appointed house, the family has achieved the pinnacle of success in traditional terms—all that can really be hoped for in this life within the village. The life-chances of one's children are also enhanced. The rule of equal inheritance by all children, regardless of sex, makes it difficult for a family to maintain its position over more than one generation. But the children of large landowning families have a chance to inherit larger amounts of land because the initial estate is larger and the "pie" can be cut into several still-sizable pieces. The ownership of land and orchards, as pointed out above, gives a family the capital to increase the size of its estate by loaning money, and also by purchasing rice mills. The four rice mills in the village are owned by large landowning families and their children. In a wealthy family, the estate is often larger when the family head reaches his later years than it was when the family cycle began, and more is available to give the children a good start in life.

Villagers are well aware of the advantages of having only one or two children. Some of the landowning families of the village, even before modern means of birth control were available, deliberately limited by abstinence the number of children they had. They were aware of the importance of land in establishing their social preeminence and did not want their estates liquidated when they died.

Of paramount importance at the present time is that the children of large landowners are the only village young people who have the means and are encouraged to continue on to higher education in the town of Saraphi and in Chiengmai city. The four young people now attending the teachers' training college in Chiengmai city all come from wealthy families. Better education increases the life-chances of these young people. For the girls of wealthy village families, education will assure high-status, salaried positions as schoolteachers, and it may enable them to meet and marry young men from the town with the education and knowledge to enhance a family's status and increase its estate. For the men, education leads to white-collar jobs in the government bureaucracy. These are the ideal jobs in the eyes of villagers because they are prestigious, they get them out of the village, and they have an assured monthly salaried income which offers wealth and security. The children of the larger landowning families of Chiangmai village are the only ones who are given the advanced education which enables them to compete in the changing society of modern Thailand.

Landed wealth and the possibility of a sizable inheritance make the sons and daughters of wealthy landed villagers more attractive marriage partners. A man likes to marry a wealthy girl who will be able to help him establish himself in the future or maintain his existing position in village society. A young woman wants to marry a man of status and wealth who can care for her and her children.

The landowners who are a step below the elite of the village (and whom I will call "rich peasants" because they own and work enough land to make a good living and rent out surplus land to others) also benefit from land ownership because they are able to attract hardworking and ambitious men to marry their daughters and help them on the farm for a few years before they set up their own households. It is easier to keep one's daughters and even one's sons in the same village if one has enough land to bind the children to the family. If one's daughters and sons remain in the village, one can enjoy a secure old age. If one is poor or without land, one's daughter may have to move out of the village and go to live with her parents-in-law, or at best set up a new household apart from the compound of her parents.

The ownership of some land or, at least, the control of some land through renting is a prerequisite for full citizenship in village society. Only people with land to farm can participate in cooperative labor-exchange groups with their neighbors, friends, and kinsmen. The ties cemented through labor exchange in the planting and harvesting of rice assure a family aid in other endeavors such as building a new house. When there is a life crisis in the family, such as marriage, a birth, an ordination into the wad, a sickness, or a funeral, one can be sure that other families will come to help.

Only people who control land go with their fellow village citizens to build the weirs across the Mɛɛ Ping River in the dry season to back up water for their common irrigation canals. Landless men who do not even rent land can participate in such activities only as hirelings of a landowner. The same is true of many other occasions during the year, as when landowners are called upon to send a member of the family to cut the grass in the canals or to clear a small canal with farmers whose fields are close by. All this is labor, to be sure, but participation in such activities gives a feeling of comradeship with one's peers. Those who cannot participate are really not full citizens of the community.

Without control over land through ownership or renting, the granary full of glutinous rice, which assures the family of a food supply until the next harvest and which is considered the minimum standard of security by village families, is out of reach. Lacking this, families have to make arrangements to help plow the rice fields of landowning families so that at harvest time they can go to the landowner's fields and be given a share of the harvest, which will help feed the family during the coming year. Helping in rice agriculture does not earn enough rice for a poor family. In addition, a poor man must hire out to dig the irrigation ditches or the garlic fields of the landowners and mound up the furrows for the planting of peanuts. For this he is paid 10 or 20 baht a day (50 cents to $1 in U.S. money), if he is lucky. This work is not available except during the cash-crop planting season in the winter, and it is still not enough to support a family. Family members have to hire themselves out throughout the year to secure additional income. The women and girls of poor families plant rice and peanuts and garlic. They also hire out to help pull the garlic and peanuts and prepare the soybeans for sale in the market. The men of poor families hire out to cut and thresh the rice of landowning families, and the women and girls help transport it on carrying poles to the landowner's granary. In addition, in the slack season of agriculture, a poor man must hire out as a sawyer of wood, a construction laborer in the town, or a housebuilder or music player in the countryside.

If one does not own or rent land to grow the family's rice, one must buy it in the market. The villagers consider this to be shameful because it symbolizes (or once did) the poverty of a family.

If a man owns no land and is poor, he does not speak out in village councils and is not considered of much account. His lowly position in this life is explained by bad deeds in his former life and (more often) by lack of hard work in this one; and in a sense his poverty is considered his just due. The children of landless families are not sought after as marriage partners by the better village families. The sons of poor families often leave the village to marry into the families of their wives. Such a man lives in a position completely subject to the authority of his wife's father and her family. With no inheritance, the daughters of poor families are not able to attract able young men to come live with the family. No young man in his right mind wants to marry into a poor family, where he will have to support the parents and younger siblings of his wife.

For the landless or those with insufficient land, life is a constant struggle without even the security of an assured food supply. Such families have no reserves to meet crises; they live on the very margin of existence. It is not uncommon for men who were formerly poor to accumulate land and improve their position in the village, but it requires a lifetime of diligent labor and scrimping to save enough money to buy land. Money is difficult to come by in the village, and the climb up from landlessness to respectability is a long and hard one. Still, most poor families in the village spend most of their lives trying; and enough of them succeed to give heart to the rest.

## The Distribution of
## Land Ownership

Given the overwhelming importance of land ownership in village society, the central fact of village life is that there is insufficient land, that it is unevenly distributed, and that many families are landless or own very little land. In this society the stark insufficiency of land is more important than its uneven distribution, although, as we will see below, that is also a problem.

The 206 households of the village own a total of 739 tax raj (1 tax raj = .40 acre) of land (see table 4), or 291 acres. The modal landholding was "0" tax raj; the median fell in the 2–2.9 tax raj range (approximately 1 acre); and the mean average holding was 3.62 tax raj (1.4 acres) per household.

The salient facts about village land ownership can be summarized in a brief statistical litany: 32.5 percent, or one out of every three families, owns no land at all; almost 55 percent of the families own less than 2.9 tax raj, a little over one acre; and about 71 percent own less than 5 tax raj, or about 2 acres of land.

This last figure is significant because the average village family requires about 5 tax raj of multicropped fields to make a living by village standards. In human terms this stark statistic means that 71 percent of village families do not own enough land to provide them with an average living by village standards.

Many more families than indicated by land ownership figures, of course, manage to make a living by renting land and by engaging in supplementary

**Table 4**                    The Distribution of
                               Land Ownership in
                               Chiangmai Village

| Amount of Land Owned, in Tax Raj* | Number of Households Who Own This Amount | Percentage of Households in Chiangmai |
|---|---|---|
| 0 | 67 | 32.5 |
| 0–0.9 | 1 | .5 |
| 1–1.9 | 19 | 8.3 |
| 2–2.9 | 28 | 13.6 |
| 3–3.9 | 20 | 9.7 |
| 4–4.9 | 13 | 6.3 |
| 5–5.9 | 14 | 6.8 |
| 6–6.9 | 9 | 4.4 |
| 7–7.9 | 4 | 1.9 |
| 8–8.9 | 5 | 2.4 |
| 9–9.9 | 3 | 1.5 |
| 10–10.9 | 3 | 1.5 |
| 11–11.9 | 5 | 2.4 |
| 12–12.9 | 4 | 1.9 |
| 13–13.9 | 2 | 1.0 |
| 14–14.9 | 1 | .5 |
| 15–15.9 | 0 | 0.0 |
| 16–16.9 | 2 | 1.0 |
| 17–17.9 | 1 | .5 |
| 18–18.9 | 1 | .5 |
| 19–19.9 | 0 | 0.0 |
| 20–24.9 | 3 | 1.5 |
| 25–29.9 | 1 | .5 |
| Totals | 206 | 99.2 |

*1 tax raj = .40 acre.
1 acre = 2.5 tax raj.

income-producing activities. Tenant farmers must work much harder to make a living because half the income from the rented land goes to the landlord. Thus, if a village family can make a suitable living farming 5 tax raj of their own land, the same family would need to farm 10 tax raj of rented land.

A breakdown of village households on the basis of the size of farm worked is indicated in table 5. Whereas 67 village families *own* no land, only 39 *farm* no land; 28 of the landless families rent all their farms from fellow villagers or from persons in neighboring villages. In a great many cases landless families are able to rent only a fraction of a tax raj to grow a small cash crop of peanuts, soybeans, or garlic in the winter after the

**Table 5**　　　　　　　The Distribution of
　　　　　　　　　　　　Farm Size in
　　　　　　　　　　　　Chiangmai Village

| Size of Farm, in Tax Raj | Number of Families Whose Farm is This Size | Percentage of Families in Chiangmai |
|---|---|---|
| 0 | 39 | 18.9 |
| 0–0.9 | 7 | 3.9 |
| 1–1.9 | 10 | 4.8 |
| 2–2.9 | 20 | 9.7 |
| 3–3.9 | 19 | 9.7 |
| 4–4.9 | 25 | 12.1 |
| 5–5.9 | 18 | 8.7 |
| 6–6.9 | 11 | 5.3 |
| 7–7.9 | 13 | 6.3 |
| 8–8.9 | 17 | 8.3 |
| 9–9.9 | 3 | 1.5 |
| 10–10.9 | 11 | 5.3 |
| 11–11.9 | 3 | 1.5 |
| 12–12.9 | 3 | 1.5 |
| 13–13.9 | 1 | .5 |
| 14–14.9 | 1 | .5 |
| 15–15.9 | 1 | .5 |
| 16–16.9 | 2 | 1.0 |
| 17–17.9 | 1 | .5 |
| 18–18.9 | 0 | 0.0 |
| 19–19.9 | 1 | .5 |
| 20–over | 0 | 0.0 |
| Totals | 206 | 101.0 |

rice harvest. The shortage of land makes it difficult if not impossible to rent new land on a yearly basis. Much of the land rented in these minute quantities is rented from one's close relatives or family. Land is in such short supply that most of the families who own land work it themselves.

**Village Social and Economic Levels**

If the families of Chiangmai village are classified according to their social and economic status, they can be categorized as follows. Landlord families are defined as those who usually do not work land themselves but own enough land so that they can be supported by land rent and associated activities like the operation of rice mills, moneylending, and fruit-growing.

Rich peasants are defined as those families who own more land than the average and who may rent out some of their land while farming the rest; they are much better off than most of the families in the village, but they work in the fields and do not own as much property as the landlords. Middle peasants are those farm families who own enough land to be fairly self-sufficient and who are able to support themselves from the land alone. Poor peasants are those who do not own or rent enough land to support themselves at a minimally accepted level in the village. They *have* to supplement their farm income with agricultural or nonagricultural labor. Landless laborers, as the name implies, are those village families who neither own nor rent land and who make a living working for landowning families of the village or working in jobs outside the village.

Some of the village families—sons and daughters of landowners who help their parents farm and who eat from their granary, and aged widows and others—are difficult to classify in this scheme. There are about twelve families in the village who work full-time in nonagricultural occupations. Thus the terms are approximate only, and all village families do not fit neatly into my categories. Also, these terms as used here do not necessarily have all the connotations associated with them when they are used in political polemics. In particular, the "landlords" of Chiangmai village are not hated figures, as they are in many societies; they are in reality landlords only on a relative scale and a Lilliputian stage. In table 6 I have indicated the amount of land which I used to define each category. Since the rent paid for rice fields in Chiangmai village is half the crop, I counted 2 rented tax raj as 1 owned tax raj in figuring economic status. The figures in table 6, therefore, do not correspond with the figures on farm size in tables 4 and 5. Keeping these strictures in mind, the families of Chiangmai

**Table 6**

A Classification of
Chiangmai Village
Households by
Socioeconomic Status

| Status | Tax Raj Owned Equivalence | Number of Households |
|---|---|---|
| Landlords | Over 15 | 9 |
| Rich peasants | 10–14.9 | 16 |
| Middle peasants | 4– 9.9 | 71 |
| Poor peasants | 1– 3.9 | 71 |
| Landless laborers | 0– 0.9 | 39 |
| | Totals | 206 |

village can be classified to give some indication of their social and economic standing within village society (see table 6). Let us now look at individuals who exemplify each of these categories.

Pɔɔ Nɔɔj Kɛɛw,
a Landlord

Of the Chiangmai landlord class, there is no doubt that Pɔɔ Nɔɔj Kɛɛw is paramount in village society ("Pɔɔ" means father or adult man of middle age or beyond who has children; and "Nɔɔj" signifies that he is a former novice). He is sometimes called Caw Nɔɔj Kɛɛw, the term "Caw" indicating a connection with the former royal family in Chiengmai. It is questionable whether Pɔɔ Kɛɛw is of aristocratic lineage, but the important thing is that the villagers and he himself believe that he is and act accordingly.

Pɔɔ Kɛɛw is an impressive figure, who at the grand age of seventy-two looks and acts patrician and whose presence frightens village children. Even the twenty-year-old daughter of the powerful and progressive village head of Chiangmai Two stands in awe of him. Now in semiretirement, Pɔɔ Kɛɛw lives with his wife, Mɛɛ Saa ("Mɛɛ" means mother or married woman with children who is middle-aged or older), and one of his two granddaughters, at the north end of the village in a large and impressive semimodern teak house set back in one of the most beautiful gardens in the village. Each July his lamjaj trees bear fruit worth a small fortune by village standards. Pɔɔ Kɛɛw is now slowing with age and spends the heat of the day asleep on the cool and shaded mat-covered platform underneath his house, surrounded by the multicolored shrubs and plants of his carefully tended garden. He was the headman of Chiangmai One for eighteen years but has long since retired from that post to take up a role as the elder statesman of the village, leaving the active post of village headman to a younger man who, not by accident, lives next to Pɔɔ Nɔɔj Kɛɛw. Pɔɔ Kɛɛw still plays a most important role in village affairs as a member of both the all-important temple committee and the school committee. Since he is the most respected man in the village, he is entrusted with the position of treasurer of the temple committee. In effect, Pɔɔ Kɛɛw keeps and spends the village's money and makes sure, to the best of his ability, that it is spent properly.

Pɔɔ Kɛɛw is the peacemaker and compromiser of the village. Although almost every other public figure in the village is the subject of malicious gossip and even public accusations against his honesty, not once did I hear Pɔɔ Kɛɛw's integrity questioned. He is held in great esteem—even in awe—by most of the villagers, who are a bit afraid of him. Pɔɔ Kɛɛw is as old as Methuselah, as rich as Croesus, and on the village scene he could be as powerful as Caesar if he really sought to exert his will.

Pɔɔ Kɛɛw embodies all the qualities that make a man a village leader. He has character and integrity; he is a religious man who served as a novice in the temple; and, most important, he is the head of an extremely rich family that owns land, rice fields, and orchards.

Pɔɔ Kɛɛw retains the ownership and management of 18 tax raj of land, which he rents out as follows: 10 tax raj are rented to a fellow villager from whom he receives 300 thaŋ of rice per year as rent, plus a cash rent from the man for planting peanuts and soybeans on some of the rice fields after he harvests the rice. Four raj Pɔɔ Kɛɛw rents to his older brother's son, from whom he receives 147 thaŋ of rice plus a share of the peanuts which his nephew grows. And 4 raj he rents to a distant relative of his wife, from whom he receives 96 thaŋ of rice per year, plus cash rent.

In addition to this sizable income in rice, most of which is sold for cash, Pɔɔ Kɛɛw owns an orchard of twenty-one large and excellent lamjaj trees which yield fruit worth 6,000 or 7,000 baht per year. Since 1 thaŋ of glutinous rice sells for about 7 baht in average years, the income from his lamjaj is equivalent to that derived from 1,000 thaŋ of rice, the average yield of 20 tax raj.

Mɛɛ Saa, his wife, adds to the family coffers (although they hardly need it!) by selling produce in the local markets, of which there are several within walking or bicycling distance of Chiangmai. She specializes in buying at one market and selling at another where prices are higher. Her main stock in trade is the fruit and banana leaves (used as wrapping material in Thai markets) of her daughter. Market activities also contribute to Mɛɛ Saa's real calling as the village gossip; she always knows and tells everything of interest in the village.

Another important activity of Pɔɔ Kɛɛw, it is said, is moneylending. He lends money to families who live on a small margin and need cash to make ends meet. He also sometimes lends money to villagers who have misused public funds, so that they can save their reputations. In all cases, Pɔɔ Kɛɛw is fair and is much respected for activities which also yield a handsome profit.

All this still does not complete the inventory of Pɔɔ Kɛɛw's wealth. In the middle of the village, west of the temple, in an enormous orchard, lives Pɔɔ Kɛɛw's only daughter, Pii Kham, with her husband and one of her two daughters; the two daughters take turns staying with their grandparents. Pii Kham's husband is a teacher in the local school and a rider of one of the finest motorcycles in the village. Both of Pɔɔ Kɛɛw's granddaughters, young women of about twenty, are now studying in the teachers' college in Chiengmai city. Formerly they commuted daily in one of the local truck-taxis, but now Pɔɔ Kɛɛw rents a house near the college, where the girls and their grandmother stay. This arrangement allows them more time to study and gives their grandmother a chance to see the sights of the city. The three come home on the weekends. One girl stays with her parents, and the other always stays with her grandparents. It is the custom in the village always to have a young girl in the house, if possible, to care for an older couple—to get up at dawn to cook, draw water, wash clothes, and sweep the courtyard.

Pii Kham, "Older Sister Kham," as she is called even by villagers older than she because of her position in village society, owns only 3 raj of land, given to her by Pɔɔ Kɛɛw and Mɛɛ Saa, and rented out to a village man. But she also owns an enormous orchard of eighty productive lamjaj trees, fifty coconut palms, and forty banana trees. The income from the lamjaj trees alone are enough to make the family rich. In addition, Pii Kham operates the family rice mill, given to her by her father, from which she gets a sizable income; and her husband receives a government salary from his position as teacher in the Chiangmai village school.

Pii Kham and her husband are, or will be after they inherit the remainder of Pɔɔ Kɛɛw's property, by far the wealthiest couple in the village. Since Pii Kham is an only child, the property will not be divided during her generation. Her two daughters will still be the wealthiest people in the village in their generation if the family's fortunes continue to rise. Her husband will become executive head of the richest estate in the village and, having high status as a teacher, will have a capital position in village society. Even now, he entertains friends, some from the Saraphi district office, several times a week at his house with "cin laab," the "raw buffalo meat" that is the delicacy of northern men, and whiskey. This expenditure would be unheard of by any other village family. The daughters of the family have been carefully brought up to be shy and soft-spoken young women. They speak Central Thai whenever possible, to show that they are really above the social level of this village.

The family of Pɔɔ Kɛɛw, at the pinnacle of village society, gives some insight into the human dimensions of social stratification in the village from the highest viewpoint. The other landlords in the village are similar but have less status and less wealth. There are three other traditional landlords who are near peers of Pɔɔ Kɛɛw and who serve with him on the temple committee and the school committee.

## Pɔɔ Luaŋ Taa,
## a Village Headman

Pɔɔ Luaŋ Taa, literally "Big Father Taa," whose title signifies that he is the village headman of Chiangmai Two, is the head of a family whose prominence illustrates a different aspect of social stratification in village society. Pɔɔ Luaŋ Taa's family owns but 6 tax raj of land, which, by the criteria used here (see table 6), would make them lower-middle peasants. In reality, the family is about equal in social standing to some of the village landlords, and just below Pɔɔ Nɔɔj Kɛɛw. Pɔɔ Luaŋ Taa's social position is based upon different status determinants: his power base is the Thai government, outside the village; and his wealth is based upon his role as a buyer and seller of agricultural produce.

Pɔɔ Luaŋ Taa is a powerfully built man, an ex-boxer who at forty-four years of age is tending toward portliness. He can still, however, fell a man with one blow and carry out his duties as peace officer much better than most village headmen. His skill got him into trouble several years ago when he hit a drunken man who was causing a disturbance in the village and seriously injured him. He had to sell some land to pay the money necessary to placate the man's family. This episode certainly did not enhance his public image in village society, especially among his enemies.

Pɔɔ Luaŋ Taa is a modern and progressive-minded man, who is without doubt one of the best village leaders in all of Thailand. He has applied himself to bringing about progress in the village, especially in recent years when the Thai government has also set this as a primary goal. He genuinely believes in the idea of progress, but he has been clever in using the village progress program to improve his own position. He was so anxious to know what was modern and new that he sent his daughter to work for foreign anthropologists to learn their ways. Not unexpectedly, his activities have met with determined resistance from many of the traditional leaders of the village, who say they favor progress but who are still a little confused with the new things going on in the village and are afraid that their own position might somehow be challenged. They are dizzy with the speed and sometimes angry at the manner in which Pɔɔ Luaŋ Taa has gone about his task.

Pɔɔ Luaŋ Taa was clever and opportunistic enough to see which way the political winds were blowing and has, unlike most village leaders in the district, actively sought to attract government programs like Rural Development, Accelerated Rural Revelopment, and the Thai equivalent of the American Peace Corps. He has been successful beyond belief. For five years Chaingmai village has been a "Muubaan Phadthanaa," a "progressive village," with new roads and bridges and other programs launched by the Rural Development Program. Chiangmai Two was chosen as a pilot village for the Accelerated Rural Development Program in Saraphi District, largely because of the enthusiasm of Pɔɔ Luaŋ Taa, who impressed the government people in charge of the program with his leadership. Furthermore, in November 1972, along with the launching of the Accelerated Rural Development Program in the village, four members of the new and still very small Thai "ʔAasaa Phadthanaa" ("Progress Corps"), modeled on the American Peace Corps, came to live in the village to help with the program of Accelerated Rural Development (see Moore 1974, pp. 176–77). The volunteers were allowed to live in Chiangmai Two in the small house vacated by the foreign anthropologists.

Chiangmai was a village chosen to bear the full brunt of the government's efforts to transform rural Thai society by instituting better cooperation among the villagers, fostering leadership, teaching group sports and singing, and improving the livelihood of the young people by developing new occupations such as weaving rugs, sewing garments, and making cigarette lighters. The program was in full swing by mid-September of 1972, with busloads of rural people and their leaders arriving in Chiangmai from all over the country to observe the village's accomplishments. The villagers were hard-pressed to weave enough rugs and make enough cigarette lighters to have on display. The program ran into some initial snags because of the local government functionary's lack of knowledge about the conflict between Chiangmai One and Two, which caused an uproar until Chiangmai One was also included in the program; and because of a lack of tact in Pɔɔ Luaŋ Taa's leadership. But the workers immediately regrouped and went ahead again. Pɔɔ Luaŋ Taa was in danger of running too far ahead of the villagers, but he always has managed to survive such crises and probably will continue to do so.

Pɔɔ Luaŋ Taa lives with his wife, Mɛɛ Luaŋ Kɛɛw, his two daughters, Saaj and Nop, and his son, Maa, in a new, modern teak house in the southeastern part of the village. Like the other wealthier villagers, he has fluorescent lights in his house, wooden furniture, and glass cabinets with family photographs. The underneath part of the house is cemented to form a patiolike area that is spacious enough to entertain a large party and still have room for an orchestra of traditional type and dancing. There is also a fenced-in area underneath the house which serves as a garage for the Honda motorcycle. Off the patio is a newly built pastel-colored building which serves as an office for Pɔɔ Luaŋ Taa and as an occasional shed in which to store garlic until the price rises.

Mɛɛ Luaŋ Kɛɛw is an attractive, plump woman who, like all members of Pɔɔ Luaŋ Taa's family, has a warm and engaging smile. She sells "beverages" at her house at night to increase the income of the family, and she is a strong and active woman who assists her husband in most of his activities.

Her mother, ʔUj Pan ("ʔUj" means "grandparent") lives with them— or rather they live with ʔUj Pan, in approved Khonmyaŋ fashion, in which one of the daughters (usually the youngest) stays at home and her husband comes in to reside with his wife's family. ʔUj Pan is a sprightly lady of seventy who always has a twinkle in her eye. She gave birth to a total of seven children in her lifetime, but only four of them are still alive.

ʔUj Pan and her husband owned about 8 tax raj and many lamjaj trees. After her husband's death she divided the property among her two daughters and two sons, three of whom had the misfortune to have enormous families and thus started out in life poor. Dividing her estate, she hedged her bets by keeping ownership of 1½ tax raj of land, which she now rents to her other son, the poorest of her children, for the small amount of ten thaŋ of rice per year. Her other needs are cared for by Mɛɛ Luaŋ Kɛɛw, her youngest child. Pɔɔ Luaŋ Taa underwent a vasectomy some time ago to limit his family to a size that he could take care of. Perhaps he learned a lesson from the experience of his wife's older siblings, whose many children have kept them impoverished.

Pɔɔ Luaŋ Taa's son, Maa, known as ʔAaj Maa (Older Brother Maa), is a handsome and engaging young man of twenty-two, who farms the family's fields while his father is busy carrying out his official duties and buying and selling to make a living to supplement his 200 baht per month

salary as village head. He is a popular "baaw," as young unmarried men
of the village are called, and many a local "saaw," young unmarried girl,
of Chiangmai and nearby villages would like to marry him.

Saaj, nineteen, the older daughter, is short and plump and at present is
concerned about catching a husband, as are all village girls of her age.
Saaj believes her father to be the greatest man in the world, and a young
man will have a hard time winning her away from him. She is not sure
that her father loves her as much as he loves her younger sister, or that
her mother loves her as much as she does her brother. Saaj was chosen
in July 1972 by the Progress Department of the provincial government of
Chiengmai to go at state expense to study dressmaking and designing at a
well-known boarding school for women in Bangkok, whose owner had
studied in Paris. This was part of the Accelerated Rural Development
Program in the village. When Saaj returns after six months she is to teach
the other young women in the village to sew in order to pay the state
back for her expensive six-month course.

Going to Bangkok to learn to sew was a traumatic experience for Saaj.
She wanted to obey her father, who got her the appointment and whose
idea it was, and she liked the prestige it gave her among the girls in the
village, but she didn't relish the thought of Bangkok, which she had visited
only once before. Also, she was afraid she would lose her "fɛɛn," or "boyfriend," from a nearby village to some other girl. The latter fears were not
unfounded.

The government managed to make Saaj's trip from the village to the
Bangkok school a misery. Her parents took her to Lamphun, where a
government woman was supposed to meet her and take her and another
girl to Bangkok on the train. No one was there to meet her, and after
waiting for three hours she took the bus by herself to Bangkok. She arrived late in the evening, and the school did not want to let her in, since
they had not been told by the government that she was coming. Finally,
they relented and let her stay, and eventually everything was straightened
out.

In the days that followed, Saaj learned some important facts about Thai
society that she had not really known before. One was that she was from
"up-country" and was considered almost a foreigner by the people around
Bangkok. She spoke a funny foreign language, and her attempts to use
her school Central Thai were thought hilarious. To avoid ridicule, she
learned to keep her mouth shut and not say anything. She also found out
that *all* expenses were not paid by the government. She had to buy all the

expensive material on which she learned to sew, and even had to pay a fourth of a baht for every glass of water she drank. She soon had to send for money from home. After one week in the school she wanted to go home and continue sewing straw hats on her sewing machine, as she had done before. She stuck it out mainly because she was ashamed to admit defeat and to humiliate her father by returning home with nothing. After a few months she returned to the village, told all the village girls with a knowing glance what sophisticated Bangkok was like, and began teaching them to make dresses.

Nop, eighteen, Saaj's younger sister, is quiet and shy and soft-spoken, as a proper young Thai girl should be; in this she is similar to the older granddaughter of Pɔɔ Nɔɔj Kɛɛw. Nop, who can speak Central Thai and some English, attends the teacher's training college in Chiengmai city. She is her father's favorite, according to Saaj, and she is the family's hope of rising in the wider society of Chiengmai Province. They hope she will be able to marry some nice young man from a city family who has a prestigious and well-paying job in a government office.

Pɔɔ Luaŋ Taa himself is from a village which is across the wide expanse of rice fields from Chiangmai. A small trail, suitable for bicycles and motorcycles, now connects the two villages, and Pɔɔ Luaŋ Taa frequently buzzes over to see his friends and relatives there. Several other men living in his part of Chiangmai village have married in from the same village, forming a small colony and all supporting Pɔɔ Luaŋ Taa strongly. His enemies in the village (mainly in Chiangmai One) use this fact against him, saying that after all he is really not a Chiangmai village person, as all important leaders in the village should be. When Pɔɔ Luaŋ Taa was a young man courting at Mɛɛ Luaŋ Kɛɛw's house, her parents knew he came from an impoverished family. But since Mɛɛ Luaŋ Kɛɛw fell in love with him and since he was likable and hardworking, her parents reluctantly agreed to the marriage. After marriage he lived with his wife's parents and helped work their fields like any good son-in-law of Chiangmai village. To obtain money of his own he worked as an agricultural laborer, digging ditches, cutting rice, building houses, and he soon got a reputation for hard work. He accumulated a little money to buy more land for his family and to start buying and selling on a small scale. His family's fortunes began to improve, although slowly.

Since he was an ex-boxer and had a likable personality, the Chiangmai Two headman at that time, who was also the kamnan, "the chief official in the commune," chose him as his assistant. When the kamnan retired he recommended that Pɔɔ Luaŋ Taa succeed him as village headman of Chiangmai Two, and his wishes were respected, giving Pɔɔ Luaŋ Taa's fortunes and his social position a boost.

Pɔɔ Luaŋ Taa was an active and efficient village headman who soon became well known all over Saraphi District and its environs. With contacts from his official position, and with a government salary that freed him from working in the fields, his buying-and-selling business became very profitable and his family became wealthier. Soon he was able to buy more land, build a new house, and eventually buy a new Honda motorcycle when they became popular in the village. (Pɔɔ Nɔɔj Kɛɛw's son-in-law was the first man in the village to buy a motorcycle, and Pɔɔ Luaŋ Taa bought his soon after that.) He began to buy crops of garlic and quantities of lamjajs, acting as an agent for the Chinese middlemen in Saraphi and Chiengmai city, who paid him a commission and then shipped the produce to Chinese wholesalers in Bangkok. Pɔɔ Luaŋ Taa's business was improved by a patron-client relationship that he established with a rich Chinese from Chiengmai city who is well known in the surrounding countryside. This man financed Pɔɔ Luaŋ Taa's activities in return for a cut of his profit. Soon Pɔɔ Luaŋ Taa was buying large crops of garlic, which he kept until the price rose late in the season, when the supply of garlic had run low, and speculating in futures of lamjajs from large orchards over several years. Pɔɔ Luaŋ Taa's present financial well-being comes from this source.

Pɔɔ Luaŋ Taa is a capable village headman who is dedicated to the idea of progress (as he understands it) and to making his village, Chiangmai Two, the most modern in all of Thailand. He is also a Khonmyaŋ entrepreneur on a larger scale than the traditional hawker of handicraft goods and buyer and seller of chickens and water buffaloes (see Moerman [1975], who points out that Northern Thai men do participate in commerce). Usually these higher positions are held by Chinese, and it is still problematical if Pɔɔ Luaŋ Taa will ever be able to become a large merchant with his own direct contact to Bangkok. Chinese merchants are certain to oppose any such attempt. His leadership in the village is based on the force of his personality, his ability to lead men, and most importantly upon the backing of the Thai government, which will support leaders capable of carrying out its modernizing programs in the villages. His position in village society is based upon new criteria and not upon values like landed wealth, a religious education in the temple, and an ability to compromise. Pɔɔ Luaŋ Taa is a modern-minded man in an extremely traditional and conservative setting.

Pɔɔ Tan and Mɛɛ Tii,
Rich Peasants

The family of Pɔɔ Tan illustrates the level of living of rich peasants in the
village. His is a prosperous family which now owns some 13 tax raj of
land to the north of the village and rents 3 tax raj from a man who lives
in a neighboring village, making the family's farm the equivalent of 14½
tax raj of owned land (the 3 rented raj being counted as 1½ owned raj).
This puts the family near the upper limit of the 10–14.9 tax raj class, which
we have defined as rich peasant status.

Pɔɔ Tan is a thin and sinewy man of fifty-six, who is still strong and
works harder than most young men of the village. Since he married twice
and his second family is still young, he has to work in the fields at an age
when many other village men have given over this work to their children
and spend their time weaving bamboo or doing other light tasks around
the courtyard. Pɔɔ Tan would probably work anyway because hard work
has been his entire life, and he is too old to change now. He is up before
dawn every day of the year to go to the streams to empty his fish traps of
the fish for the day's meals, the crabs to feed to the ducks, and the tiny
freshwater shrimp that his wife sells in the market. Then he works in the
fields or at buying and selling buffaloes until dark every day.

Pɔɔ Tan started out in life as a poor man, and his life's work has been
dedicated to improving his family's position in village society by accumulat-
ing land and houses. On the way he has had two wives and has sired seven
children. By his first wife he had a son, who died, and a daughter, who is
now grown, with a family of her own.

The tone of Pɔɔ Tan's family is different from the quiet, dignified,
patrician life-style of Pɔɔ Nɔɔj Kɛɛw's family and from the intelligent,
rollicking, and sociable style of Pɔɔ Luaŋ Taa's family. All three families
are acquisitive; but in Pɔɔ Tan's family acquisitiveness has become an ob-
session. Each baht is squeezed between the fingers of Mɛɛ Tii, the keeper
of the family coffers, before being released. The best food available to the
family—the freshwater shrimp which Pɔɔ Tan takes from his traps each
morning, and the duck eggs and chicken eggs—is sold in the market for
the handful of cash it brings instead of being eaten by the family, who do
not have an adequate diet, although they could afford to eat well. Each
morning, at the exact instant when it becomes light enough to see in the
kitchen built to the side of the house, Mɛɛ Tii switches off the sole electric
bulb, under which her daughter has been preparing breakfast. "A baht
saved is a baht earned" hardly does the family justice.

Pɔɔ Tan has spelled out this Spartan policy to the family members. At New Year the family can expect no new clothes. Three years ago, when Pɔɔ Tan built the new teak house, all the daughters of the family who had gold necklaces had to give them to their father, who sold them to raise money to complete the house.

The house is the family's pride and joy. It is of the size of the large old village houses (1,690 square feet), and it is made of very beautiful and very expensive honey-colored teak wood. The floors are solid teak an inch and one-half thick. The house is modern in style, although not as modern as some of the garish buildings following the city style that are currently being erected in and around Chiangmai village. The furniture is of solid wood, uncomfortable but lasting. The roof tiles are not the cool clays of the older houses but the new wood boards impregnated with cement, which make the house hot as an oven in the summer, cold in the winter, and damp in the rainy season, but are durable and long-lasting. The house has a spacious central hall which runs from front to rear, passing a front room where the Buddhist altar is located and where guests are entertained, and two sleeping rooms, one on either side of the hall, and ending in a back kitchen (see fig. 1).

At the north end of the east sleeping room are the mattresses and mosquito nets of Pɔɔ Tan, Mɛɛ Tii, and Thaa, their eleven-year-old son. On the other side of some glass storage cabinets, at the south end of the room, sleeps Sin, the third daughter, who is seventeen years of age. On the other side of the hall is the bedroom of Kham, the oldest unmarried daughter of the family. The family would be pleased if a new son-in-law came to share the room with her (I learned that she married in September 1974). Saajthɔɔŋ, twelve, the youngest daughter and the child who will eventually inherit the house, lives in the next compound in a house that belongs to the family, with Pan, twenty-four, the married eldest daughter of Pɔɔ Tan and Mɛɛ Tii, and with Pan's husband, thirty, and their three-year-old son, Pɛɛŋ.

At the rear of the house, beyond the two bedrooms, is a long room used for storing the family's bicycle and other odds and ends and for holding dried garlic, which wealthier village families keep until the price rises later in the year. Beyond the storeroom is a small lean-to with open floor-slats, through which scraps fall to the chickens below. The room is used as a kitchen. Ladderlike wooden steps lead down from the kitchen into the courtyard; a landing with cement steps is at the front entrance.

At the front of the courtyard, near the house, is the family's granary,
fourteen by eighteen feet, which like the house is raised about eight feet

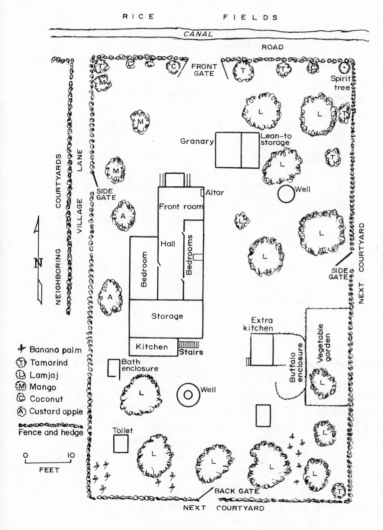

**Fig. 1**                        Village house and
                                  compound

off the ground on cement pillars and is reached by a removable wooden ladder. The interior of the granary is divided into three bins. The largest bin holds the glutinous rice that Pɔɔ Tan's family eats during the year. The second and smaller bin holds the ordinary rice that is grown as a cash crop on the wet northern fields in the dry season, after the glutinous rice harvest. This ordinary rice is held back and either fed to the family's ducks or sold to a buyer who comes to the village in a truck and hauls it away. The third bin is where the specially selected seed rice, six thaŋ of glutinous and two of ordinary, is stored until the fields are planted the following year.

In the space beneath the granary near the front gate, which opens onto the road, in August 1972, Pan set up a small restaurant, where she sells liberally spiced noodles cooked with greens to the occasional passerby or to villagers who come with containers in hand. Like almost all village women, Pɔɔ Tan's wife and daughters are adept buyers and sellers of goods. When Mɛɛ Tii was a younger woman and she and Pɔɔ Tan were just starting out in life, she had a small store in the same location as Pan's, where she sold spices, candies, matches, and other oddments, which she hauled in from the market town.

At the rear of the courtyard is another large shed which sometimes houses the family kitchen; attached to it, under the same roof, is a stall for Pɔɔ Tan's large, powerful pink-colored water buffalo. Unlike many villagers, Pɔɔ Tan uses his buffalo rather than tractors hired from the city to plow his rice paddies and peanut-growing fields; the reason is simple—tractors cost more money.

Pɔɔ Tan's father and mother lived in his compound before him, with Tan and his older brother, a strangely shy and withdrawn man who was the abbot of the village temple for over twenty years. Pɔɔ Tan's father was a man from Chiangmai One who married Pɔɔ Tan's mother and came to live in her parents' house. Pɔɔ Tan does not know much about his father because he died when Tan was only twelve or thirteen years old. He remembers that his father was a cattle merchant who bought cattle in Chiangmai village and sold them elsewhere. He also once went to India through Burma with five friends, each of whom had a boy along as a rice carrier. In India they bought gold and brought it back to sell at a profit in Chiengmai city. Chiangmai villagers once engaged in wide-ranging commerce like many other northern Thai men (see Moerman 1975).

After his father died, Pɔɔ Tan lived alone with his mother in the old house which stood in the present courtyard; his older brother had gone to the village temple to live as a novice. Tan and his mother were very poor, but they did their best to make ends meet. They worked the eleven large fields that lie in one strip near their house to the north of the village. To supplement their income, Tan at seventeen began to sell oxen and buffaloes, which he has continued to do until the present day. He never had a chance to go to school and is today illiterate, not even being able to sign his name.

Tan married his first wife when he was twenty-one, and he had two children by her: one is a daughter who lives with her husband and children up the road about a quarter of a mile; and the other was a boy who died from malaria when he was only a year old. When Tan was about twenty-nine, tragedy struck again with the death of his wife, again from malaria.

A short time later, Tan married Tii, his present wife, who had just been divorced by her first husband, Pɔɔ Can, for barrenness after a marriage of seven years during which the couple had failed to have children. In the village, it is appropriate for a widower and a divorcee to marry.

Tan was thirty and Tii twenty-seven when they married and began a new life together. Pɔɔ Tan's mother had died by that time, and he had been left with his small daughter. Pɔɔ Tan did not move into Mɛɛ Tii's house, as is usually the custom, because he had no sisters to inherit his mother's house. Instead, he brought Tii to live with him in the house he had inherited from his mother, on the site of their present house. They lived in the old bamboo house for two years after their marriage and then built another, in which they lived until they became prosperous enough to build their present house a few years ago.

Mɛɛ Tii added to Pɔɔ Tan's holdings by buying two rice fields located to the north of the village, not far from her new home. She raised the money by selling her half of the land that she and her first husband had accumulated during their marriage. Since Pɔɔ Tan's brother had become a monk and planned to make the Buddhist priesthood his life's career, he did not take his half of the inheritance, and so Pɔɔ Tan inherited all eleven of his mother's fields. Together with Tii's two fields, they now had a total of thirteen.

Mɛɛ Tii also came from a poor family, poorer than her new husband's, and she had led a hard life until her second marriage. Both Tan and Tii were ambitious people who were willing to apply themselves to better their position in village society. They worked very hard growing rice and planting cash crops in the dry season. To supplement their income, Pɔɔ Tan bought and sold buffaloes each year to farmers who needed draft animals, and Mɛɛ Tii opened the small shop. After the children started to come, she was tied to the house most of the day.

As the years went by, Pɔɔ Tan and Mɛɛ Tii increased the size of their farm. First they rented eight rice fields from Pɔɔ Nɔɔj Kɛɛw, who lives near them. Later they saved enough money to buy seven rice fields adjacent to the ones that Mɛɛ Tii had purchased north of the village. When Mɛɛ Tii's parents sold their house and land in Chiangmai village to emigrate to Fang, where cheaper land was available, Pɔɔ Tan and Mɛɛ Tii managed to buy ten paddy fields from them adjacent to their other holdings north of the village. This completed their present farm holdings of 13 tax raj of land owned plus the 3 tax raj rented.

A farm of 16 tax raj means that Pɔɔ Tan's family are rich peasants who are high in the economic and social hierarchy of the village. Only 11 of the 206 village households own as much as 13 tax raj. While by no means landlords and certainly not members of the elite of the village, Tan and his family have through hard work raised themselves from poor peasants to rich peasants, and they are very proud of this fact. "If I had not worked so hard," Pɔɔ Tan says, "I would still be like my neighbor, who has nothing." The culmination and symbol of the family's good fortune is the beautiful new teak house, complete with flluorescent lights, which they built several years ago.

?Aaj Nid and Pii Saj,
Middle Peasants

The family of ?Aaj Nid and Pii Saj ("Pii" means "older sister" or a mature woman who does not yet merit the term "Mɛɛ," or "mother") is an example of the middle-peasant level of living in the village. ?Aaj Nid is a quiet, unobtrusive man of thirty-six who comes from a poor family in a village near Chiangmai. He lives with his wife and four daughters in a small bamboo house in the courtyard of his wife's parents, a rich peasant family of Chiangmai Two.

?Aaj Nid married into his wife's village because his parents were poor and he had no prospects in his own village. Because he was poor, his wife's family did not encourage his courtship of their daughter, Saj. Even after she became pregnant and they had to get married, her grandfather, who was alive then, would not let him come to live in their house or courtyard, as it is customary to do. ?Aaj Nid then took his wife to live in his own village, where she became ill because of the malevolence of his family's matrilineal spirits. (The "illness" was probably a reflection of her inability to get along with her husband's family.) She insisted that they return to Chiangmai village, but her family still would not allow ?Aaj Nid in their house, and so he and his wife moved in to live with a neighboring woman who was a close matrilineal kinswoman of his wife. After a time his wife's grandfather relented, possibly because of unfavorable village gossip, and built them their present small bamboo house within his courtyard.

?Aaj Nid and his wife and children have lived in the small bamboo house for fifteen years, right up to the present time. For the first few years, he spent all his time helping work the land of his wife's family. In return for his help, he was allowed to take rice to eat from his wife's family's granary. During the dry season after the rice harvest, he was also allowed to grow cash crops on a few raj of land that his father-in-law was not using. He and his wife worked hard to save enough money to start a more independent household. He hired himself out as a farm laborer, and she became a market woman and went daily to sell banana leaves, coconuts, and assorted fruit, which she bought in the village and sold in the large morning market in Chiengmai city.

Together they scraped up enough money to buy 2 tax raj of land, which is the nucleus of their present farm. After a few more years, through his father-in-law's contacts in Chiangmai village, he was allowed to rent 3 tax raj of land from a neighboring villager. The couple continued to help the wife's family in the fields but were able to spend more time on their own farm. Also, they established their own granary, a tiny structure made of galvanized tin, built on the ground underneath the granary of the father-in-law and mother-in-law. In two years, again through the social contacts of his father-in-law, ?Aaj Nid was able to rent an additional 3 raj of land, which brought the total size of their farm to 8 tax raj, with 6 tax raj rented and 2 owned.

?Aaj Nid and Pii Saj's family has plenty to eat and decent clothes to wear, but they cannot afford luxuries or any of the new material things like motorcycles or electric fans. They do not have the money to install an electric pole, so they tap the electric supply of the main house for their one light bulb. ?Aaj Nid and his family live just above the poor-peasant level, near the bottom of the middle-peasant range; most of the families in Chiangmai village live as they do.

They are not satisfied with their present status. To ensure that no more children come along, Pii Saj takes birth-control pills, which she obtains from the government health post in the village; she has gained weight since taking the pills, but she has not become pregnant again, and she continues her occupation of market woman. ʔAaj Nid works as a construction laborer in Chiengmai city for 20 baht per day in the agricultural slack season, when such work is available. They are trying to save enough money to purchase additional land and, eventually, to build a new house. When their second eldest daughter was thirteen, they sent her into town to work as a clerk in the shop of an acquaintance. This did not work out to their satisfaction because she spent all her earnings in town and did not bring any of the money home to her parents; so she was scolded and brought back home. Now, like her older sister, she helps her father and her grandfather work in the fields.

Pɔɔ Pɛɛŋ and
Mɛɛ Sii, Poor Peasants

The poor-peasant level of living in Chiangmai village can be illustrated by the family of Pɔɔ Pɛɛŋ, fifty-four, and Mɛɛ Sii, fifty-one, who live in Chiangmai One. Pɔɔ Pɛɛŋ and Mɛɛ Sii have had five children during their married life, all of whom are alive. Their younger daughter and her husband, who were married during our stay in the village, live in the house, as do their two sons: In-taa, seventeen, an agricultural laborer, and Lad, twelve, who is still going to school. Their oldest son lives in a neighboring village with his wife's family, and their other married daughter lives in Chiangmai Two with her husband.

Mɛɛ Sii is from a poor peasant family in an adjacent village. When Pɛɛŋ married her, he went to live with her family in her village. He stayed there one month but had to leave because the matrilineal spirits at her house did not like the new young couple and made him continually ill. (Again, the spiritual illness suffered by Pɛɛŋ was probably due to his not getting along with his wife's family and their not having enough land to motivate him to stay.) After one month they moved into their present house in Chiangmai village, and Pɛɛŋ became well again.

Pɔɔ Pɛɛŋ inherited 2 tax raj of rice land from his parents. He is not very able or ambitious, and neither is his wife. During the years they have been married, they have not increased their landholdings. Each year they farm 2 raj of glutinous rice and get a yield of about 140 thaŋ. They grow two fields of garlic on the same land during the dry season and make about 900 baht. In addition, during the year I was in the village, they rented 3 tax raj for peanuts at 300 baht, and made a net profit of 300 baht after paying the rent. The family's basic income from agriculture for one year was roughly 2,000 baht, or less than U.S. $100 per year at the 1972 rate of exchange. If, as the villagers told me, the average amount of glutinous rice consumed per person per year is 30 thaŋ, the six members of the family would have consumed about 180 thaŋ of rice, or 40 more than they produced. They had to spend about 300 baht to have enough rice to eat. To supply money for their other needs the middle son worked as an agricultural laborer on the fields of landowning villagers. The married daughter living at home also hired out occasionally; the son-in-law worked in a carpenter shop in the city; and Pɔɔ Pɛɛŋ and Mɛɛ Sii made coconut dippers and rope to sell. The family lives only a little above subsistence level.

The family's poverty is one of the reasons that their older daughter went to live with her husband on the other side of the village after a short period of residence with them, and why their younger daughter and her husband will go to live with his parents after he helps the family for a few months. The family is so poor that they do not have land to support a son-in-law, and there is no prospect for anyone to inherit property from them.

Two Landless
Laborer Families

Landless laborers are the poorest people in Chiangmai village. Village families who fall into this category are of two types: one type is an independent household that is landless and has no other prospects save their own labor; the other is a household of a married couple who live in a dependent relationship with the wife's parents. The second type is in a much better economic position than the first because the patron house next to which they live may be rich and prestigious and the younger couple will some day inherit part of its property and perhaps succeed to its position of prestige in village society. For dependent households of the second type, landlessness is only one stage in the family's life cycle.

The family of Mɛɛ Kham, sixty-three, and Pɔɔ Khoom, sixty-four, and their five unmarried daughters is representative of the first type of landless laborer—one that is not attached to a patron house. Pɔɔ Khoom is a man from a poor family in a village next to Chiangmai, who married Mɛɛ Kham forty-six years ago when she was seventeen and he was eighteen. Over the years they had a total of eleven children born to them, only six of whom are now alive. Their house is one of the poorest in the village, being made entirely of bamboo, set precariously upon crooked bamboo stilts, and topped with a thatched roof. The house contains little in the way of furnishings; the family owns very few material goods of any kind. Unlike most houses in Chiangmai village, this house does not have electricity because the family could not afford the initial outlay of erecting an electric pole and installing the necessary wiring.

The economic resources of the family consist of their labor and Pɔɔ Khoom's water buffalo. They own no land other than their house compound and its few fruit trees, nor do they rent any. They used to rent some farmland, but the children of their landlord grew up and took over the land themselves several years ago. Because of the increasing number of people in the countryside and the shortage of land, the family have been unable to find any more land to rent.

Their main source of income is the rice that Pɔɔ Khoom earns from hiring out with his water buffalo to plow the fields of village landowners who can afford his services at five thaŋ of rice per tax raj plowed. Khoom is paid, like many other laborers on the village rice fields, at harvest time. When the farmer harvests his rice Khoom goes and gets his wages. Since his family eats about 180 thaŋ of rice per year, Pɔɔ Khoom would have to plow 36 raj per year with his buffalo just to make enough rice to feed his family. He does not come close to plowing this much land because the work is very hard and he is getting old.

To supplement their income from plowing, the family members hire themselves out as farm laborers throughout the year when work is available. They uproot and transplant rice; cut, thresh, and carry harvested rice back to the landowner's granary; dig ditches to prepare the fields for growing garlic; plant garlic; dig ditches and use the dirt to mound up planting places for lamjajs; pick lamjajs; and uproot peanuts. Sometimes the parents and their daughters contract as a single labor team to work so many raj for a fixed sum of money; sometimes they hire out separately. It is a hard and unrewarding life.

Their oldest daughter, aged thirty, works in Chiengmai city as a servant for about 150 baht ($7.50) per month plus board and room. She saves most of her meager salary and brings it home to help her family.

The other type of landless laborer household—the type attached to the house of a parent-in-law—is represented by that of ʔAaj Taa, thirty, and Pii Kɛɛw, twenty-four, and their son, who is three years of age. They live in the northern part of Chiangmai Two in a large but very old and dilapidated wooden house set in a courtyard adjacent to the house of Kɛɛw's family. Their house and the compound in which it is built belong to Kɛɛw's father and mother. Before Taa and Kɛɛw moved in after their marriage five years ago, the house was inhabited by Kɛɛw's older sister and her husband, who lived there until they had saved enough money to purchase land and build their own house. Taa and Kɛɛw are probably only temporary tenants in their house because, according to custom and her parents' expectations, they are supposed to save enough to go out on their own, thus freeing the house for Kɛɛw's younger sisters when they get married. The youngest sister, Sii, now ten, is expected to marry last and to inherit the parental house.

Taa and Kɛɛw own no land at all, and little property of any kind. Taa is a poor man who brought only the clothes on his back when he married into Kɛɛw's family. Actually Kɛɛw was not such a great catch for him; for five years she had been working as a servant in Chiengmai city and Bangkok (according to her story), but other villagers—how correctly I do not know—claim that this was not her true occupation. She gave her earnings to her father, who used them to build his handsome new house. Taa was supposedly not aware of his wife's history when he married her but found out about it later and has been furious ever since. Relations between Taa and Kɛɛw are strained at best, and they quarrel frequently and loudly.

Taa and Kɛɛw work on her father's large farm under her father's direction and control. Taa gets his orders from his father-in-law through his wife. He is almost entirely under the old man's thumb. This situation is so potentially explosive that Taa never speaks to his father-in-law or mother-in-law; he seldom even comes across the fence into their compound. The strict avoidance taboo prevents arguments between him and his wife's family.

In return for their help on the farm, Taa and Kɛɛw and their son are allowed to have rice from her father's granary to eat throughout the year; in addition, food prepared at the big house is often carried over to their dwelling. The two households are still one for the most part. In addition, Kɛɛw's father usually lets her and Taa have 3 tax raj of land on which they can grow a cash crop of peanuts or garlic during the winter dry season, allowing them to make 1,000 baht or so a year if they are lucky. The use of the land is not guaranteed; during the year I was in the village, Kɛɛw's father decided that he would use the land himself that year.

Whenever he is not working in the fields for his father-in-law, Taa works as a laborer in a small factory not far from Chiangmai village. He makes 20 baht ($1.00) for a day's hard work. He and Kɛɛw save as much

of their income as possible in the hope that they will eventually be able
to buy their own land and achieve some independence from her family.
There is also the expectation that they will inherit a few tax raj of Kɛɛw's
parents' land sometime in the future—after her father dies, or whenever
he decides to give it to them. Until then, they remain landless laborers.

# 5          Irrigation

## Traditional Irrigation
## Systems in the
## Chiengmai Valley

The Chiengmai Valley, like other valleys of northern Thailand (Moerman 1968, pp. 50–51), contains many small-scale traditional irrigation systems which are operated and maintained by peasant villagers.[1] In Saraphi District alone there are four such peasant irrigation systems, which water a total of some 13,500 tax raj of land.

These traditional systems are similar to those established in the valley by King Meŋraaj, founder of the city of Chiengmai in the thirteenth century. Accounts of the ancient Chiengmai irrigation systems given in the book *The Laws of King Meŋraaj, King of Lannathai,* written in 1292,[2] are sketchy and incomplete but are still apt descriptions of the irrigation works as they exist today. This fact was brought home to me forcefully when I visited villagers rebuilding a large weir across the Ping River in 1972. While there I asked about the spirit of the weir, which I had read about in the ancient manuscript, and I was astonished to find that the same deities are worshiped today in the same way! Since it is known that King Meŋraaj first established his capital near the present town of Saraphi and remained there for several years before moving to Chiengmai, it is not inconceivable that the irrigation canals which water Chiangmai village's fields today run in some of the same channels as King Meŋraaj's.

An effective state could not long exist in northern Thai valleys like Chiengmai without a productive agricultural base, and productive rice agriculture presupposes an irrigation system. Rainfall alone, though it is heavy during the summer and fall, is not sufficient. Without an effective water management system, the villagers' fields would become marshes and shallow lakes during the floods at the end of the rainy season and would turn into dusty and parched patches at the height of the dry season. Such a situation exists at present in some of the frontier villages which I visited in the Fang Valley north of Chiengmai city near the Burmese border, recently settled by emigrants from Chiangmai village, who have not yet had a chance to build and perfect their water control systems.

The Chiengmai Valley irrigation systems have long been under the direction and control of a central state authority. *The Laws of King Meŋraaj* mentions royal officials whose task it was to oversee the operation of the valley's irrigation systems and to see that they were maintained properly. The heads of the local systems under the old Chiengmai kingdom were men living in the countryside who were somehow connected with the royal family of Chiengmai, either by distant kinship (real or putative) or as appointed officials (see McGilvary 1912, p. 195).

At the end of the nineteenth century, when Chiengmai became part of the modern Thai nation, the irrigation systems came under control of the Thai government. The central government has not changed the indigenous systems very much except to ordain that the headmen of the local systems are to be elected by the villagers under the supervision of the district officer. The Thai government has been satisfied with building large concrete weirs and water gates on the main river channels and has not yet interfered much with the internal operation of the local systems, probably because the government officials recognize that the systems are managed quite well by long-established principles.

**Chiangmai Village's**
**Three Irrigation**
**Systems**

Chiangmai villagers participate in three separate irrigation systems. One is a traditional type, one is a modified traditional system, and one is part of the government's modern Old Ping River Irrigation Project. This latter project dates from 1939, when the Royal Irrigation Department constructed a large concrete weir across the Ping River near Chiangmai village to divert water from the present Ping River bed into one of its older channels. New, concrete water gates were built to improve water control for the local irrigation systems which draw water from the old channel of the river. The government planned the Ping River Irrigation Project to water land to the south in Lamphun Province, but it was persuaded by a former headman of Chiangmai village to extend a lateral canal a short distance north to water 600 raj of low-lying fields south and southeast of the village.

At the village level, the social organization of this government canal system is much like that of the more traditional systems. The headman of Chiangmai Two is the irrigation headman of the subcanal, and he oversees the maintenance of the canal much as the irrigation headman of the traditional systems did. The main difference between the operation of the government canal and the older canals is that Thai government workmen instead of the villagers themselves build and maintain the main weirs and water gates. Irrigation system X, the second irrigation system which waters Chiangmai village's fields, branches off from the Ping River in the outskirts of Chiengmai city, ten or fifteen miles north of the village. Operated as a modification of the traditional irrigation system, irrigation system X is the largest in Saraphi District, with many subbranches which spread out over the valley floor, east of the river, and then run south following the gradient of the land. Some branches enter the Kwang River, which runs parallel to the Ping along the eastern side of the valley far from the village. The branch of the system which waters the village's fields runs due south from the point where it leaves the Ping River. It flows through the village's northern and eastern fields before emptying into the Old Ping River through the same exhaust canal as that used by the government subcanal.

Like all the other villagers who participate in system X, Chiangmai village farmers who use its water elect a village irrigation headman. He supervises the distribution of water at the village level, mobilizes the farmers to clean the canals, represents Chiangmai villagers' interests to the leadership councils of the entire system, and transmits orders concerning irrigation from the higher officials to the villagers. The present village irrigation headman, like almost all other village leaders, is from a good family; he is the son-in-law of one of the four most wealthy and powerful men in the village.

Irrigation system Y is the most traditional of the three systems which supply village farmers with water. Because I was interested in learning about the old systems before recent modifications, I studied irrigation system Y in more detail than the government system or irrigation system X. Most of the following description of traditional irrigation in Chiangmai village is based upon my study of irrigation system Y, although I believe irrigation system X operates in much the same way.[3]

Irrigation system Y's main canal comes off the Ping River just south of where the irrigation system X's canal separates off, ten miles or so north of the village. System Y's main channel runs south, parallel to and just east of the Ping River, through the countryside all the way down to Chiangmai, the southernmost village in the system. Along the way its branches water the fields of villages from three communes of Saraphi District: commune A, the commune where it originates; commune B; and commune C, in which Chiangmai village is located. The farmers of seven administrative villages in commune A and seven administrative villages in commune B—almost all the villages in these administrative units—use system Y's water; but Chiangmai One and Two are the only two administrative villages in commune C which do so.

**The Physical Structure
of Irrigation System Y**

Irrigation system Y is intricately segmented into progressively smaller canals. At the highest level, it is divided into two large segments which, borrowing a page from Evans-Pritchard's book *The Nuer* (1940), I will call maximal canals: commune A maximal canal I and the communes B and C maximal canal II. As pictured in the sketch (map 5), there is a junction about midway in the system where the main canal forks. The right fork is a short exhaust canal which leads back into the Ping River; the left fork carries the water into maximal canal II. Along maximal canal I are the seven villages of commune A; and along maximal canal II are the nine villages of communes B and C.

If we take Chiangmai village's population figures as a base and estimate 100 farmers per administrative village, maximal canal I would service about 700 farmers, and maximal canal II about 900. The total population which draws water from the system I would estimate to be at least 6,400 (calculating four persons per family, the average family size in Chiangmai village). Approximately 2,800 people draw water from maximal canal I, and approximately 3,600 from maximal canal II. The maximal canals are thus fairly evenly balanced in the number of users of each.

Each maximal canal is divided into major canals, each of which feeds water to the fields of farmers in two or three administrative villages. There are seven major canals in the total system, three in maximal canal I and four in maximal canal II. Each major canal has a recognized name. This name also designates the weir that is located at the junction of each major canal with the maximal canal, either to back up water for the major canal or to let it flow freely downstream, as the situation requires.

Major canals are, in turn, divided into smaller canals which I call minor canals. At rough estimate, there are about one hundred minor canals in the system. The major canal of Chiangmai village, for example, divides into six minor canals, which take water to various sections of the village's

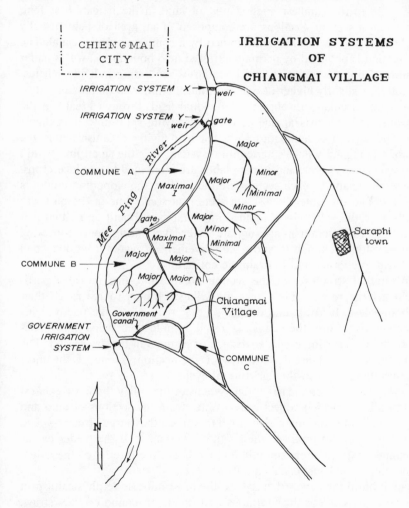

**Map 5**

fields. On the average I estimate that each minor canal supplies water to sixteen farmers. This number, of course, varies a great deal. In Chiangmai village one minor canal supplies water to fifteen farmers, and another supplies the fields of only one farmer.

At the lowest level of segmentation, there are myriads of very small feeder canals which I call minimal canals. Minimal canals lead from a minor canal to the smallest integral unit of land in the irrigation system, which I call a section. Sections are composed of an area of fields usually owned by only a few farmers and drained by a common exhaust canal. The entire section is bounded by permanent raised field boundaries, with smaller and more temporary internal field boundaries separating individual fields. The section is slightly higher at one end than the other so that water enters at one point, circulates through the individual fields through breaks in the field walls, and exhausts at one or two lower-lying spots into an exhaust canal. The section is analogous to a cell in a living organism; it is the "cell" of Chiangmai village's agricultural system. It is the small unit within which plants, soil, water, and human labor are combined to produce crops. The size and shape of each section are dictated by the slope and contours of the land and the water flow. Each section at some time in the past was carved out of the valley floor, molded into shape, and built up so that it is level enough to maintain an appropriate water level during the rice-growing season but sloped enough to allow the movement of water from one small paddy field to another and to drain the entire unit.

The internal structures of the section are flexible, like movable partitions in a large room. This allows the village farmers to rearrange their mud boundaries, furrows, and ditches so that they can make paddy fields for rice and then, after the rice is harvested, remold their fields into shapes appropriate for growing garlic, soybeans, or peanuts in the dry season. The rearranging of the internal structures of the section is one of the most time-consuming tasks in the agricultural cycle.

At every level within the irrigation systems of the valley there are exhaust canals of all sizes which collect excess water from the sections of land and empty it back into the main river or into some other large stream, which carries it away downstream to the south of the valley. If the feeder canals at maximal, major, minor, and minimal levels are the arteries of the irrigation system, the exhaust canals are its veins.

In addition to the canals themselves, the most impressive physical aspect of irrigation system Y is the enormous weir, made of bamboo stakes, straw, and sand which the villagers maintain across the Ping River just a few yards below the point where the main canal of the system diverges from the river. The purpose of the weir is to back up a head of water into the system's intake canal during the dry season when the water level in the river is low. There are smaller weirs at each canal junction in the system to regulate water flow. Some of those at the junctions where major canals branch off are made adjustable by building a frame into which boards can be placed or removed. At lower levels in the canal system the weirs and dams are nothing more than makeshift structures of straw and mud.

The physical structure of the irrigation system is completed by water gates which regulate the entrance of water into the system, the internal distribution of the water, and its exit. By opening and closing the water gates and regulating the water flow internally by weirs, farmers can adjust the level of water in the system to meet their requirements during the different seasons of the year. During the winter dry season, after the main rice crop of the year has been harvested, the water level of the river falls and there is not sufficient irrigation water to permit the planting of cash crops such as garlic, peanuts, and soybeans, or a second crop of rice (if the price of rice is high enough that year). To build up a head of water for irrigation during the dry season, the peasants rebuild irrigation system Y's major weir across the Ping River which is washed away in the flood season of the preceding fall.

After the main weir is rebuilt and water again enters the irrigation system, the exhaust gates are closed to back up the water and fill all the canals in the system. If the year is unusually dry and the water is still not sufficient, a rationing system is put into effect by the leaders; internal weirs are used to circulate the water among the various canal branches. This policy is maintained during the dry months until June, when the rains begin again.

After the planting of the rice crop in early summer, gates and weirs are manipulated to adjust the water level in the paddy fields for the requirements of growing rice.

During the height of the rainy season in the fall, the river and the canals overflow their banks and flood the fields. At this time of year, the main problem is how to get rid of unwanted water, and so the leaders of the irrigation system manipulate the system in order to reduce its water level. The main gate at the Ping River is closed to prevent river water from entering the canals. The internal weirs are removed to allow water to flow through and out of the system. The exhaust gates are all opened to let the water out as quickly as possible. In an extremely wet year rainfall fills the canal system so rapidly that it is impossible to exhaust the water quickly enough, and the fields flood.

In December and January, after the rainy season is over, it is time to harvest the rice. During harvest the water is drained out of the canals to dry the fields and to make harvesting easier.

## Social Organization of Irrigation

Irrigation system Y, described above, supplies water to approximately 6,500 villagers. Without such a system, agriculture as the villagers now know it would be impossible. If the irrigation system is to operate effectively there are certain yearly tasks that must be carried out, and to carry out these tasks the villagers have to organize themselves. The first task of the peasants and their leaders is to maintain the physical structure of the system: the weirs and canals.

Since the floods wash away the main weir across the Ping River every fall, they must rebuild it each year. The Ping River is an enormous water-course—one of the major rivers of Thailand—and great numbers of men have to be mobilized to gather the materials and furnish the labor required to build a weir across it. Two weeks of concentrated labor by all the farmers who use the system must be devoted to the task.

The entire earthen canal system also must be cleared of mud, debris, and vegetation. Each year, especially during its flood stage, the Ping deposits enormous quantities of silt in the irrigation canals. If the canals were not dug out at least once a year, they would silt up and eventually be inoperable. The smaller canals and ditches must be dug out even more often, usually several times in a year. To clean the canal the peasants first have to drain the entire system of water and keep it that way for several weeks. During this time the entire system, from the maximal canals to the smallest minimal canal, including the exhaust canals, is dug out and cleaned; and all the gates and weirs are repaired.

The successful completion of these maintenance and repair tasks requires the cooperation of large numbers of men; the supervision of these men and the coordination of their activities require leaders who have the authority to make decisions. These leaders also need effective sanctions to ensure that each member of the irrigation association fulfills his obligations. Such a system of authority has existed for centuries in the Chiengmai Valley.

In the days of the old Chiengmai kingdom, according to older villagers, the "Kɛɛmiaŋ," the headman of irrigation system Y, was chosen by the villagers with approval of the king of Chiengmai or one of his officials. At present, the headman is chosen by the three kamnan, or heads of the three communes (tambon) served by the irrigation system. The present head of irrigation system Y, a man who lives in commune A, has been head for about two decades. He is one of the richest and highest-status men in this part of Saraphi District, and owner of an enormous traditional Thai house with a beautiful garden and a large private lake for fish. His granary, mounted on giant teak timbers, is as large as most village houses. The size of his lamjaj orchards is legendary in the countryside. He is a man whose social status gives him the respect necessary for the head of an entire irrigation system.

The head of irrigation system Y has two assistant heads, with whom he consults on all important matters concerning the system. One of the assistant headmen is the kamnan of commune B; the other is the village headman of Chiangmai One. Irrigation officials may be and often are the same people who serve as village and commune heads. The head of the entire irrigation system is also in charge of all activities which concern maximal canal I of the irrigation system. The assistant heads from commune B and Chiangmai village (in commune C) divide between them the supervision of maximal canal II, which runs through their area. All major decisions which concern the system as a whole involve consultations between these three highest officials in the system. If the system needs to be represented to the government or to other irrigation systems, the head represents it.

In addition there is a second level of leadership which consists of the heads of each major canal. For the commune A maximal canal I there are three secondary heads in charge of its three major canals, and for maximal canal II there are another three. Decisions in commune B involve the kamnan and his two assistants.

At the third level of leadership are the village irrigation headmen, who are in charge of all irrigation matters in their village. The village irrigation headmen are often, but not always, headmen of administrative villages as well. They are chosen by the farmers of their village who draw water from the irrigation system. Usually these leaders serve for life or until they retire. They represent their village's interest to the higher officials in the system, and transmit orders and decisions from the top down. During the work of digging out the canals and repairing the weirs, they serve as foremen in charge of the men from their village.

Finally, at the lowest level of leadership are the assistant village irrigation headmen. These men, usually two in number, are selected by the village irrigation headmen. They are runners who transmit messages from the headman to each of the farmers. They also coordinate the irrigation activities of farmers in the various sections of the village, although at this level things usually operate in an informal manner.

In addition to the above officials, two gatemen are hired to guard the water gates and to open and shut them when ordered to do so by the irrigation officials. One watchman tends the main gate of the canal and also keeps watch on the Ping River weir. A second man tends the gate which separates maximal canal II from maximal canal I. The main gate watchman is paid 150 thaŋ of rice per year, and the second watchman is paid 50 thaŋ. Rice to pay the watchmen is collected by the irrigation headmen from each farmer who uses irrigation system Y.

The officials of the irrigation system have many duties, and their jobs are time-consuming. At each level of the system, from that of assistant village irrigation headmen in charge of minor and minimal canals to that of headman for the whole system, each leader represents the water needs of his constituency to higher branches of the system and in turn transmits information, decisions, and orders down from higher levels. Village irrigation headmen and their assistants come together to discuss problems at the village level. When a meeting is held by irrigation headmen at the major canal level, which usually includes several villages, the village irrigation heads come together to discuss the needs of the various villages. Finally, all the leaders attend meetings of the entire system, like the one held each year, usually in January, at the main water gate to discuss when to drain the system for cleaning, when to rebuild the weir, and how to ration water during the dry season. The irrigation headman of Chiangmai village was constantly busy throughout the year, buzzing back and forth across the countryside on his Honda motor scooter, tending to the affairs of the irrigation association.

At each level the irrigation officials have the authority to make decisions. The assistant village irrigation headman helps resolve disputes over water use between two farmers who draw water from the same minimal canal. At the village level (minor canals), the village irrigation headman has the authority to ration water in times of scarcity, to adjudicate disputes, to report people who try to steal water or evade regulations to the district officer, and to mobilize the farmers in his village to clean the canals. The head of the system and his two assistant heads make the same kinds of decisions for the system as a whole; they resolve disputes between the farmers of different major canals and ration water among the maximal and the major canals in times of scarcity.

Irrigation officials are responsible for keeping records of the amount of land farmed by those who use the system's water. Records are necessary because the amount of labor each farmer is required to perform and the amount of rice he has to contribute to the gate watchmen depend upon the amount of land he farms with irrigation water from the system. Irrigation officials act as labor foremen and supervisors when the men are mobilized, telling the farmers when and where to assemble for work. More specifically, irrigation headmen do the following.

1. They decide when to clean the system and rebuild the weir.
2. They regulate water use at all levels during periods of scarcity.
3. They give orders to the water gate watchmen to open or shut the water gates.
4. They keep lists of farmers who owe labor obligations and fine the farmers if they do not furnish the prescribed labor.
5. They adjudicate all disputes over water between members of the irrigation system.
6. They supervise all labor and inspect the work.
7. They decide how deep to dig the ditches in the various sections of the canal system and how to construct the weir.
8. They report all who violate rules of the irrigation association to the government for punishment.

In return for their duties, the irrigation heads are excused from paying taxes on thirty raj of land, they do not have to furnish irrigation labor, and they manage to keep some of the fines levied.

## Cleaning the Irrigation Canals

The best way to describe the social organization of irrigation system Y is to relate how the villagers and their leaders annually clean their irrigation canals and reconstruct the main weir across the Ping River, a process I witnessed in 1972. They carry out these tasks in such an efficient and well-organized way that anyone who witnesses it will forever scoff at the notion that Thai peasant society can be characterized as "loosely structured."

Each year, the leaders of system Y hold a meeting at the main water gate on the Ping River to discuss the annual cleaning of the canal system and the rebuilding of the weir. By this date the rainy season has ended, the rice has just been harvested, and the farmers are planting garlic, soybeans, peanuts, and a second rice crop. Since the water level in the river is low at this time of year, it is easier to empty the canal and clean it and it is possible to rebuild the weir across the river. At their 1972 meeting at the water gate, the head of irrigation system Y, along with all the other administrative officials of the system, decided that the main water gate would be closed on January 25, so that the system would be entirely drained by January 27. From January 27 to February 4 all the canals would be dug out and cleared of debris. Seven days is the usual time allowed each year to clean the system; the dates vary from year to year, depending upon the water level in the river and the planting dates for the dry-season crops.

At the same meeting, arrangements were made to rebuild the Ping River weir in the eight days immediately after the canals were cleaned. These eight days, added to the seven it takes for cleaning and the three days it takes to refill the canal afterwards, make a total of about three weeks—the cleaning and maintenance time per year for the larger canals. In addition, a total of at least a week is spent cleaning the minor and minimal canals at the village level. These must be cleaned several times a year. Since many Chiangmai village farmers use water from more than one irrigation system and have to help clean all they draw from, as much as a tenth of the farmer's yearly labor is directly devoted to maintaining his irrigation system.

Each year after the meeting at the main weir, the irrigation leaders return to their villages and inform the farmers of the year's schedule. This allows the farmers to make plans to be free when their labor is needed, and it also allows them to adjust the planting of their cash crops so that the three-week absence of irrigation water does not damage the crops.

I will describe how Chiangmai village farmers clean the canals, but first it is necessary to point out a few principles which govern the process of canal maintenance. The basic principle is that a farmer has to help maintain all irrigation canals and structures through which the water travels to his fields. He has to help clean lengths of the canal system in proportion to the area of land he farms which draws water from the system. Because Chiangmai village lies at the tail end of irrigation system Y, the water the villagers use travels through the entire length of the main canal (that is, the two maximal canals), so Chiangmai villagers have to help clean the entire maximal canal system, from their fields right up to the main weir at the river. Because of their location, Chiangmai village farmers clean more of the main canals than farmers of any other village. The commune A villagers whose major canals come off the maximal canal near the river have to clean as many major, minor, and minimal canals as Chiangmai, but they are responsible for cleaning only a short length of the main canal, that portion upstream from where their major canal branches off. They do not clean the big canal below that point.

Like the farmers of other villages, those of Chiangmai village start the annual canal cleaning at the border of their village. They clean their major canal up to commune B. Then they help commune B clean up maximal canal II. Finally they help clean maximal canal I right up to the river. Only after all this do they clean the minor and minimal canals within the borders of their village. In sum, they start at the boundary of the village and work up through larger and larger canals; then they go back to their starting place and move down through smaller and smaller canals until they reach their own fields.

On January 25, at the same time that the main water gate was closed and the exhaust gates were opened to drain maximal canal I, the gate where maximal canal II divides off was also closed and maximal canal II was allowed to drain. On January 27, the Chiangmai villagers who used irrigation system Y's water started cleaning where the canal is crossed by the boundary between communes B and C (see map 5).

Every farmer who uses water from the canals must contribute his fair share of labor and materials to clean and repair the system. If he does not contribute labor, he must send someone in his stead or pay a fine which his irrigation headman can use to hire someone to replace him. Careful and exact records are kept of obligations and contributions; everyone in the system wants to be sure that everyone does his fair share and no more. If a farmer does not fulfill his obligations he will be fined by the irrigation officials. If he continues to be negligent, he will ultimately be taken to the district officer for punishment.

The traditional northern Thai measures used in calculating the appropriate work load per farmer are the "waa" and the "soog." The waa is the distance from fingertip to fingertip of a man's outstretched arms. A soog is one-fourth this, or the distance between the fingertips of a man's outstretched arm and his elbow. When the canals are being dug, a bamboo pole is brought by one of the irrigation leaders, and in front of the assembled men a young man of average stature stretches out his arms to measure a waa, and this length is cut on the bamboo pole, with the soog also being indicated. Then the distance that people have to clean is measured off with the bamboo measuring rod, one waa or soog at a time by the irrigation headmen on the ground along the canal.

To determine the length of canal to be dug and cleaned by each farmer in any particular segment of the canal system, the villagers divide the total number of tax raj of land which this length of the canal supplies with water into the length of the canal. This gives them the length to be dug per tax raj owned. Then they multiply this figure by the number of tax raj worked by each farmer who draws water from the canal; this gives the length of the canal to be dug by that particular farmer in that part of the canal. The obligations per tax raj do not change much from year to year, since the amount of land farmed has been constant for some time now, and most farmers know what their obligations will be on any given segment of the canal. Since the lengths of the different segments of the canal are fairly well known, calculations and measurements do not have to start from scratch each time the canals are cleaned.

Nevertheless, the exact length that each farmer is to dig on any particular day is measured out with the bamboo rod by the irrigation officials at the bank of the canal. The leaders of any given unit have a paper with the names of the peasants who have obligations to clean this part of the canal. Beside each man's name is the figure indicating the amount of the man's land which uses water from the canal. After determining, by formula, the length of canal to be cleaned per unit of land, the irrigation leader reads off the man's name and his helper marks off the appropriate distance. The man then enters the canal at that point and starts shoveling out mud. Everyone crowds around the leaders at the beginning. As places are assigned, the crowd gradually thins out as men enter the canal and begin shoveling mud at a prodigious rate.

Unfortunately, marking off equal lengths of canal does not always ensure an equitable amount of work per unit area of land. The depth of the canal, its width, and the amount of tree roots and vegetation to be cleared away vary at different points along the waterway. The further upstream one goes toward the river, the deeper the canyon cut by the canal becomes, and the more difficult it is to clean the mud from the bottom. To allow for this variation, adjustments are made in the length of the traditional measures;

in some places a waa for a difficult stretch is only half or three-fourths as long as a normal waa.

Another method the villagers use on some sections of the canal is to divide the length of canal into the same number of sections as there are groups participating and then draw lots to see which groups clean the difficult highland sections and which clean the lower, less difficult sections. In still other parts of the canal, the order in which the various village groups dig is fixed by tradition. On one segment of the canal dug by Chiangmai villagers, the canal length is always divided into three sections: Chiangmai digs the lowest section, another village the second, and a third village the furthest upstream. This arrangement is an attempt to compensate for the additional length of canal that the villages further downstream have to dig.

To return to the day-by-day reporting, the Chiangmai villagers rested on January 28, while the farmers from the other villages finished cleaning their major canals up to where they join the maximal canals. While digging maximal canal II, the farmers are under the supervision of the assistant heads from commune B and Chiangmai village (commune C). The village irrigation headmen and the assistant headmen walk up and down the canal bank supervising the labor of their men on the job.

In addition to assigning villages and men the proper length of canal to dig and keeping records to ensure that everyone fulfills his obligation, the irrigation supervisors and foremen also inspect each length of canal to make sure that it is dug to a proper depth. Difficulties with drainage in various parts of the system and the measures necessary to correct these difficulties are discussed at the main meeting of the year at the weir and at other meetings at different levels within the system. Inspection is not pro forma; the Chiangmai villagers, for example, were required to go back a second day and redig part of their major canal, because their first efforts did not make the canal deep enough to suit their leaders. No groups are allowed to dig their canal too deep, however, because they would then draw too much water, robbing the other groups. If a certain part of the canal system is not clean, the farmers who depend upon it for their water are at a disadvantage because the water flows more slowly through their part than through others.

In 1972, the villagers from Chiangmai spent from January 27 to February 4 digging and cleaning maximal canal II up to the point where it joined maximal canal I. As they moved up the canal from their own major canal, they picked up other farmers from the commune B villages. The group working in the channel of maximal canal II grew larger and larger until near the junction all the villagers from commune B and Chiangmai village were working.

After maximal canal II was cleaned, the commune B and Chiangmai villagers proceeded to clean their share of maximal canal I. The arrangements for dividing up the work on this part of the canal are similar to the ones described above for maximal canal II. At this higher level, however, commune B and Chiangmai were treated as one group, on the same level as commune A, when the length of canal they were to dig was determined.

As the canal cleaning proceeded upstream toward the river, the number of men working in the canal continued to grow as the groups of farmers from the major canals, one by one, joined the large group moving up the main canal channel. The last section near the river brought together all the farmers who drew water from the system. They bent to their work, throwing mud from the bottom of the canal up onto the bank; the air was literally black with the bottom mud.

As I witnessed the size of the work groups in the canals increase as the men moved upstream day by day to ever-higher levels of segmentation in the canal system, I was reminded of the process of ancestral worship in the Chinese lineage in Hong Kong, in which the groups grew larger and larger as they worshiped ancestral tombs at ever-higher levels of segmentation in the lineage (see Potter 1968, pp. 22–27). The process of group formation in a system based upon segmentary opposition is the same whether it is based upon the common descent of blood through the generations or shared irrigation water down through a branching canal system.

Later, when Chiangmai village cleaned the six minor and the many minimal canals within the boundaries of the village, the process was reversed. The entire group of village men who used water from the system started out together. Then as they moved down the canal, the groups became progressively smaller as men reached their branch canal and hived off at that point along with the men who shared that branch with them. Finally, each farmer was left with only a few neighboring farmers who shared the smallest canals in the irrigation system.

Those farmers who share water from the smaller canals are, in general, more closely related to each other by ties of kinship or common residence than to those with whom they share less water. These farmers walk to their adjacent fields together in the morning with their hoes and plows over their shoulders, and return together in the evenings; because they share water from the same minimal canal, they plant and harvest at the same time. It is the same as the principle of blood relationship in a kinship system; one cooperates most with, and is most closely related to, those men with whom one shares the most "blood." Common interest in descent is analogous to common interest in irrigation water; these are two of the oldest principles of human association.

The annual cleaning of the canals serves a symbolic social function as well as an instrumental one. As the formers cooperate with other farmers in cleaning their canal system, moving from smaller canals up to higher levels of segmentation within the system (see fig. 2), they recognize those to whom they are most closely related. And the fact that they share this important experience reinforces their feeling of solidarity.

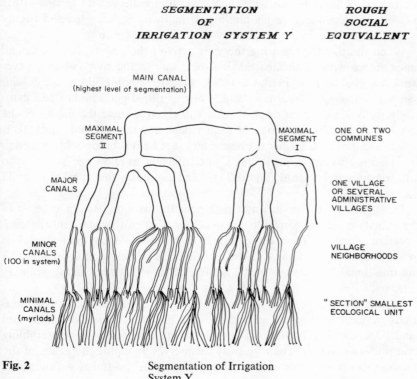

SEGMENTATION
OF
IRRIGATION SYSTEM Y

ROUGH
SOCIAL
EQUIVALENT

MAIN CANAL
(highest level of segmentation)

MAXIMAL
SEGMENT
II

MAXIMAL
SEGMENT
I

ONE OR TWO
COMMUNES

MAJOR
CANALS

ONE VILLAGE
OR SEVERAL
ADMINISTRATIVE
VILLAGES

MINOR
CANALS
(100 in system)

VILLAGE
NEIGHBORHOODS

MINIMAL
CANALS
(myriads)

" SECTION" SMALLEST
ECOLOGICAL UNIT

**Fig. 2**                    Segmentation of Irrigation
                             System Y

## Rebuilding the Weir

It took the villagers seven days to clean the canals. It took seven more days to rebuild the main weir across the Ping River.

The weir is constructed by pounding six- and seven-foot-long sharpened bamboo stakes across the river bed with large sledgehammers. Between the many rows of bamboo stakes drawn across the river bed are placed what the villagers call "crocodiles," rice-straw bundles filled with sand and ballast.

In rebuilding the weir the Thai countrymen exhibit the same penchant for organization they show in cleaning their canals. Each farmer who uses system Y water must furnish bamboo stakes, crocodiles, and labor in proportion to the amount of his land which is watered by the system. For each tax raj of land, a farmer must bring ten bamboo poles of the appropriate length and ten crocodiles of straw and sand. If a farmer has under ten tax raj of land, he has to furnish one adult male unit of labor—either himself, his dependent, or his hireling. If he owns between ten and twenty tax raj he has to furnish the labor of two men, and so on.

When the day for repairing the weir arrives, the countryside roads and lanes are crowded with men making their way to the weir (women never work on the weir or in the canals). Oxcarts rumble along filled with bamboo and sand. The atmosphere is one of ribald good humor and camaraderie. When the men reach the bank of the river near the mouth of the canal, the irrigation headmen of each village call the roll and check their lists to see that each farmer is present and that he has brought his material. If a man is absent, he has to pay a fine sufficient to allow the headman to hire someone in his stead. The roll is called every day that it takes to build the weir.

Meanwhile, at the main water gate near the weir, the senior officials of the irrigation system gather to discuss the design of the weir and the construction schedule. Their more formal dress—white shirts and slacks—is in keeping with the dignity of their position as leaders and contrasts with the traditional blue jackets and wide-legged short trousers of the ordinary villagers.

During the days of weir construction the river bank is thick with hundreds of men working in village groups, busily unloading bamboo and sand. One can hardly walk without bumping into peasants or stumbling over piles of bamboo. The men busy themselves wrapping the heads of the bamboo stakes with thin strips of bamboo so that the stakes will not split when they are pounded. They sharpen the opposite ends of the poles so that they can be more easily driven into the river bed. The air flashes with the glint of busy machete-like knives hacking away at the bamboo stakes. While some of the men are thus engaged, others tie up bundles of sharpened bamboo stakes, carry them a short distance upstream from the weir construction site, toss them far out into the river, and then dive in and ferry their bamboo-bundle rafts down to the appropriate work place on the weir.

The weir is neatly divided into two halves which correspond to the two maximal canals of the system; the right half (facing downstream) is commune A's, and the left half is the combined responsibility of communes B and C. Each half is in turn subdivided into sections assigned to individual villages. Chiangmai village's section has sections of commune B villages on both sides of it. Each village is responsible for furnishing the material and labor for building its section of the weir under the supervision of its irrigation headman. The head and the two assistant heads of system Y design the weir and supervise its overall construction.

Since the working space for any one village on its section of the weir is crowded and the footing precarious at best, all the men of a village cannot work there at the same time. So each village divides itself into work groups of friends and relatives which correspond roughly to the men who draw water from the same minor canals. These groups take turns going onto the weir and driving in the bamboo stakes; about an hour on the weir per shift is a common schedule. While one group is on the weir, the other groups are resting, sharpening the stakes, or transporting the material out to their section of the weir. As can be imagined, rebuilding the weir is a scene of feverish activity, with hundreds of men sharpening and driving stakes at the same time.

After the weir is completely rebuilt, the leaders make on offering of flowers, puffed rice, raw rice, and a boiled pig's head at the two shrines of the spirits of the weir—one spirit guarding the commune A half of the weir on the right bank, and one guarding the communes B and C half of the weir on the left bank. They thank the spirits of the weir for allowing them to rebuild successfully and entreat the spirits to protect the weir and prevent it from being swept prematurely downstream. The countrymen told me that if offerings were not made to the protective spirits of the weir, the bamboo stakes would jump out of the river bed and the entire structure would be swept away.

**Opposition, Conflict,
and Central Authority**

Farmers who share water from irrigation system Y are unified by their common interest in this basic economic resource. If anyone is to benefit, all have to cooperate in maintaining their system, combining to protect the interest of their irrigation system when it is in conflict with other local systems, and submitting to a common central authority. The irrigation systems would soon break down without cooperation and the allocation of authority.

However, conflict is possible between farmers who have fields in the same section of land and who draw water from the same minimal canal. Such conflict rarely breaks out into the open because there are many ties which bind people together at this level and prevent open conflict.

Within this overall framework of cooperation, conflict constantly occurs between larger segments over the use of scarce water, particularly in the dry season, when there is not enough water for everyone to draw as much as he wants and needs. Since the social organization of the irrigation system follows the segmentation of the canal system, conflict takes place at every point of segmentation. The structuring of this opposition is evident in figure 2.

In times of scarcity, farmers from different village neighborhoods who draw water from the six different minor canals of irrigation system Y come into conflict over the use of the water from the major canal that supplies the village. When this occurs, the irrigation headmen of the village ration the water of Chiangmai village's major canal, allowing each minor canal to use the water for a specified period of time and then closing off that minor canal and letting another minor canal open up and draw water to its fields. Again, open conflict is not common at this level because the ties which bind the farmers together as members of the village community cushion the conflict and prevent it from becoming severe. Open violation of irrigation rules at this level is also difficult because detection of the culprit would be almost certain and the guilty person would lose face in the village. However, open conflicts do sometimes occur at this level.

It is at the next level within the irrigation system—between different major canals and different villages—that open conflict frequently occurs. Chiangmai village has trouble with the villagers from commune B, who live just upstream from them. In dry years and at other times of water scarcity, commune B villagers block the canal and divert the water into their major canal, depriving the Chiangmai village farmers downstream. They do this at night or whenever they think they can get by without being caught. Conflict between Chiangmai and the other villages has been endemic for decades and still occurs today. The head of irrigation system Y has to be called in to mediate disputes between the users of the major canals and to enforce the water-use regulations.

One branch of irrigation system Y, I was told, is no longer in operation because conflict between the different villages which drew water from the canal became so intense and hatreds so bitter that the farmers would no longer cooperate to maintain the canal. Some of them left system Y and joined system X.

Conflict also occurs between the two maximal canals of the system. In mid-January, 1972, after the general meeting of all system Y leaders at the main weir, at which they decided upon the timetable for draining and cleaning the canal that year, a second meeting was held by the leaders of maximal canal II. At this rump meeting, the leaders of maximal canal II said that in past years their part of the canal had not been dug deeply enough and water was not flowing into it as fast as it should; this meant that the other half of the canal system was using more of the water than it should. This year they asked all the subordinate leaders to have their men dig the canals deeper in their section to ensure that they would get a greater share of the water. These plans were carried out. The Chiangmai villagers had to dig at least one of their segments over again to conform to these plans of their leaders.

I heard no further stories of conflict between the two major canals of irrigation system Y, but I am almost certain that such conflict occurs during the dry years. It is significant that offerings are made to two different guardian spirits of the weir, one for the commune A villagers and one for the people of communes B and C, who use maximal canal II. There is no one deity who symbolizes the unity of the entire system.

During extremely dry years conflict also occurs between the different large irrigation systems like system X and system Y, two of many which draw water from the Ping River. A year or two before I arrived in Chiangmai village, the government agreed to build system X a new, permanent concrete weir across the Ping River to replace the traditional weir which, like System Y's, had to be rebuilt once each year. When the System Y people down the river heard about the plan, they were afraid that the proposed concrete weir would hold back all the water in a year of scarcity, and allow little or no water to flow downstream to their weir. Even the traditional weirs of bamboo sometimes deprived systems downstream; a concrete weir would certainly do so. The members of system Y were up in arms at this possibility. They told the system X people that if they tried to build anything other than the weir of traditional design, they would tear it down!

Since this was a conflict between two entire traditional irrigation systems, the government had to be brought in to try to resolve the dispute. The district officer and his irrigation officer acted as mediators. Thirteen meetings were held between the leaders of the two irrigation systems in the neutral ground of the district office. Finally a compromise was reached whereby the concrete weir was built with a section at one side which could be opened in time of extreme water scarcity to allow sufficient water to pass downstream. The government irrigation officer in charge of the Old Ping River system was selected as the man to whom system Y's chief could go to get the wooden section of the weir opened if required.

As Wittfogel (1957), (following Marx [1965, pp. 33–34; 1969]), and Steward (1955, chap. 11) among others, has pointed out, the governance and maintenance of wideranging irrigation systems in the same valley require a state-level authority to organize and mediate. Irrigation systems like X and Y would have inevitably come into open conflict in times of water scarcity if the traditional Chiengmai state had not existed to organize and govern the irrigation system on a valley-wide scale. Since the downfall of the Chiengmai kingdom, the Thai government has had to furnish this necessary central authority.

My analysis of the remarkable traditional irrigation systems of the Chiengmai valley supports essential parts of Wittfogel's and Steward's theory about the relation between irrigation and the state. At the lower levels, the necessity for organizing irrigation activities stimulates peasant social organizations that are not found in parts of Thailand where locally run irrigation systems do not exist. One reason why peasant social organization in the Chiengmai Valley differs from that in other parts of Thailand is the presence of irrigation.

# 6      Courtship and Marriage

## Baaws and Saaws

In Chiangmai village, marriage is ideally based upon the romantic love that develops between two young people during courtship. It is sometimes like this in practice. But the "baaws" and "saaws" ("unmarried young men and women") of the village are not unaware of such practical considerations as the wealth and social standing of the prospective spouse's family, whether or not he or she is a hard worker, how many brothers and sisters will share in the inheritance, and so on. And if the young people are sometimes carried away by their emotions and lose sight of these practical considerations, their parents are there to step in and remind them. It is rare for a girl to marry a boy in Chiangmai village in the face of her parents' strong disapproval, although such cases are not unknown.

### Patterns in Courtship

The Khonmyaŋ take their courting seriously and go at it with great gusto, as they have as far back as anyone can remember. Courting customs in Chiengmai, unlike those in many parts of Asia, have not been borrowed from the West or from the Central Thai of Bangkok, although the villagers have been quick to adopt certain modern embellishments from the West, filtered through the capital. They read romantic novels, listen to soap operas on the radio, idolize popular movie stars whom they have seen on the screen in Chiengmai city, and now talk about "fɛɛns," borrowed from the English "boyfriend," although with a somewhat different meaning. A "fɛɛn" is a young man to whom one is engaged, and not simply an acquaintance or a sometime caller at one's home; in meaning it is the equivalent of the French and English word "fiancé" rather than "boyfriend."

The village girls have been quick to adopt new weapons in the war between the sexes. They try to remain or become "slender" (the last syllable, as in many borrowed words, has a strongly accented falling tone), and they make great use of "cutek"—Cutex, or fingernail polish. They also have modern-style haircuts and permanents, and when they go out or go to town they wear slacks and modern over-the-pants shirts instead of their traditional "sarongs."

The traditional Khonmyaŋ courting institution is called "ʔɛwsaaw," "ʔɛw" meaning to go for an outing, and "saaw" being the word for an unmarried nubile girl.[1] So ʔɛwsaaw means to go visiting the girls or to go courting. And, as the name implies, it is the boys and young men who take the initiative by going to the girls' houses to visit them at night after the day's work is done. ʔɛwsaawing also takes place at temple fairs, ordinations, funerals, and any other occasion where boys and girls gather and talk to each other. It is usually at these occasions that boys and girls from different villages become acquainted and make the contacts that later lead a boy to go visiting a girl at her home.

After dark on almost every evening of the year when the weather is good, the roads and paths of the countryside near Chiangmai village are filled with groups of men, ranging from teen-agers still wet behind the ears to experienced young men in their twenties, all going to visit girls in the same village or in neighboring ones. Boys are always seen in groups of at least two or three; they never go alone because men from other villages have been known to waylay boys who are courting girls from their village. Sometimes these encounters are deadly, since the boys take along knives and guns to protect themselves or for other less praiseworthy reasons. Also, gangs of boys from different villages not infrequently stage pitched battles over girls and to express high spirits. Chiangmai fought a neighboring village in 1971, and relations have been strained between the two villages ever since. One of the first orders the new acting district officer gave when he assumed his post in 1972 was that the carrying of knives and other instruments of war by boys going to ʔɛwsaaw had to stop. This was duly read to some of the villagers by the village headman and then duly ignored by everyone, as are most government pronouncements of this kind.

When a young man of the village visits the house of a girl, both parties engage in a ritualized conversational duel which is humorous, filled with double entendres, and sometimes ribald. The conversational duel furnishes a framework within which the boy and girl can look each other over and converse in an approved fashion. The double entendre also allows the boy to tell the girl and the girl to tell the boy how they really feel about one another. The ritual conversational dueling is called "ʔuubaaw" and "ʔuusaaw," literally, "talking to the boys" and "talking to the girls." Young men and women are judged according to how skilled they are at this bantering. Those able to give witty and amusing retorts which put the other person down are admired and sometimes feared by those on the butt end of the thrust.

For example, if a young boy comes in and starts talking to a girl, she might pointedly call him "nɔɔŋ" ("younger sibling"), the word for husband being often "pii" ("older sibling"), and say that she is too old for him. The boy might then take up the challenge and say that "old coconuts are riper and sweeter." The girl might come back with the rejoinder, "Are you calling me a coconut?" whereupon the boy might give in and, sighing dejectedly, say, "I guess I'll have to study some more."

Or if a boy comes ʔɛwsaawing to a girl's house and she invites him to come up the stairs into the house, he might say, "Just a minute, I'm too hot and have to cool off first," meaning that she has so excited him that he dare not go up until his ardor passes.

Boys and girls from the same village have known each other all their lives, and there is no need for introductions. Boys and girls from different villages, as mentioned above, usually meet at public events such as marriages, temple affairs, and funerals; and there are innumerable events like these throughout the year. Many young people go to these events not so much out of piety or social conscience as interest in meeting prospective spouses or friends. If a girl meets a boy and they flirt and talk together a bit and she likes him, she may tell him where she lives and invite him to call. If she wants to discourage him, she may lie to him about where she lives.

If the boy does come calling, he always comes after dark; "the daytime is the time for work, and nighttime is the time of courting." Just as important, night forms a cloak that covers the comings and goings of boys or girls. A boy would be too shy to come to visit a girl in the daytime when everyone in the neighborhood would know what he was about; but he can do it at night. Also, this anonymity makes it possible for the boys to have a girl in literally every village, and they try to convince each girl that they are in love with her and want to marry her, in hopes of making a sexual conquest.

The girls are fully aware of this attitude and are extremely wary about believing the protestations of young men. The interplay between men and women in the courting situation reflects a similar mistrust among all people in the village on almost all matters. "You can never tell what is in a person's heart" is a saying frequently heard. In their readings of TAT drawings (a kind of psychological projective test), the villagers are loath to read any kind of meaning into the actions of others. "He is going somewhere, but where I don't know" and "What he is thinking, I don't know" are repeated again and again. Distrust of others is inbred into every villager at an early age and permeates courtship as well. Young women are just as active in trying to deceive young men, but the villagers usually talk as if it is the men who do most of the deceiving in hopes of seducing the girls. The catch to this game is that if the girl tells her parents of the young man's seduction they may try to exert every pressure possible to make the boy marry their daughter; and often, if both the man and the woman come from the same village, such pressure is effective.

The double standard is fully operative in village society, and the girl stands to lose most in these encounters because, if she loses her virginity, she ruins her reputation and no boy will want to marry her. The girls are also under supernatural sanction from their matrilineal ancestors to remain chaste. The belief in the village is that if a girl loses her virginity and does not tell her mother so that her mother can make offerings to the lineage spirits and beg their pardon for this transgression, then the spirits will make a member of the girl's family, often her mother, ill. This fear puts pressure on the girl to avoid premarital sex and, if this is not possible, to inform her mother and father—an added sanction. For a girl to engage in premarital intercourse is "phidphii," "an offense against the spirits."

The stereotype that is most often used by women in talking about courtship and marriage is that of the false young man. He is on his best behavior when courting the girl, not drinking, swearing, or engaging in any vices, but playing the upstanding young man that any family would want as a son-in-law. Then a month or two after marriage, and especially after the woman becomes pregnant and he is sure of her, he drops the mask and begins to drink and gamble and go philandering. An image seen by the men is that of the deceiving woman whose affections are fickle and who deserts one man for another. After marriage, when the boy goes to live in the house of his wife, he finds himself the object of hostility from his wife's siblings and is under the domination of his wife's father, to whom his wife is often apparently more attached than to him. From the male perspective, there may be good reason for despairing of it all and taking to drink. Also, a woman is not above deceiving a young man by telling him that she is pure and that she has had no other "feens," a falsehood that he does not discover until his wedding night.

## The Bittersweet Years

Almost all village boys and girls (see table 7) become baaws or saaws between the ages of fifteen and seventeen, with more girls than boys waiting until they are seventeen to begin courting. Baawhood and saawhood are recognized social statuses in village society, and to ask someone when he became a baaw or saaw is a meaningful question which any villager will answer. A girl becomes a saaw when her body matures enough to be noticed by young men, who validate her new status by coming to call and starting to flirt with her.

**Table 7**                    Age of Beginning
                    Courtship for
                    Chiangmai Village
                    Men and Women

| Age at Beginning Courtship | Men | Women | Total |
|---|---|---|---|
| 14 | 2 | 3 | 5 |
| 15 | 10 | 11 | 21 |
| 16 | 27 | 16 | 43 |
| 17 | 8 | 12 | 20 |
| 18 | 2 | 1 | 3 |
| 19 | 2 | 3 | 5 |
| 20 | 1 | 0 | 1 |
| 21 | 0 | 1 | 1 |
| Totals | 52 | 47 | 99 |

NOTE: Figures are based upon a questionnaire given to a randomly selected sample of 10 percent of village households.

During the first few years of courtship, both boys and girls stay in the background, don't talk very much, and learn how to ʔuubaaw and ʔuusaaw. A young boy at first is afraid to open his mouth lest a girl skilled at ʔuubaaw make a fool of him. A boy is helped over the initial hurdle of first going to see a girl by arriving ostensibly to help a group of saaws peel garlic, shell peanuts, or perform some other task commonly done during the evening. The task at hand also helps smooth over any lulls in the conversation if it is less than brilliant and stimulating.

In the old days a young man took a simple stringed instrument, made from a hollowed-out half of a coconut, to serenade his girl, but this custom has now been given up. Besides using music, generations of village men all over northern Thailand had their bodies, especially that part covered by shorts, tattooed by a skilled specialist in magic with signs designed to win a girl's heart the minute she laid eyes on a man, even though she didn't see the tattoos. The tattoos also protected the boy or young man against injuries from a knife or gun when he went courting and ensured his fertility after marriage. The last generation or two of young men have given up the tattoos because they were made fun of by the Central Thai and also because they were terribly painful. Some young men died from infections incurred during the tattooing process.

The girls have their version of group cooperation in the courting process which matches the boys' going forth in groups for mutual protection; they have the equivalent of labor-exchange groups which are found in agriculture, in which one offers a day and then gets paid back a day in return. In the case of the courting girls, it is the giving and returning of an evening. Whenever a girl has some task like shelling peanuts or preparing boiled soybeans for the market, or peeling garlic and breaking the heads into cloves to be planted, or making decorations for a festival, she will invite several of her girlfriends to come and help her. Of course boys are somehow always informed of these events and show up to "help the girls." When one of these invited young ladies has a similar event at her house, she invites the girl who had her, thus returning the favor. It is considered highly improper for any girl to crash one of these affairs uninvited. Each girl in a neighborhood will thus take turns in hosting her friends in a group courting situation, which will get the other girls away from the watchful eyes of their parents for a while.

The coming of the boys to court after dark is always heralded by the barking of the house's watchdog. The popularity of a young lady can accurately be measured by the volume of canine barks, growls, and howls which meet each new arrival during an evening. Good parents screen carefully the young boys who come to call on their daughters. When a boy comes the first time, they carefully inquire about his family and his relatives and so on. If they are satisfied that he is a proper suitor, they give him their approval and ask him to come again, or tell their daughter to

ask him. If the young men visiting their daughters are regarded as trust-
worthy, the older people may tell them they are welcome to stay and talk
with the girls of the family while the parents retire to their room. The
young couple are then free to talk to each other, but everything is proper
and not much privacy is afforded the young people because the bamboo
and wooden walls of village houses are not very thick and almost everything can be heard.

If a young woman does not like the boy who has come to call, she will
let him know through the verbal dueling that takes place between them,
or, if this does not work, she will simply retire to her room and not come
out until the boy has gone. If the parents do not approve of the young man
they may tell their daughter not to see him again—sometimes within ear-
shot as the boy is leaving. The daughter usually, but by no means always,
respects her parents' wishes because she knows that after marriage the
young couple will live with her parents; if her parents reject him, the situation is difficult for all concerned.

If a boy who has come courting lives far away and it is late or the
weather is bad, he may be allowed to sleep on the front porch because it
would be too dangerous or uncomfortable for him to return home that
night. He sleeps alone, however. Premarital sex, as discussed above, is
unacceptable in the mores of this society, and although it does take place
it is not encouraged. It is not so bad if the couple follow with marriage
soon after.

As in all societies which allow young people some choice in their marriage partners and which have institutionalized dating, the years of courtship in Chiangmai village are bittersweet. There is the fun and excitement
of the ?uubaaw and ?uusaawing and the eternal flirting and gossiping and
giggling and teasing. But there is also the painful lack of confidence of
unsure young people thrown on their own devices. And there is the fear
that one may never get married and have a wife or husband and family.
The false smiles, the misunderstandings, the deceit, and the trifling with
sensitive and tender affections result in much suffering. Those who are not
attractive, who do not come from families with status, and who are not
skilled or clever in the word games do not find this "freedom" amusing.
The boy too painfully shy to go to the houses of girls he likes, even under
the cloak of darkness, and the girl so unattractive that the dogs are always silent before her house suffer great misery from this institution.

The distrust, animosity, aggression, and unsureness of all Chiangmai
interpersonal relations come full-blown in courtship. The boy tries to act

the model young man when he is courting. He is proper, hardworking, and in general acts like the ideal husband and son-in-law. He does not smoke, drink, gamble, fight, or keep bad company. The girl has the upper hand in courtship because she can give or withhold her affection and her hand. Only by being on his best behavior can a boy make a conquest or gain his favorite's hand in marriage. A girl knows how frequently boys deceive, and so she is mistrustful and cautious. She knows that if she weakens she will lose her reputation and reduce her chance of marriage—unless, that is, she deceives some other boy. The girl knows, too, that well-behaved suitors often become spendthrifts, gamblers, drunks, and good-for-nothings a few months after marriage, when they are sure of the girl. To hear older people and women and girls in the village talk about courting and marriage is often to have this stereotype of the deceitful male raised. Stories are told of seductions, after which a woman finds out that the man is already married and that she has become a "little wife."

The girl who gives in to boys and makes love to them soon becomes a matter of village gossip, first among her lovers and the other young men to whom they boast, and then among her girlfriends and the other villagers. "Men like girls like that, and they always find out who they are and they like them; but they will not marry them," was a comment of an old lady of the village about a particular village girl whose bestowal of favors had become a village scandal and shamed her family. A girl like this can make a good marriage with a suitable young man only by deceiving him. Usually she has to marry a widower or a divorcé. The village, like all villages, has a memory that lasts through the generations; nothing is ever forgotten. But, like all villages, there is a closing of ranks against anyone outside the group. Boys coming from far away to court are not always told about the girl's reputation in her own village.

Given such distrust on the part of the girls (some girls go to the point of offering their suitors whiskey to test their self-control) and on the part of the boys, it is no wonder that many matches do not develop into warm love relationships that last through the years. The relations between husband and wife in Chiangmai are often strained and distant.

Men in Chiangmai usually court the girls for five or six years before they marry for the first time. Chiangmai village's young women are saaws for one to five years, with a sizable minority waiting as long as six to nine years (see table 8). The age at first marriage has a wider variation than the age at beginning courtship, but the greatest number of men get married at the age of twenty-one or twenty-two. This is partly due to the

Table 8                 Number of Years
                        Between First Courtship
                        and First Marriage in
                        Chiangmai Village

| Years | Male | Female |
|---|---|---|
| 0 | 0 | 1 |
| 1 | 4 | 9 |
| 2 | 2 | 2 |
| 3 | 1 | 10 |
| 4 | 5 | 6 |
| 5 | 8 | 8 |
| 6 | 13 | 3 |
| 7 | 5 | 1 |
| 8 | 2 | 3 |
| 9 | 4 | 3 |
| 10 | 5 | 0 |
| 11 | 0 | 0 |
| 12 | 1 | 0 |
| 13 | 0 | 0 |
| 14 | 0 | 2 |
| 15 plus | 1 | 0 |
| Totals | 51 | 48 |

NOTE: Figures are based
upon a questionnaire given
to a randomly selected
sample of 10 percent of
village households.

exigencies of the Thai draft law: if one is not drafted at twenty-one, then one will not be, and so he can marry without the worry of being separated. The girls get married one or two years younger than the boys, mostly between the ages of seventeen and twenty-one, although, as with the men, there is much variation (see table 9).

## A Typical Courtship

The institution of courtship can best be understood by describing an actual courtship and the resulting wedding that took place in the village in 1972. The bride was a girl of Chiangmai named Can, and the groom was Laa, a boy from an adjacent village who was brought up in Chiangmai village by foster parents.

Laa's father, Pɔɔ Taa, was a Chiangmai village man who had married Mɛɛ Cuu and had gone to live in her village. Pii Naa, Laa's father's

**Table 9**                     Age at First Marriage
                                in Chiangmai Village

| Age | Male | Female | Total |
|---|---|---|---|
| Below 15 | 1 | 0 | 1 |
| 15 | 0 | 0 | 0 |
| 16 | 0 | 2 | 2 |
| 17 | 2 | 5 | 7 |
| 18 | 2 | 5 | 7 |
| 19 | 3 | 8 | 11 |
| 20 | 0 | 4 | 4 |
| 21 | 17 | 8 | 25 |
| 22 | 10 | 1 | 11 |
| 23 | 3 | 2 | 5 |
| 24 | 3 | 1 | 4 |
| 25 | 1 | 7 | 8 |
| 26 | 3 | 1 | 4 |
| 27 | 3 | 0 | 3 |
| 28 | 1 | 0 | 1 |
| 29 | 1 | 0 | 1 |
| 30 | 1 | 1 | 2 |
| 31 | 0 | 0 | 0 |
| 32 | 1 | 1 | 2 |
| Unmarried after 32 | 1 | 0 | 1 |
| Totals | 53 | 46 | 99 |

NOTE: Figures are based
upon a questionnaire given
to a randomly selected
sample of 10 percent of
village households

younger sister, had married a Chiangmai village man but remained child-
less for many years. When Laa was eight, Pii Naa came to her elder
brother and asked for a child to be adopted by her, and Laa was given
over. He left his father's house to come to live with his aunt in Chiangmai
Two. He went to school in Chiangmai, and after finishing school he helped
his foster parents work their fields and gardens. However, he never lost
track of his real father and mother and visited them often.

When Laa was sixteen he started to court the girls, and since he was a
tall and handsome young man he became acquainted with many of them;
but none caught his fancy to the exclusion of the others. In terms that
would not be used in Chiangmai village but which would be understood
there, he was playing the field and doing rather well at it. Then one day
at a housewarming celebration in Chiangmai he met Muun, the seventeen-

year-old daughter of Pɔɔ Tan, and they talked together. Muun was an easy girl to talk to. She invited him to come courting at her house. According to his account, he was a little interested in Muun and went to her house to see her off and on for quite a while. But, again according to Laa, he found out that Muun liked other boys as well and was making love with one or two of them (as well as him), so finally he stopped going to Muun's house and began to go elsewhere—to all the surrounding villages. (Muun tells a different story. She says that she loved him and he told her he loved her, so she let him make love to her. Muun told her parents that she was carrying his baby. To escape this trap, it is said in the village, he hurriedly began to go courting at Can's house. Muun's parents now claim that she just said that she was pregnant because she was a crazy young girl, but that it was not true. No one to this day, except Muun, and maybe her parents, knows the truth of the matter. Muun did not give birth to a child. Whether she had an abortion or a miscarriage is not known outside her immediate family circle.)

According to Laa, in December 1971, after he had stopped going to court at Muun's house, and after going to see many girls, he went to the house of Can, a Chiangmai village girl who lives in the south part of the village, to help a group of boys and girls peel garlic for planting. At first, Laa said, there was no special relationship between them; he didn't know that he liked her more than any other girl.

Then toward the end of December he realized that she was a very special girl and began to talk to her in the special language of courtship. He told her her eyes were like honey, that her hair was beautiful down her back, and so on. Each asked the other whether he had a fɛɛn, and each said no—an obvious untruth on both sides. In effect, they soon became fɛɛns. After this Laa came visiting every evening for three or four months, and they also met when the occasion offered at temple fairs, housewarmings, funerals, weddings, and other such affairs in Chiangmai and in the adjacent villages. They probably slept together.

When Laa began to call on her, Can already had a special relationship with Pradid, a boy from a nearby village who had been calling on her for some time. When Pradid saw that Can was being won over by Laa, a man from her own village (a situation in which Laa had the advantage), he became angry and stalked away from Can, saying that it was obvious that she had found a new fɛɛn and that he was leaving and never coming back.

Can was afraid for some time that Pradid was a "witch," a "phiika," who would come back to do her harm, as not infrequently happens in

Chiangmai. If a boy who has been scorned is a witch, he will harbor hatred for the girl and will come back in the form of an owl to sit in her room looking at her while she is asleep. If she becomes weakened or ill, she is vulnerable and the witch can enter her body and harm her or kill her by eating her insides. But Can saw no owl after Pradid went away, so she knew he wasn't a witch. (If she had been possessed by Pradid she would have called in an old man with magical powers, who would have whipped her with a crocodile tail until the spirit identified itself and then was forced to leave her body.)

According to the later accounts of both Can and Laa, they were both in love with each other during all this time but didn't say so openly for fear that their love was not returned. Then on May 28, 1972 (about the time that Muun created the furor in the village by claiming that she was pregnant), Laa came to Can and told her that he loved her more than anything in the world. Laa said that after he said this she didn't say anything but that a boy can tell when a girl loves him, and he was sure she did. Can told him that if he felt this way, he should talk to her parents. (If she had not loved him at this point, she would have had to tell him so.)

Laa left, saying that he would have his foster parents come to ask for her from her parents; it is the custom in Chiangmai village for the boy's parents to arrange the marriage at her house. His foster parents told him that this was such an important matter that they had better go tell his real parents in the adjacent village, which they proceeded to do with alacrity. His real father, Pɔɔ Taa, then came to Chiangmai village and went with the boy to talk to the girl and her father.

Can was eighteen years of age, about two years younger than Laa. Her mother had died when she was fourteen, and after that she took on the responsibilities of caring for her father, running the house, and raising her younger siblings. She became a saaw at sixteen, and, according to her own admission, had met lots of boys before Laa came to call.

The meeting took place between the "khonjaj" ("big people") of the two families: Can's mother's father and her mother's older brother talked with Pɔɔ Taa and Laa's foster father. The boys' khonjaj said that the two children were in love and asked Can's father if his side liked the boy and if he was acceptable to them.

The girl's khonjaj said that he was a very nice young man, that he was more than acceptable to them, and that since the couple were in love in any case, they could not be more happy with the marriage. The young couple were then brought in and were asked if they were in love and wanted to get married, and they answered yes. Then the girl's family told the boy's family to choose an auspicious day for the marriage ceremony and feast.

Pɔɔ Taa and Laa's foster father asked the birthdate of Can and armed with this information went to see Pɔɔ Sii, a very old man of the village who has the learning and the occult books necessary to choose auspicious days for almost everything. Pɔɔ Sii took the birthdates of the two young people, consulted his book, and divined that Saturday, June 10, at four in the afternoon was the best time for the marriage ceremony to be held.

After this Laa's foster father gave 25 baht to the girl's father as the "kaa saj phii," the "price to be paid to the ancestral spirits of the girl's lineage for raising the girl." Until the "phii," the "ancestral spirits" of the girl's lineage, had been informed, the marriage could not take place. Also, since the young couple would reside at least initially with the parents of the bride, her ancestral guardian spirits had to be informed so that they would protect her husband.

The phii of Can's matrilineage were fed and informed on June 5 by the "kawphii," the old woman "elder" of Can's lineage. This is the crucial step in traditional marriage for the villagers. In the old days, and some-times even now, the boy would simply move into the girl's house on a propitious day after her spirits had been informed, and they would be considered married; a young man would pack his bundle of possessions and his sword (the "symbol of a man") and would go to the girl's house in the dead of night. Nowadays the villagers have adopted the custom of having a banquet and an elaborate ceremony of tying the two wrists to-gether. The same principle still holds, however; the crucial event in Chiang-mai village marriages is the offering of the spirit price to the girl's matri-lineal ancestors. Once that is done, the couple is married. This is a point worth emphasizing because some Central Thai and others have believed that a young couple just goes and lives together without any ceremonial recognition of the fact. Nothing could be farther from the truth. There is the ceremony of asking the khonjaj of both families to approve the mar-riage. And there is always the paying of the spirit "bride price" for the girl. The first Christian marriage attempted in Chiengmai city had to be postponed because a khonjaj of the bride's family insisted that he would not recognize the legality of the union until the spirit price had been paid (see McGilvary 1912, p. 207).

On June 5 the spirits were consulted; and on June 6 Laa came to live at Can's house. The next day they went to Chiengmai city to buy the necessary mattresses and bedding. They also had invitations of a formal kind, new-style and expensive, printed in Chiengmai city to send to the relatives and friends of both sides, inviting them to the wedding feast on June 10. All this was not done formerly except in extremely rich families. Can and her family paid for the feast and reception. Fortunately, the donations of money which would be given by the guests would pay back a large share of the expenditure.

A month after the engagement, at 4:00 P.M., the new-style wedding ceremony, a custom apparently borrowed from the Central Thai and the Chinese, began. The young people's club of Chiangmai village had brought the chairs and tables for the feast from the temple and had helped Can and her family set everything up in the courtyard. They also helped cook and serve the food and refreshments, and several of the boys took on the task of parking the many motorcycles and bicycles of the guests. These numbered about two hundred, mostly men representing their families, as is the custom. By 4:30 the men were seated at the long tables talking, drinking rice whiskey, and consuming vast quantities of peanuts.

Meanwhile up inside the house were Can and her "bride's attendants," all prettily dressed in Thai silk, with flowers in their hair in traditional Chiengmai fashion. The house was aswarm with old ladies who had come to see that all was done properly, and they were saying how nice Can looked, and what a nice boy Laa was, and how happy they all were for everyone. While Can was in her room getting ready, the notables of village society were arriving in the main hall of the house, where the actual ceremony was to take place. There was the village headman of Laa's native village, and the two village headmen of Chiangmai village, together with rich and respected members of the community.

At this time Laa, together with a group of his friends, appeared at the gate of the compound, merrily and a bit drunkenly carrying a cardboard suitcase with his belongings, symbolizing the loneliness of the man's trip to his bride's house and his dependence on her family.

The groom's party arrived amidst a great popping of firecrackers, and then there ensued a haggling over the proper price that the groom would have to pay to the relatives of the bride before he was admitted. The proper price turned out to be a bottle of rice wine, which was hoisted aloft and waved as Laa and his friends poured into the compound. A last-ditch defense was made at the door to the bride's house by her mother's brother, a member of her matrilineage, but he was not able to stem the tide, and the party entered, sobering a bit when they saw the big men of the village assembled before them. Laa had on pants, white shirt, and a thin tie to mark the formality of the occasion, although he appeared to be quite casual and joking about it all.

After a short wait the bride made her entrance. After greeting the guests, she and her attendants took their positions, kneeling behind pillows at the front of the hall facing the assembled audience. There then followed, as at all formal Thai gatherings, a succession of endlessly monotonous speeches by the three village heads and the main relatives of both sides, telling what an important occasion marriage was and what a good wife and mother, and husband and father, should be. The groom looked a bit bored by the proceedings, and the bride looked scared.

After this, all the notables and relatives tied the couple's hands together with white cords and said good words over them to bring them luck. And after this Laa, with his suitcase, and Can were ceremonially ushered into the bedroom, where they were stared at by all and sundry.

After a while the banquet got under way. All the guests were seated in the courtyard below and were served the meal of greens and salt pork plus raw minced buffalo meat and more alcohol. At the conclusion of the eating, as the evening was wearing on, the bride and groom, together with their attendants, walked around the assembled company to all the tables, carrying a large silver bowl filled with scented handkerchiefs. Everyone was offered a handkerchief and then was expected to put a contribution into another, similar container.

At several points along the circuit of the tables on the money-gathering expedition, men, by now under the table figuratively but not yet literally, waved envelopes of money in the air and demanded that the bride and groom stand on chairs in front of everyone and that they hug and kiss each other before they were given the money. By this time the bride was beginning to pale but managed to get through this ritualized teasing of bride and groom which is so common in many places of the world. The couple were not enjoying this very much; but then they were not expected to. The affair finally petered out late in the evening, and everyone went home.

Such are courtships and weddings in Chiangmai village.

# 7        Family, Inheritance, and Kinship

Familial and kinship groupings and institutions are no more loosely structured than the other aspects of village society that we have already discussed in this book. The ideals which define the form of the family and guide an individual's behavior toward family members and kinsmen are just as clearly formulated in Chiangmai as they are in any other society. That these ideals are not completely realized in actual life makes rural Thai society no different from any other culture. And like all other peoples in the world, the Thai villagers of Chiangmai have some choices and flexibility in their social patterns which they can exercise to maximize their own personal interests. But talk of loosely structured families and nebulous kindreds simply does not square with what we found in the village.[1]

## The Family

Matrilocal Residence
and Endogamy

After marriage, Chiangmai village couples go to live in the bride's parents' house.[2] If the bride is the youngest daughter, who will inherit the parental house, the couple will reside there permanently; if not, they usually live a year or two with the bride's parents and then reside permanently nearby, often in the same courtyard. This is the universally expressed ideal, and it is observed in almost all marriages, even if the period of residence with the wife's family is only a token one of a few months. Matrilocal residence and the labor that the groom performs for the bride's family is a form of bride-service, a way of repaying the matrilineal spirits of the girl and her family for raising her to maturity. Village women explain their strong emotional preference for matrilocal residence by claiming that they could not possibly live harmoniously with the husband's family, especially his mother.

Nevertheless, under certain circumstances the ideal residence pattern is not followed. When the man's family is much richer or of much higher status than the woman's family, and the couple decide that it would be greatly to their advantage to cast their lot with his family, they may move there after a token stay of only a few months with the woman's family. Or a couple may decide to reside with the man's family if his parents have no daughters to perform the woman's work of the household, to care for them in their old age, and to inherit the house and the matrilineal ancestors. In such cases the couple go, after a short stay, to live with the groom's family. Also, a couple may choose to reside with the husband's parents (patrilocally) if there is a personal conflict with the wife's family so extreme as to make life with them absolutely impossible. Such conflicts occasionally occur; one son-in-law I heard of was run out of his wife's family's household at gunpoint.

The rule requiring a young man to live with his wife's family puts him in a weak position. During the early years of his marriage he is an outsider to the people surrounding him, and he is under the authority of his wife's father. As well as living in his father-in-law's house, a newly married man may even have to sleep in the same room as his parents-in-law if the family is extremely poor and the house is small. He works the rice fields of his wife's family under the supervision and direction of his father-in-law, eats rice from the granary of his wife's family, and is dependent on his father-in-law for assistance in such important matters as obtaining land to rent. In the early years of his marriage he does not speak up in family councils, and his own wife and children are under the authority of his father-in-law, whose demands have priority over his own.

McGilvary, the early American missionary already mentioned above, a keen observer of the Khonmyaŋ villagers around Chiengmai city over a lifetime, puts it succinctly: "After marriage, the almost universal custom of the country has been that the husband lives with the wife's family. He becomes identified with it, and for the time a subordinate member of it, almost to the extent of becoming weaned from his own family" (1912, p. 178).

When the young man marries into his wife's family from a different village, his position is even weaker than that of a young man from the same village. He is further cut off from the support of his own family in the course of his daily life, and he is at the mercy of his wife's family, her relatives, and her fellow villagers. However, many men avoid village exogamy: 140 of the 294 Chiangmai village marriages on which I have information were village-endogamous, marriages in which both the man and the woman were from Chiangmai village. In such marriages, the boy still has to move into the house of his father-in-law and is still in a weak position, but because the members of his wife's family are fellow villagers and because he remains close to his own family, kinsmen, and friends, his move does not cut him off from all his previously formed solidary relationships as marriage into another village does.

These are the ideals. If we compare ideals to the actual behavior of the villagers and describe behavior in statistical terms, the results are as follows. Of the 140 village-endogamous marriages, 88 were matrilocal, following the ideal pattern in which the man initially moves to stay with the woman's family and then continues to reside in their house or nearby, usually within the same courtyard. Eighteen were matri-neolocal; after an initial period of living with the wife's family, the couple set up their own household away from the wife's parents' house and courtyard, but still in the same village. Sixteen of the 140 endogamous marriages were matri-patrilocal; after an initial period of living with the woman's parents, the couple took up residence with or near the man's parents, but still in Chiangmai village. The remaining eighteen cases were neolocal marriages, in which the newly married couple did not reside with the wife's parents at all but instead immediately set up their own house apart from either family somewhere in Chiangmai village. If there is no land at all available, a situation which became more common with the population explosion of the past fifty years, then the young couple have to seek their fortune elsewhere—even out of the village.

The nominal violations of the rule of matrilocal residence which occur when couples reside matri-neolocally or neolocally within the village are not structurally significant because the same kind of superordinate-subordinate social relationship between the wife's parents and the daughter's family can be and is maintained even if the married daughter does not live in her parents' courtyard but does live in the same village. If residence is patrilocal, a patrilocal extended family is formed and the usual pattern of relations between son-in-law and wife's parents cannot be maintained.

But such marriages are infrequent and are usually made only to fill a gap in the establishment of normal family relations caused by the absence of a daughter in the husband's family.

When one considers the 154 marriages (out of the 294 on which I have information) in which village exogamy occurred—that is, marriages in which a Chiangmai man or woman married someone from another village —48 were marriages in which men from outside married Chiangmai women and came to live in the village with their wives; 46 were marriages in which Chiangmai men married outside the village into the village of their wives—an almost even exchange of men. Thus, 94 of the 154 exogamous marriages observed the ideal matrilocal residence rule. Fifty-nine of the 154 exogamous marriages involved women of Chiangmai who married out or women of other villages who married in. Hence, in these 59 cases, the rule of matrilocality was not observed. Like the exchange of men between villages, the exchange of women was also evenly balanced, with 29 women marrying into Chiangmai and 30 Chiangmai women marrying out into other villages. Women who marry outside their own village do so under great duress—usually because they are poor and stand no chance of inheriting house or property in their own village. One additional marriage was a rarity—one in which both the man and woman were from other places and came to Chiangmai to live.

In spite of these exceptional cases, over the past several decades the vast majority of the men and women of Chiangmai—79 percent of the men and 86 percent of the women, to be exact—have married within their village. Village society is socially inbred in the sense that most families are related by marriage ties (recognized or not) in many diverse ways simultaneously.

The Family Cycle

The dynamics of family life in Chiangmai can be understood only in the context of the domestic group cycle (see Goody 1962); in Chiangmai as elsewhere social structure is a process in time.[3]

An ideal-type domestic cycle in Chiangmai village would be as shown in figure 3. The cycle begins with the marriage of a young couple and the subsequent birth of children, which forms a new nuclear family (see Phase I of figure 3).

As the children grow up, the sons marry out of the family and go to live with the families of their wives; they are expected to leave the family into which they were born to seek their fortunes. Daughters ideally marry in sequence of age. Each daughter and her husband lives in her parents' house for a period which varies from a few months to several years. When a son-in-law moves in to live with his wife's family and has children, adding a new nuclear family to the original couple, the structure of a Chiangmai family changes from the nuclear one just described (Phase I) to a multigenerational extended matrilineal-stem family composed of parents, unmarried sons and daughters, and the married daughter and her husband and children (Phase II).

If there is only one daughter in the family, she, together with her husband and children, remains to live with her parents for the rest of their lives, and ultimately inherits the house. If there is more than one daughter in a family, the first married daughter and her family usually move into a separate house when the second daughter marries and brings her husband to live in her parents' house. Two married daughters are not supposed to live in their parents' house at the same time, although occasionally

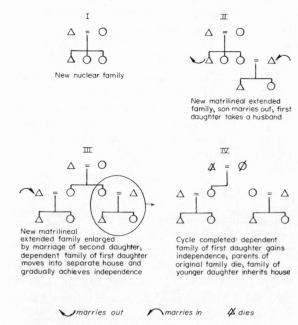

**Fig. 3**                    Phases in the family and
                              household cycle

this happens for a short period of time if two daughters marry close together. The older daughter and her family move into a smaller house in the courtyard of her parents or as near the parental house as possible. They remain under the domination of the parental house, since the father-in-law controls their labor, but they attempt to gain independence, often by seeking to buy their own land as soon as they are able. The parents like to retain their primacy as long as possible, and the process by which a dependent household gains independence is usually long-drawn-out and conflict ridden.

Phase III of the family cycle is represented in figure 3 as that point at which all the sons have married out and gone to live with their wives' families; a second daughter has married and lives with her husband and family in the parental house; and the older married daughter and her still-dependent family are living in the same courtyard nearby.

Phase IV of the family cycle begins when the youngest married daughter and her husband take over formal control of the household from her retired parents. If the parents desire to do so, they may divide up their property among their children at this time, giving the dependent daughters' families independence. The cycle ends when the youngest married daughter and her family inherits the deceased parents' house and (if it has not happened before) the property is divided and the dependent families achieve complete independence and start the cycle over again.[4]

Family And
Household Types

In 1972, our census showed 875 persons in the village living in 206 households, an average of 4.25 persons per household. As shown in table 10, 129 of the village households were nuclear families, 8 were nuclear families plus matrilineal relatives, 43 were matrilineal extended families of three generations living under the same roof, 10 were patrilocal extended families, and 16 were of diverse types.

Many of the nuclear family households mentioned above are actually not independent; they are connected in varying degrees of subordination and dependence to the household of the wife's parents. The most subordinate households are still under the authority of the parental household, work its rice fields, and eat from its granary. The less subordinate households are independent in terms of food production, have their own granary, and manage their own fields; but they do not have formal ownership of

**Table 10**                    Household Types in
                                Chiangmai Village, 1972

| | |
|---|---|
| 1. Nuclear family households | 129 |
| (husband, wife, and unmarried children) | |
| 2. Nuclear family plus matrilineal relatives | 8 |
| 3. Matrilocal extended families | 43 |
| (husband, wife, married daughter, daughter's husband, and daughter's children—3 generations) | |
| 4. Patrilocal extended families | 10 |
| (husband, wife, married son, son's wife, and son's children) | |
| 5. Miscellaneous* | 16 |
| Total households | 206 |

*Included under the category "miscellaneous" are households containing the following types of people: widower; widow (2); unmarried man; brother and sister; a man, his younger sister, and his older sister's daughter; a man and his son; a widow and her son and his daughter; a widow and her daughter's son; a widow and her son's daughter; a widow and her friend's daughter's son; a widow and her brother's daughter's daughter's son; a woman and her sister's son's daughter; a widow with her son and her daughter's daughter; and an abandoned woman and daughter (2).

their land, which still lies in the parents' hands. These dependent households are actually members of matrilineally extended families, even though they do not live under the same roof as the wife's parents' family. In other words, there are more matrilineally extended families in Chiangmai village than there are matrilocal households. Household (a living and property owning unit) and family (a jural unit which organizes labor and sometimes shares rice) do not always coincide (see also Mizuno [1968] and Keyes [1975] for a similar analysis).

Family Relationships

Key relationships in Chiangmai village families are between parents and daughter, a woman and her husband, and between father-in-law and son-in-law.

During the early years of her marriage, when she lives in the house of her parents or in a dependent satellite household near them in the village, a woman remains loyal to her parents and under the authority of her father. If a man wishes to transmit a message to his son-in-law, he does it through his daughter or granddaughter. A man can order his married daughter and her husband and children to work on his farm and to represent him in labor-exchange relationships with other families in the village. One way that a man can build up a village entourage is to have his daughters attract sons-in-law to him.

The relationship between a mother and her married daughter living in the same household or nearby continues to be close throughout their lifetime (see a similar case in Burma in Nash [1965], p. 51). The line of descent through women is the family's thread of structural continuity from one generation to another. The house, the garden, part of the family rice land, and the matrilineal spirits pass down from grandmother to mother to daughter and then to granddaughter, in a direct and unbroken line of succession. The core of women have common interests that last more than one generation. They bring men into the family to perform the necessary labor in the rice fields, to act as executive heads of the family, and to give them children. Keyes (1975, p. 291) describes how women in the northeastern village of Nong Tuen express filial piety by dedicating a small portion of their temple offerings to their parents; a similar practice is followed in Chiangmai.

As Sulamith Heins Potter (1975) points out, the villagers solve the problem of succession to jural authority in the family in a way different from the classical patrilineal mode, where authority passes from father to eldest son; and different from the classical matrilineal mode, where authority passes from mother's brother to sister's son. The mode in Chiangmai is one of *affinal succession*, where authority in the family moves from father-in-law to son-in-law, men who are connected only by ties to their wives, a line of women.

A man is supposed to be a willing worker for his father-in-law and submit to his authority. In return for his help in the rice fields, the son-in-law and his family earn the right to eat rice from his father-in-law's granary. The son-in-law and father-in-law are two unrelated men who are connected only by affinal ties—the fact that they both married into the same family line of women. The father-in-law is able to exploit his son-in-law's labor and to exercise control over him, a situation which is resented by the younger man. This relationship is potentially explosive, and to prevent trouble there is an avoidance taboo between a son-in-law and his parents-in-law; they almost never speak to one another and avoid each other's presence if possible.

A dependent family tries to save money and to buy its own house and land and thus become independent of the parental household as quickly as possible. As time goes by, a young son-in-law begins to make money of his own. There are several economic possibilities open to him. He may grow winter cash crops on land given to him or rented to him for a nominal sum by his father-in-law; in other words, he may begin to reap material rewards from his relationship with his wife's family. He may work his own rice land, if he inherits any. He can work as an agricultural laborer for wages on the fields of other villagers. There is also the possibility of working as an unskilled laborer in the city. His wife may earn money by becoming a market woman or by opening a small village shop.

If a man marries a young woman who is to inherit her parents' house and compound, he continues to live in her house with her parents and gradually assumes more authority as his father-in-law ages. A constant struggle occurs in almost all village families between young people who wish to take over formal authority in the family and the wife's parents who wish to retain control over the family and formal ownership of their land as long as possible. Control of the family is dependent upon retention of the land, and so older people like to retain ownership of their land to ensure that they will be well-treated in their old age. When the father-in-law retires or dies, the resident son-in-law succeeds to his position as male head of the family.

Relations between father and son are quite different from those between father-in-law and son-in-law. Relations between village fathers and sons resemble in some ways the warm and nonjural relations between Trobriand fathers and sons, as described by Malinowski; and relations between a man and his father-in-law resemble the relations between a man and his mother's brother in the Trobriands, in that the father-in-law is an authority figure from whom a man succeeds to jural authority. When a boy is small his father is responsible for teaching him to plow, to fish, to weave bamboo mats and baskets, and to do all the other things men are expected to do in this society. If the father has the means, he sends his son into the temple for a year or so to serve as a novice and to make merit for his parents' souls in the afterlife. In return for his education in the ways of manhood and in return for his livelihood, a son owes his father love, respect, and obedience; and he has to work on his father's farm.

Ties between mother and son are even warmer than those between son and father. Mothers want to retain their sons' affection, and they are proud to have land for their sons to inherit in their village so that they do not have to marry into another village.

Relations between parents and sons, however affectionate, do not have the structural significance of the ties between parents and daughter— especially between parents and the daughter who will inherit their house and care for them in their old age. Sons do not have a long-term, permanent interest in their natal family because they must eventually leave it and marry into another family. Sons do not have as much status in their natal families as do sons-in-law; the situation is as described by Keyes (1975, p. 290) in the northeast, where sons-in-law take precedence over sons in families where the male head has died, when the family has to be represented at meetings in the temple. The loyalty and the economic interests of a man lie with his wife's family and the new nuclear family that he and his wife will establish. As young sons grow to adulthood this structural fact is manifested in conflict between father and son over the son's labor on his father's farm. Young men become increasingly more interested in making money of their own and in courting the girls than they are in working for their natal family. Still the parent-son tie continues to be fairly warm and strong, and the tie is important because sons will inherit their parents' land equally with their sisters. This is the major difference between father-son relations in Chiangmai and in the Trobriands; in Thailand a son may inherit land from his father, even though he succeeds to his father-in-law's jural authority. If it were not for this fundamental economic fact, the parents-son tie would be just as weak in Chiangmai village as the parents-daughter tie is in a society like traditional China, where the daughter inherits no property, marries out into her husband's family, and is never considered a real member of her parents' family— even while she is growing up.

In Chiangmai a man makes his career and, he may hope, his fortune in the context of his wife's family. Village men dream of marrying beautiful and wealthy girls who have few younger siblings to support or to divide the inheritance. A rich woman with no brothers and sisters, who will inherit her parents' house and estate, is the best possible catch for a young man.

## Inheritance

The ideal and general rule usually followed in Chiangmai village inheritance is that all children, sons and daughters, inherit equally the rice fields, orchards, and gardens of their parents. Inheritance can be delayed until both parents die, but sometimes parents divide the property after they retire; or if one member of an old couple dies, the surviving member frequently divides his property. He may or may not retain a portion for himself as security. Parents often retain formal title to the property long after they have retired and have given its management over to the succeeding generation. When I was soliciting answers for my household census and questionnaire, parents and their children frequently claimed ownership of the same fields, the children anticipating their inheritance.

The main exception to the rule of equal inheritance is that the youngest married daughter, who brings her husband to live in the house of her parents, inherits the house and its grounds, in addition to her share of the rest of the property. According to village testimony, this is to repay her for caring for her aged parents. If there is no daughter to inherit the parental house, one of the sons is expected to bring his wife in to live with his parents. If there are no married children, a child is adopted from within the bilateral kindred to inherit the property. In the few cases of adoption I know about, a daughter was usually adopted from the wife's sister.

The reality of inheritance is much more complicated than the ideal and reveals more detailed rules and options, as is brought out in the following actual cases of inheritance in the village (compare Mizuno 1971 and Keyes 1975). These cases also illustrate variations in family and residence patterns.[5]

*Case 1.* ʔUj Can, an elderly village lady, together with her deceased husband, once owned 8 raj of rice land and a sizable lamjaj orchard in the village. The couple had seven children, of whom four—two daughters and two sons—survived to adulthood and figured in the inheritance. After ʔUj Can's husband died, she divided up her property among her children. She retained 1½ raj of land for her own use; this she now rents for a nominal sum to the son who lives nearby, but after her death it will go to her other married son, who is a schoolteacher in Chiengdao, a town north of Chiengmai city. He will probably sell it to one of his sisters in the village.

The remaining 6½ raj was divided equally among the married daughter with whom ʔUj Can is now living, the older married daughter who has a house in the same compound, and her married son who lives nearby.

In addition to the rice land, each of the three children who are living in the village near their mother received a portion of the parents' lamjaj orchard. The married son brought his wife to live with him near his mother because his wife was an older daughter of a poor family and would not inherit her parents' house, nor did her parents have sufficient land to give them a house site to build on. Since ʔUj Can's son inherited a lamjaj orchard, he built a house there and brought his wife to live with him. In this case, special circumstances made it inadvisable to follow the norm of matrilocal residence.

Case I suggests the following additional rule governing inheritance in Chiangmai: sons who marry out of the village do not necessarily inherit property; sometimes (rarely) they relinquish their inheritance, or they take money or some other compensation. They sell their inherited share of land to one of their sisters who remains at home.

*Case II.* A long time ago, the mother of ʔUj Taa, who had been separated from her husband since ʔUj Taa was one year old, owned 5 raj of rice land and 1 raj of house garden. ʔUj Taa's mother on her deathbed told her two daughters, Taa and Tib, that the property was to be divided equally between them. Since at that time Taa was twelve and Tib was fifteen, their mother told Tib that she should keep Taa's share of the inheritance in trust for her until Taa married, and that she should take care of her younger sister.

So the two sisters lived together in their mother's house after her death. Tib married first, at the age of twenty-one. Taa, the younger sister, continued to live with Tib until she too married, at the age of nineteen. When her younger sister married, Tib divided the property and gave her younger sister her half of the inheritance. Each sister got 2½ raj of rice land and ½ raj of house garden. When Taa married she had the right to inherit the parental house as the younger married daughter, and so Tib, her older sister, built a new house for her family on her half of the garden and left the parental house to Taa and her husband.

A few years later, Tib's husband inherited a garden from his parents, and he wanted to go and live there. Taa bought back Tib's ½ raj of garden compound for 300 bhat. As the years went by, Taa and her husband bought 2½ raj additional rice land from Mɛɛ Peŋ, Taa's mother's mother's sister. Taa and her husband now owned 5 raj of rice land and 1 raj of garden, in addition to the parental house. They had five children before he died.

After his death, Taa married another man, one who owned 5¼ raj of rice land and ½ raj of garden in another part of the village. She had two more children by her second husband, both of them boys. During the final few years of their marriage, ʔUj Taa divided the property he brought to their marriage between their two sons. ʔAaj Hian, the bachelor younger son, received 2¾ raj of rice land, plus his father's house. ʔAaj Maa, the married older brother, received 2½ raj of land and ½ raj of garden. After the property had been divided in this way, Hian, the younger brother, decided to give his father's house to his older married brother. He moved into his brother's smaller house and never married. People think that he will leave his property to Dɛɛŋ, his brother's oldest son, "because he loves the child so much."

The children of ʔUj Taa's first husband had no right to inheritance from their mother's second husband and received nothing. This suggests another rule in village inheritance, namely that children usually inherit only from their natural parents; if a man or woman is married twice and has children by both spouses, each set of children inherits only from their natural parents.

ʔUj Taa has not yet divided her property from her first marriage, but she says that each of her five children by her first husband will receive equal shares, 1 raj of rice land each. In addition, her married youngest daughter by her first husband, who is now living with ʔUj Taa, will inherit the parental house. Theoretically, it would seem, ʔUj Taa's two sons by her second marriage would also have some inheritance rights over the land she brought to her first marriage, but since they have received an adequate inheritance they will not be given a share of ʔUj Taa's earlier property.

*Case III.* Pɔɔ Kham was a man from a neighboring village who married Mɛɛ Pan of Chiangmai village and came to live with her there. Mɛɛ Pan had been married before and had a son, Aj. At the time of the marriage of Mɛɛ Pan and Pɔɔ Kham, Pɔɔ Kham's parents divided their property. Since Pɔɔ Kham was to live in Chiangmai, and property in his native village would be inconvenient for him to work, he sold his share to his sister; he did not inherit much property, so there was not much money.

Mɛɛ Pan was poor and did not have much money either, but they worked hard, saved, and finally pooled their money to buy their own land—1½ tax raj of rice land and 1 raj of garden. They had six children, three boys and three girls. Not long ago Mɛɛ Pan died, and Pɔɔ Kham died the following year. Before Kham died, he made arrangements for the house to go to his eighteen-year-old granddaughter, Cancuum, who had lived with her grandparents for years, ever since her widowed mother, Kɛɛw, Pɔɔ Kham's daughter, had remarried and had gone to live with her new husband elsewhere in the village. Kɛɛw's first husband, Cancuum's father, had left Cancuum a large water buffalo as her inheritance. Pɔɔ Kham left his house to Cancuum because when the family recently built their new house, they ran out of money halfway through construction and had to sell Cancumm's buffalo to get the money to finish the house. All her aunts and uncles agreed that she should have the house, since if it had not been for her buffalo there would have been no house.

As for the 1½ raj of rice land and the 1 raj of building land and garden, Pɔɔ Kham told his children to divide it up as they saw fit. The children had no difficulty dividing the rice fields; each of the six children received ¼ raj. When it came to dividing the 1 raj of garden, however, there was trouble because, with the land divided six ways, each sibling would receive an insignificant amount. In such cases it is customary for some or all of the heirs to sell out to one or more of the others, so that a family living compound, house plot, and garden can be maintained. Usually brothers sell to sisters.

The matter was complicated by a dispute over the proceeds from the Chiangmai village funeral society and the consolidation of the land between Laa (one of the daughters) and her husband, and ʔAaj Pan, one of the sons. Laa and her husband, Sɛɛn, had been living in the parental house with their parents and Cancuum, their niece. Since Laa was the youngest married daughter and had lived with and cared for the parents, she had a strong claim to the house, which they lost to Cancuum because of Cancuum's water buffalo. Furthermore, Laa and Sɛɛn had the money to buy out some of the other shares. Pɔɔ Kham had belonged to the Chiangmai funeral association but had been unable to keep up the required 2-baht payment every time someone died. His son-in-law, ʔAaj Sɛɛn, kept up the payments for him, so that, when Pɔɔ Kham died, Sɛɛn and Laa got the 2,000-baht death proceeds from the funeral society. The usual practice in such cases is to spend about 1,000 baht on the funeral and keep the other 1,000. The funeral actually costs over 2,000 baht because the family has to make a coffin and feed the priests and all the people who come. The balance of the funeral expenses is by custom paid by all the heirs, who in this case were the six children. ʔAaj Pan, one of the sons, was angry that Sɛɛn and Laa had made so much money off the death of his father, and he claimed that all the 2,000 baht should be spent for the funeral expenses. After some quarreling and much bad feelings, ʔAaj Pan gave in and agreed to pay his share of the remaining funeral expenses.

Since he had no cash, he had to agree to sell his part of the garden inheritance to Sɛɛn and Laa. At first he agreed on a price of 450 baht.

Later he came back and demanded an additional 50 baht. His sister was
furious, but her husband said, "Never mind," and they gave the additional
50 baht.

The inheritance of the garden land is still not resolved with the other
heirs, but the situation of the family members is this: of the three sisters
and three brothers who inherited shares, one brother lives with his wife
in another part of the village; another is married into a neighboring village;
and the third, ʔAaj Pan, lives in the same village but some distance away.
It appears that all three brothers have now agreed to sell to their sister
Laa and her husband Sɛɛn. Of the other two sisters, Kɛɛw lives with her
second husband in another part of the village. Her share will go to her
daughter, Cancuum, who inherited the house. The third sister, Kham, is a
widow who lives in a small house in the same compound as the parental
house; she inherited the strip of compound and garden on which her house
is sitting. Since she has no children, it is unclear what will happen to her
share after her death. Probably it will go to Laa and Sɛɛn, or to Cancuum
and her husband, if she marries. In spite of the conflicts and the com-
plexities, it seems that the compound and garden will be consolidated into
one or two family living units by a daughter and a daughter's daughter of
the deceased. In accord with preferential matrilocality and matrilineality,
the house and the compound tend to pass down to females through females.

*Case IV*. Mɛɛ Naa told me that her grandmother's (her mother's
mother's) name was Kham. ʔUj Kham had three daughters: Tum, Bua,
and Muun. Muun inherited 4 raj of rice land and 1 raj of garden from
Kham, but Muun's husband brought no property to his marriage. Muun
died before her husband, leaving him to live with their only child, a
daughter, Naa. After a while he remarried. When Naa herself married, her
father gave her the 4 raj of rice land and the 1 raj of garden that he had
held in trust for her. He had no claim on this property, since it belonged
to his wife. This case suggests another principle of Chiangmai inheritance,
that when a man and a woman marry the property that each one brings to
the marriage remains his separate property. At his death the property goes
to his or her natural children, not to the spouse, to dispose of as they wish.

*Case V*. Pɔɔ Aj was one of the two children of ʔUj Laaj, who owned
15 raj of rice land and 1 raj of garden. Before ʔUj Laaj died she divided
her property between her two children: her son, Pɔɔ Aj, received 6 raj
of unproductive lowland fields and 4 raj of good highland; his sister, Mɛɛ
Kɛɛw, who had lived with her parents until their death, received 5 raj of
good rice land and 1 raj of garden, plus the parental house and the granary.

Pɔɔ Aj married Mɛɛ Suu and went to live with her parents. After the parents died, Aj and Suu bought their present house plot and built their house; Mɛɛ Suu's parental house plot nearby, which she inherited, is now inhabited by one of her daughters. Pɔɔ Aj and Mɛɛ Suu had six children—three daughters and three sons. At present Pɔɔ Aj is still actively working his land, and so Aj and Suu have not divided it. They say that the rice land will be divided equally among their six children. They are discussing the disposition of their house and garden with their children at present. They wish to leave them to their youngest daughter, Khamnɔɔj, who is now living with them, if the other children will agree.

This case, again, illustrates the desire of the people of Chiangmai to maintain the integrity of the parental house and compound and pass it on to the youngest daughter.

*Case VI*. When ʔUj Sɛɛn and ʔUj Khankɛɛw married, she had 15 raj of rice land. She died giving birth to her first child, a daughter named Taakham, who inherited all 15 raj of rice land and 1 raj of garden from her mother. Not long afterwards, ʔUj Sɛɛn remarried. He had no children by his second wife.

When Taakham was a young woman, she married ʔAaj Can. Taakham, like her mother, died giving birth to her daughter, Sunaa. The baby Sunaa was taken to live with her father's mother, ʔUj Tuj. When Sunaa was eight years old Can, her father, died; and when she was seventeen ʔUj Tuj died. This left Sunaa sharing a house with her father's older brother, Pan, a bachelor who had never married.

At the age of twenty, Sunaa married Chaa, a man from a neighboring village, who came to live with her. After she married, her grandfather, ʔUj Sɛɛn, again a widower, gave over to her the 15 raj of rice land from her grandmother and mother that he had held in trust for her, with the provision that she was to feed him for the rest of his life. To this 15 raj was added 2½ raj of rice land and 1 raj of garden from her uncle Pan. Sunaa thus inherited a total of 17½ raj of rice land and 2 raj of garden, where she and her husband now live. Her husband's father owns 30 raj of rice land but has not yet divided it.

*Case VII*. Mɛɛ Saa married Pɔɔ Muun. After their marriage Saa's parents gave her 5 raj of rice land and 1 raj of garden. Muun also received his inheritance, 3 raj of rice land and 1 raj of garden, before his parents died. During their marriage, Saa and Muun bought an additional 2 raj of rice land, making a total of 10 raj of rice land and 2 raj of garden land.

Saa and Muun had one daughter, Pan, and one son, Can. Can married into his wife's village, and Pan stayed at home to live with and take care of her parents. When the inheritance was divided, Can, the son, received 5 raj of rice fields and 1 raj of garden, as did his sister. In addition, she inherited the parental house and granary.

Pan married Kham, and they had a daughter, Laa, who lives with them. In addition, before she married Kham, Pan had given birth to an illegitimate son named Sanid, who lives with Mɛɛ Laa, a woman who adopted him.

During their marriage, Kham and Pan bought an additional 4 raj of rice land together. Although they have not yet formally divided their estate, they intend to divide it as follows: (1) the 4 raj they accumulated jointly during their marriage they will leave to Laa, their daughter; (2) the property that Pan brought with her into marriage will be split equally between Laa and her illegitimate half-brother, Sanid, except that Laa will get Pan's house.

The rule that men and women retain separate control over the property that they bring to their marriage allows provision to be made for illegitimate children like Sanid. If his mother had owned no property, he probably would not have received anything. This case also suggests that legitimate heirs may receive priority over illegitimate children in inheritance. All the jointly accumulated property of Kham and Pan plus half of her own property went to Laa. Pan's illegitimate son might have been entitled to more if he had been legitimate.

*Case VIII.* Mɛɛ Laa married Pɔɔ Kɛɛw. Before Mɛɛ Laa's parents died they divided their property, and Mɛɛ Laa received 7 raj of rice land and 1 raj of garden, plus the house. Pɔɔ Kɛɛw's parents, who lived in a neighboring village, gave him a cash inheritance of only 1,000 baht, which he used to purchase ½ raj of land in Chiangmai village. Laa and Kɛɛw had one child, Sunaa, a daughter, who became a schoolteacher and now lives in a distant village, where she teaches; she is forty-two and has never married.

Since Mɛɛ Laa and Pɔɔ Kɛɛw had no son of their own and had no child of their own at home after Sunaa left, they adopted Sanid, the illegitimate son of Pan (see Case VII, above).

All their property will go to Sunaa. However, since she does not live in the village, Sanid now farms the land and cares for his foster parents. In addition, Sunaa has formally adopted him and registered him as her son, and so the property will ultimately go to him anyway after she dies.

*Case IX.* ʔUj Taa, an only child, married ʔUj Nid, a poor man from a neighboring village. Nid did not claim any of his parents' small legacy (according to his grandchildren, who related the case to us), leaving it to his brothers and sisters. ʔUj Taa inherited 5 raj of rice land and 1 raj of garden from her parents. During their marriage ʔUj Taa and ʔUj Nid purchased an additional 3½ raj of rice land, making their total estate 8½ raj of rice land and 1 raj of garden.

Taa and Nid had one child—a daughter Kham. Kham married a man from a nearby village; Pɔɔ Nan, as he came to be known, inherited ¾ raj of garden from his parents' estate. His brother and sister received 1 raj of garden and 3 raj of rice land each, and the sister also inherited the house. Pɔɔ Nan, since he had married a wealthy woman, reputedly felt sorry for his brother and sister and so did not take all the inheritance he was entitled to.

Mɛɛ Kham, as she became later, received a handsome inheritance: 8½ raj of rice land and 1 raj of garden from her mother, and 3¼ raj of rice land and 1 raj of garden from the sister of Mɛɛ Kham's mother's mother, who had died without marrying.

Mɛɛ Kham and Pɔɔ Nan have many children, only two of whom have yet married. They have not decided about inheritance yet. According to them, "There is not any need to divide up the property, since all the children are living together at home and eating together."

*Case X.* ʔUj Bua inherited 4 raj of rice land and 1 raj of garden from her mother. She married ʔUj Kham, a Chiangmai village man. Before his parents died, they gave him his inheritance—10 raj of rice land; he did not take any garden, leaving it to his sisters. So the couple had a total of 14 raj of rice land and 1 raj of garden. They had four children, three boys and a girl. Three of them married but the fourth, Siŋ, did not.

ʔUj Bua, now a widow, says that she has informally—but not really—divided her property among her children. They use the land, but each of them still brings her 20 to 30 thaŋ of rice a year for the use of the land. ʔAaj Kɛɛw, the youngest son, has 4 raj of the family's rice land; Pɔɔ Mun, the oldest child, has 4 raj also; and Siŋ, who lives with his mother, has 6 raj. (ʔAaj Kɛɛw reported in another context that he *owned* the 4 raj of land, whereas Pɔɔ Mun reported that he *rented* 4 raj from his mother, paying her yearly 25 thaŋ of rice and 40 baht for growing peanuts.) The daughter, Iin, married a wealthy man who lives in an adjoining village. She is so wealthy that she has claimed none of the property, at least so far. If her mother needs anything, Iin sends rice to her.

According to ʔUj Bua, the final division of her property has not yet been made; the present arrangement whereby the two married sons use the property is "just for eating." The uncertainty seems to be over whether Iin really will claim her part of the inheritance and what Siŋ will do with his share of the property, since he is unmarried and likely to remain so.

This family is unusual in that neither married son has sired children, and the third son has never married at all. Each of the married sons adopted a daughter of his wife's older sister to inherit his property. Also, at present living with ʔUj Bua and Siŋ is a young woman who is adopted and who will probably marry, bring in a husband, and inherit the garden.

*Case XI.* ʔUj Taa owned a total of 9 raj of rice land. She gave birth to four children, each of whom inherited 2¼ raj of land. Mɛɛ Khaaw was the first of ʔUj Taa's children to marry. She married Pɔɔ Phom, who had 3 raj of his own: she had one child with him, a daughter named Nuaŋ. After Mɛɛ Khaaw died, her husband, Phom, married her youngest sister, Mɛɛ Saaj. With Mɛɛ Saaj he had three more children: Sɛɛn, Nii, and Laan. Then Mɛɛ Saaj divorced Pɔɔ Phom, and he went to live with a new wife in Chiengdao, a town north of Chiengmai city.

When Pɔɔ Phom died, his four children by his first two wives (sisters) divided his property, each receiving ¾ raj. Nuaŋ, his daughter with Mɛɛ Khaaw, received all her mother's 2¼ raj. The second sibling group of three divided their mother Saaj's property. She had already sold 1 raj of her 2¼ raj inheritance, leaving 1¼ raj to be divided three ways.

Pii Nii, daughter of Pɔɔ Phom by Mɛɛ Saaj, then married Mun, a man from a nearby village. He owned 1 raj of land there, which he sold after his marriage. In Chiangmai village he and Nii then bought 1 raj from Nuaŋ, Nii's half-sister. They also purchased the fields and garden of Sɛɛn, Nii's brother, who in turn used the money to buy land in another village, into which he had married. Thus Mun and Nii have consolidated 3⅓ raj and have only one daughter, Toj, to inherit it.

## Kinship

### The Bilateral Kindred

The most important kinship group of any Chiangmai villager is composed of the descendants of his maternal and paternal grandparents. This group, the members of whom are called "pii nɔɔŋ kan," includes all one's uncles and aunts and their children (first cousins) through both his mother and father, on both sides of the family, males and females (see figure 4). Contrary to the image of a loosely defined, nebulous, laterally oriented kindred based upon contractual relationships, as projected by earlier writers (see Chapter 1), this group is clearly defined for each set of siblings; it is solidary, and relations between its members are no more contractual than kinship relations in other societies.

Outside one's immediate family, the members of one's bilateral kindred are the people to whom one owes the greatest respect, affection, and mutual support and cooperation. These are the closest relatives one has; and they are much closer than unrelated neighbors or fellow villagers in general. Frequent visiting takes place between the households of fellow kindred members, even if they live far away. The kindred members of one of the families we stayed with in Chiangmai village, who had emigrated to Fang years ago, came to visit several times each year, even though it was a day's bus ride.

At life crises, such as marriages, ordinations, and funerals, one's bilateral kindred always come to help. Whenever it is necessary to build a new

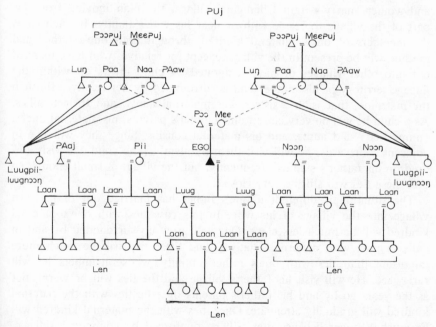

**Fig. 4**                    Kinship terms of reference

house, members of one's kindred will be the first people to offer assistance. In times of illness, scandal, or some other dreadful occurrence, one's uncles and aunts and cousins all come to visit and offer support.

When one forms reciprocal labor-exchange ties with a group of people to cooperate in rice agriculture, his bilateral kin members are almost always the first included. The labor-exchange groups of the poorest farmers, which are the smallest groups in the village, are almost entirely restricted to bilateral kin.

If one has land to rent out, one usually offers it first to a member of one's bilateral kindred before offering it to a more distant relative or an outsider. If one has land to sell, one is expected to offer it first to a kindred member before selling it to others.

And if someone kills a member of his kindred, it is incumbent upon the bilateral kin to kill that person or to see that revenge is taken in some other way.

The quality of one's relations with the members of one's bilateral kindred depends upon the residence of one's father and mother. Usually men and women marry within Chiangmai village, the man moving from his part of the village to reside with or near his wife's family. In such cases the members of one's bilateral kindred, through both one's father and mother, will be present in the village, except for relatives who have married out into other villages or have emigrated. A child grows up within the lineage territory of his mother and is surrounded by her relatives through the matriline, that is, her sisters, her maternal aunts, and their families. As a child he will be very close to his mother's parents, his maternal uncles (unmarried) and aunts, and his maternal cousins. Since they will live in adjacent courtyards, he will visit them frequently. The child will visit kindred on his father's side less frequently, but the village is small enough so that these ties will still be very close.

The situation is different if one's father has married out of his own village into the village of his wife. In this case ties with one's paternal kindred will be much less close. One will grow up surrounded by and in daily contact with maternal relatives, and these ties will be much more important than ties with one's father's family, whose members he will rarely see. He will visit his father's village and the ties will be warm, but as the years go by and his father's parents die, the ties with the paternal kindred will gradually attenuate. One's ties with the maternal kindred will be much stronger because they will be reinforced by common residence, membership in the same village groupings, and cooperation in labor exchange.

If one's mother has married into one's father's village, the situation will be reversed, with the paternal kindred being much more important than the maternal kindred.

## Kinship Terminology

The kinship nomenclature used by Chiangmai villagers is completely bilateral in nature, making no terminological distinction between relatives through the father and relatives through the mother (see figure 4, showing Chiangmai reference terms).[6] The term for one's grandfather, whether he is one's mother's father or father's father, is "pɔɔʔuj"; and the term for grandmother, whether maternal or paternal, is "mɛɛʔuj." All four grandparents can be referred to simply as "ʔuj" if the speaker wishes.

Father is referred to as "pɔɔ," and mother as "mɛɛ." With the occasional exception when the terms pɔɔ and mɛɛ, plus the personal name, are used to refer to the father's and mother's older siblings, neither of these terms is used to refer to any collateral relative (except when they are used generally for all villagers, nonrelatives included, in a polite way). The direct line of descent—grandfather, grandmother, father, mother, son, and daughter—is clearly distinguished from collateral lines. There is no merging of lineal and collateral kin types within these generations.

Mother's siblings and father's siblings—one's aunts and uncles—are treated the same in the reference terminology, with no distinction made as to whether they are related through the father or the mother. Mother's and father's siblings are distinguished by sex and by seniority—whether they are older or younger than one's father or mother. Father's older brother and mother's older brother are both referred to as "luŋ." Father's younger brother and mother's younger brother are referred to as "ʔaaw." Father's older sister and mother's older sister are referred to as "paa." And father's younger sister and mother's younger sister are referred to as "naa."

In one's own generation, one's brothers and sisters are distinguished by age relative to oneself; and one's older siblings are in addition distinguished by sex. Thus one's older brother is referred to as "ʔaaj" and one's older sister as "pii"; but one's younger brothers and sisters are all referred to as "nɔɔŋ." In one's own generation one does not distinguish the sex of siblings or cousins younger than oneself; and this holds true for all kin in the descending generations.

First cousins, the children of one's mother's and father's siblings, are referred to collectively as "luugpii-luugnɔɔŋ" ("children of older and younger siblings"). One is not permitted to marry them or anyone within the bilateral kindred.

In the first descending generation, one refers to one's own children, both sons and daughters, by the term "luug," which means "child." One's own children are distinguished from all other relatives of their generation; nephews and nieces (sons and daughters of one's own siblings) are referred to by the term "laan." This same term is used to refer to the children of one's first cousins.

The term laan seems peculiar to English speakers because it is a genuinely classificatory term, one of only two terms in the Chiangmai reference terminology that merges lineal and collateral kin into one kin category: nephews, nieces, and grandchildren are all referred to as laan. This usage was confusing to us in the village because when we asked how someone was related and were told that so and so was "my laan," we could never be sure until further inquiry whether a nephew, niece, granddaughter, or grandson was meant. The term laan, in addition to ignoring differences between lineal and collateral kin, also ignores the generational differences between nephew-niece and grandchild. The only other term that merges lineal and collateral kin and ignores generational differences is the term "len," which refers to one's own great-grandchildren, and to the children of nephews and nieces.

The terms laan and len cannot be easily or understandably translated by an English kinship term. The meaning of laan for the villagers is a "bilateral kinsman of either sex who belongs to the first or second descending generation from ego, and who is a primary relative of one's primary relatives." Thus a sibling's child and a child's child are both referred to as laan. In the same way, len refers to "all kinsmen, of either sex, who belong to the second or third descending generations from ego, and who are tertiary relatives" (primary relatives of one's secondary relatives). In simpler terms, which is the way the villagers view the matter, a len is the child of a laan. The villagers lump these nonprimary relatives of junior generations together in a few terms because it is not necessary for a senior person to make too many distinctions at this level; he ignores sex and lineality, and distinguishes relatives only according to distance of relationship within the kindred.

The Matrilineage

"Kinship is like a banana tree that starts out with one central trunk and then gradually sends out shoots around it; even after the mother trunk has died, the clump of surrounding seedlings remains." This was told to me by an elderly villager to help explain how Chiangmai village matrilineages grow and develop.[7]

Matrilineages are groups of related households which trace common descent through the matriline—through females only—to a group of sisters who lived from three to eight generations ago (see figure 5, the genealogies of two of the largest lineages in Chiangmai).[8] Each matrilineage is a coresidential group which tends to inhabit its own section of the village, as shown in map 6. Some households are scattered outside their lineage areas in other sections of the village, but this is a recent occurrence and is because population pressure and land scarcity have prevented people from building their houses in their lineage area. Even if a household that belongs to a certain lineage moves out of its area, its members continue to have important social ties with their lineage group. Since matrilineages are usually coresidence groups, the social ties between lineage members are reinforced by propinquity and by cooperation in labor exchange.

Common lineage residence results from the rule of preferential matrilocal residence, which requires daughters to remain in or near their parents' house and to bring their husbands in to live with them. As the generations pass, a core of matrilineally related women form a group of households living adjacent to one another. These groups of households form matrilineages of from three to eight generations descended from a common set of sisters who worship a common spirit or spirits. Every member of the matrilineal kin group is able to trace his exact genealogical relationship with every other member of the group; the genealogical links are actually known.

Membership in the matrilineage passes from a mother to her children; a child belongs to the matrilineage of his mother and not of his father. If a woman belongs to matrilineage X, her sons and daughters will belong to matrilineage X. The woman's husband, the father of these children, must be of another matrilineage. This is because of the rule of lineage exogamy: a man must marry a woman outside his own matrilineal descent group. If marriage takes place within the group, the villagers believe that the resulting children will be malformed or insane.

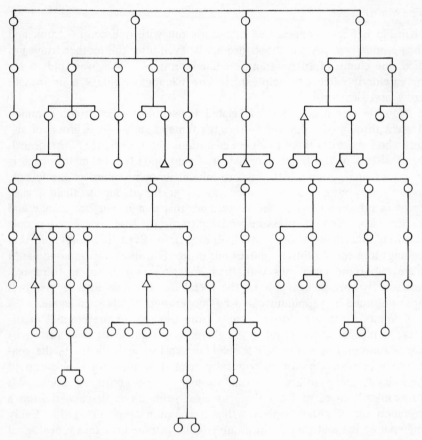

**Fig. 5**                          Genealogies of two village
                                    matrilineages

When a man marries, for all practical purposes he becomes a member of his wife's matrilineage, although he never completely loses membership in his own mother's matrilineal descent group and can return to it.

If a man's parents have no daughters, he may remain living in his parental house and bring in his wife to reside with him. In such cases, his wife may worship his matrilineal spirits as well as her own, for all practical purposes becoming a member of both groups. Her children may, then, also have dual membership. At least one of the daughters of such a couple will choose to continue her father's matriline and pass it on to her daugh-

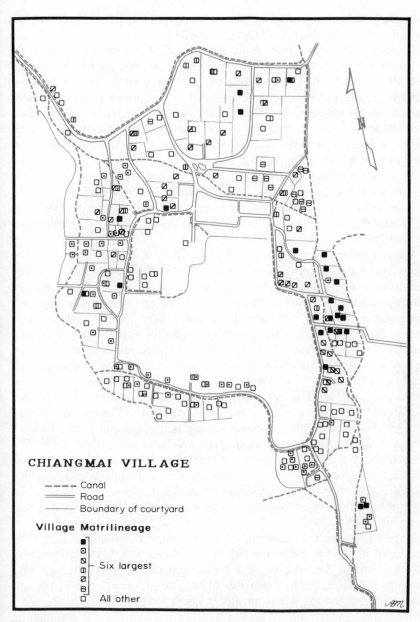

CHIANGMAI VILLAGE

‒ ‒ ‒ ‒ Canal
═══════ Road
─────── Boundary of courtyard

**Village Matrilineage**

■
▣
◨  ⎱
▨  ⎰ Six largest
▧
▤
▢   All other

**Map 6**

ters. Such an arrangement is only a stopgap measure to continue the matriline (see also Turton 1972, pp. 220–21).

Status considerations may also motivate a man to continue membership in his mother's matrilineage as well as his wife's, so that the house worships two sets of spirits at the same time and has membership in two lineages. All five of the richest men in Chiangmai village worship their mother's matrispirits as well as those of their wife (see the similar findings by Turton 1972, p. 222). It was my impression that they sacrificed to their mother's matrilineal spirits because they wanted to continue the good fortune that such spiritual protection had brought to them.

If a man divorces his wife and returns to live with his parents, or if he returns home for any other reason, such as the death of his wife, he may be reintegrated into his mother's matrilineage. As Turton (1972, p. 223) explains, a man may be a member of several different matrilineages in his lifetime.

When speaking of the groups which we have called matrilineages, the Chiangmai villagers speak of groups which have "phii diaw kan," "people who have spirits in common." Chiangmai people are vague about the exact nature and identity of the matrilineage guardian spirits worshiped by each kin group which they call "phii phuu njaa." The members of a matrilineage feel themselves to be related because they share these spirits and worship them in common. The spirits protect the members of their lineage from the depredations of living people, malevolent ghosts, disease, and death (usually caused by evil spirits). If offended, however, the lineage spirits are capable of causing their descendants to become ill (see also McGilvary 1912, p. 91, and Turton 1972, p. 233). Villagers do not take young babies out of the protective sphere of lineage courtyards because they are afraid that a malevolent ghost will take away their souls. We learned about this belief when we attempted to take our young daughter out into the rice fields; every woman from the surrounding households rushed out to stop us. In other circumstances, however, guardian spirits have been known to accompany a young man of the village to war and bring him back safely.

Once each year the members of each lineage contribute money to a woman of the group, called the "khon khyn-khon waa," "the person who rises and speaks," a woman of a senior generation of the lineage who worships the lineage spirits that live in the "baan kaaw," one of the old houses of the lineage. Many members come to participate in the ceremonies, and members of the lineage who are away in the city working, or who have married out into another village, send contributions even if they cannot be present. The offerings made to the lineage spirits are later divided among and eaten by members of the group who participate in the worshiping ceremony.

The actual ceremony (witnessed by Sulamith Heins Potter) consists of the khon khyn-khon waa of the lineage coming to the old house where the spirits of the group reside and presenting them with several trays of food as an offering. She invites the spirits to eat, reports to them any events concerning members of the group that occurred during the year, and asks them to protect the group's members. After a few minutes she takes a bowl of uncooked milled rice, raises it to her head, and asks the spirits to indicate whether they have eaten their fill or not. To determine this, she takes a handful of grain from the bowl; if she draws an even number, the spirits have indicated they have eaten their fill; if it is an odd number, they have not. In the latter case, she waits for a few minutes and then draws again, until she obtains an affirmative answer.

Occasionally, dances are given for the spirits of some lineages by their members. At these occasions, called "fɔɔn phii" ("dancing for the spirits"), one of which we witnessed, an orchestra is hired, tents and altars are set up, and many lineage members together with a few spirit mediums come together, hoping to become possessed by the spirits through dancing. The women begin by grasping a mosquito net hung from the central rafter of the tent and swinging around wildly; this is supposed to put them in the mood for being possessed by the lineage spirits. Everyone dances until some of the women begin to go into trances and exhibit wild behavior, including sword fighting, upon being possessed by a spirit. Possessed persons transmit messages from spirits to the people present.

After the dancing is over, an elaborate ceremony is performed in honor of the lineage spirits and for the fertility of the lineage. Part of the ceremony is solemn, but most of it is buffoonery. The women ritually plow the fields with a man acting as the plow buffalo, and some drunken women symbolically mount the rear of the man-buffalo as if to impregnate him. This rite is probably related to the fact that sometimes a son-in-law who marries into a family is referred to as a "work buffalo" (see Turton 1972, p. 222). After that, rice is symbolically planted, birds are symbolically shot, and an elephant (again played by the man) is symbolically captured. An important aspect of the ceremony is that people who in the past have asked the lineage spirits for help in curing an illness and wish to repay them for their help contribute money for the occasion.

The spirits of Chiangmai lineages can be subdivided and are frequently split when families move to another area. The families who left Chiangmai to settle in the Fang Valley took some of their lineage ancestral spirits with them and installed them in their new houses, forming a branch of the lineage. The division of the ancestral spirits represents the fission of the lineage group. When a woman moves to another village she contributes to the worship of her lineage spirits at the home village for a while; but as time goes by either the old ties are attenuated and a new branch lineage is formed, or she assimilates to her husband's lineage. The spirit dances of the lineages may be an opportunity for related lineages of different villages in the vicinity to come together; such a group of related lineages may be called a clan.

The village of Chiangmai is divided into twelve major matrilineages plus many odd families or small groups of two or three related families who are recent arrivals in the village. Six of the twelve lineages (the ones noted in map 6) are fairly large, and together include 68 percent of the village's 206 households and most of the long-term residents. These important lineages have 9, 13, 15, 24, 31, and 45 households as members, respectively. Chiangmai lineages are larger and more substantial than those reported by Turton,[9] and their size seems to belie Turton's data, from which he inferred that after a size of ten households was reached, the lineages in his community split. This does not seem to happen in Chiangmai and may perhaps explain why I heard nothing about lineage fission except when occurring as a result of out-migration.

Of the three largest lineages, one lives largely in one administrative half of the village, another is located mainly in the other administrative half, and the third is about evenly divided between the two administrative halves. This is a neat structural arrangement, which allows opposition between the two most powerful lineages but mediates this opposition through their relations with the third lineage which ties them together.

The matrilineages of Chiangmai own no corporate property except for the lineage spirits—ritual property; and although some have lineage shrines as separate structures, most spirits simply stay (during rituals for them) in a corner of the old house of the lineage. The only social functions the matrilineages perform are those of regulating sex and marriage and curing illnesses. They become of general importance in Chiangmai because they tend to be residential units which reinforce and are reinforced by ties of neighborliness, cooperation, and political alliance.

# 8

# Form and Variation in Thai Peasant Social Structure

Chiangmai village's social structure, which I have described at length in the preceding chapters, cannot be fitted into Embree's loose-structure paradigm. On the contrary, Chiangmai village is a highly structured society. To briefly summarize, it is a corporate group with a common identity; the temple committee and the school committee form quasi-governing boards which make decisions on behalf of the villagers as a whole and resolve disputes between community members. Village society includes cooperative groups and voluntary associations, ranging from the funeral society and neighborhood groups which send food to the temple, to labor exchange groups. Cooperation is the dominant ideology of village social relations. Notwithstanding this, the village is divided horizontally into strata which differ in wealth, power, and prestige; and into factions, centered around wealthy and powerful families, which oppose each other on most important issues, jockey for power, and engage in quarrels and disputes.

Family life is, on the whole, stable, and marriages are usually long-lasting. Divorce, although not uncommon early in first marriages, is a manifestation of Chiangmai's type of family pattern, in which the relation between the newly married-in son-in-law and his wife's family is brittle. Divorce is a consequence of a particular type of family structure rather than an indication of a lack of structure.

Family relations, residence rules, and inheritance patterns are clearly defined. Kinship duties and obligations are observed as much in Chiangmai as in any other society. Corporate extended-stem matrilocal families are present, along with matrilineal kin groups. Individual social behavior is just as regular and predictable in Chiangmai as in other societies.

Additional structuring is supplied by the larger authoritarian, centralized, and stratified society within which the village exists. Government bureaucrats who administer this society have authority over their representatives in the village: the village headmen, the head teacher of the local school, and the clergy. If the government insists, its orders will be carried out, by force if necessary.

The Chiangmai village data alone demonstrate that the loose-structure paradigm does not apply to all of rural Thailand. The present study is, however, only the most recent of many studies of rural Thai communities whose findings support and reinforce my thesis. Their cumulative effect shatters once and for all the loose-structure paradigm. Studies by Moerman (1966*a*, 1966*b*, 1967, 1968), Turton (1972), Davis (1973, 1974), Sulamith Heins Potter (1975), and the present study in the north, together with other recent works by Tambiah (1970), Keyes (1967*b*, 1975), and Mizuno (1971) in the northeast, reveal rural social patterns similar to those of Chiangmai village and not "loosely structured" at all.

The differences between these recent studies, mainly but not entirely in the north and the northeast, and the original Bang Chan study in the delta region of the central plain—the basis for the loose-structure paradigm—is not simply a matter of regional variation. A reexamination of the Bang Chan data presented by Sharp and his colleagues (see below) reveals that Bang Chan shares basic structural elements found in all Thai villages to which, because of the loose-structure paradigm, these writers did not give sufficient weight.

In the light of these new research findings, there is no longer serious doubt that the loose-structure paradigm does not accurately describe rural Thai social patterns. A new paradigm must be created. In this final chapter I sketch a new paradigm that is emerging from recent studies, including my own. I describe the basic structural uniformities present in almost all Thai villages, while giving due recognition to the variations that exist. I emphasize the word "sketch" because it is difficult to generalize about the social structure of all of rural Thailand from the few village studies that are available. Not only is there a lack of information (especially about the south), but also the various community studies were written at different times by anthropologists with different theoretical frameworks, interests, and emphases. Anthropologists in Thailand, as elsewhere, in their role as ethnographers of rural communities rarely have attempted systematically to relate their findings to other community studies. Often when an anthropologist fails to mention a structural feature such as a neighborhood, for example, one cannot necessarily conclude that neighborhoods do not exist in his community; if he is mainly interested in religion, ritual, or economic decision-making, he simply may have failed to describe them, or may not have noticed them. I mention this possibility to remind the reader how difficult it is to generalize from village studies, and to warn him that the paradigm I sketch in this chapter is tentative and will have to be modified as the results from studies already carried out as well as from future research become available.

Like the Balinese villages described by Clifford Geertz (1959) and by Hildred and Clifford Geertz (1975, pp. 72–76), Thai villages are extremely variable and no two are exactly alike. But they are recognizably Thai instead of Balinese or Indian or Chinese villages because they all are constructed from a limited number of structural principles (what Geertz, whose theoretical lead I am following here, calls "planes of social organization").

In rural Thailand, eleven structural elements may be seen to generate rural communities: the extended-stem family cycle (including the compound); the bilateral kindred; neighborliness and formal neighborhoods; cooperative labor-exchange groups; the junior-senior relationship; class and status divisions; entourages; political factions; administrative hamlets; the village community; and the wad.

These eleven structural elements are found in every Thai village. In their various permutations and combinations they form the social structures of rural Thai communities, no two of which are exactly alike. An example is the element of the community as a whole. The ideal rural community for Thai villagers is a spatially segregated, nucleated village that is separate from neighboring communities and has its own temple. Most villages in Thailand are, in fact, like this. There are, however, many physical variations. Some villages are ribbon settlements that are built in linear fashion alongside a road or canal because of ease of transportation. In areas of low population density, one ribbon village will be clearly separated from another. In areas where the population is dense, ribbon villages will tend to run together and form a continuous settlement. Some villages, like Chiangmai village, are built in circular form because this was the configuration of the high ground suitable for house building in the middle of the surrounding paddy fields. Finally, in the region southeast of Bangkok some houses are separately dispersed on their own fields, forming a continuous blanket pattern of settlement over the countryside. One reason for this is that the land was sold to individual farmers by land magnates in Bangkok (see the account by de Young 1955, pp. 8–12). Even here, however, people living on the scattered farms in a particular area consider that they are part of a particular village.

In each of the kinds of villages, villagers will construct a Buddhist temple because they believe a temple to be necessary for a civilized social existence. In the nucleated villages there will be a simple one-to-one correspondence between the temple congregation and the social community; in the ribbon settlements along roads or canals the same relationship will be found in areas of low population density, but in areas of high population density, where settlements are continuous, people who live at the edge of one village may go to the temple of the neighboring village or to both alternately. An affiliation with one or more temples will seem essential to them.

Thai villages, as structural forms, run through a cycle similar to the cycle of domestic groups. When villages reach a certain size they tend to divide, with a smaller satellite settlement setting itself off from the parent community. Until the smaller settlement's population grows enough to support a temple of its own, its residents will continue to attend the temple of the parent community; after that, the people of the smaller settlement will build their own temple and gradually cease to patronize the older temple.

The same kind of variation is found in the realization of each of the other ten structural elements which form the blueprint that Thai villagers use to construct their rural communities. In some Thai villages, like Bang Chan, there will be a higher percentage of patrilocal extended-stem families than in villages like Chiangmai, possibly because of the different ethnic backgrounds of the Bang Chan settlers, who were partly Chinese and Malay (more of this below). The relative emphases given these eleven structural elements in different communities make for a richly textured and diverse social life, but everywhere this life is woven into similar patterns from the same strands.

In addition, there are other structural features, such as irrigation societies, formal neighborhood groups organized to rotate food-sending to the temple, matrilineal kin groups, village guardian spirits, associations for financing funerals, and young people's groups, which are peculiar to certain regions of Thailand or to certain ethnic groups. These additional structural elements overlie the eleven universal structural principles found everywhere in rural Thailand, making for even more variation and diversity; there is no average or typical Thai village.

By discussing rural Thai social structure in terms of structural elements, I am not lapsing into an idealistic, emanation theory of social structure. What I am saying is that Thai villagers have definite ideas in their minds, ideas defined by their culture, as to what a proper Thai rural community should be like and how members of such a community should behave toward one another. If groups of Thai emigrate into unsettled regions of their country, as many have done in recent decades because of the pressure of population in their home villages, they will, on the basis of a cultural blueprint containing these eleven principles, proceed to construct village communities that are all recognizably Thai, though they will vary because of differences in the groups that found them, in the means available to them, and because of differences in the ecological, social, and political environments of Thailand.

Let us discuss each of these eleven structural elements in turn.

### The Extended Stem Family Cycle and Compound

The extended-stem family described above (Chapter 7), in which the youngest daughter and her husband stay home to live with and care for her parents and inherit the house, is the dominant form described in the literature. There is some variation in residence patterns in Bang Chan and presumably in other villages in the lower delta region near Bangkok, which produce more patrilocal extended-stem families than in other parts of the country; even here, however, matrilocal extended-stem families outnumber the patrilocal variety. Another variant form is described by Moerman in the north among the Thai Lue, where couples alternate their residence, living first with the wife's parents for three years, then with the husband's parents for three years, apparently producing both patrilocal and matrilocal extended-stem families (Moerman 1968, p. 107).

There are also undoubtedly other more minor variations in residence patterns and family types found among the many small ethnic groups in Thailand, such as the Vietnamese, Chams, Mons, Khmers, and Phuthai, and there is another major variant among the Malays in the south, but the matrilocal extended-stem family and its associated structural cycle is the basic *Thai* pattern.

A point that I want to stress because of its importance in my argument against the loose-structure paradigm is that the matrilocal extended-stem family cycle is the basic form of rural Thai family system, *not* because of statistical clustering which results from the random choices by individual actors pursuing their idiosyncratic material interests, but because this kind of family system is culturally defined and normatively prescribed: the Thai believe that this is the way families should be. Previous descriptions of the so-called loosely structured nuclear family, based upon preferential neolocal residence, as the typical Thai peasant family (see, for example, Sharp 1963), are wrong and based upon a fundamental misunderstanding of Thai family structure. The errors in the loose-structure argument are threefold: an inability to conceive of family structure as a cyclical process through time: and (as pointed out by Sulamith Heins Potter [1975]) a misconception that the Thai (unlike any other people known in the world) lack normative prescriptions defining their family life so that they can only be studied statistically. Third, in Sulamith Heins Potter's words, Thai family structure

> can be understood from the point of view that lineality is traced through women, rather than men, and that authority is passed on affinally, from father-in-law to son-in-law, by virtue of their relationships to the line of women. . . . The key factor is the recognition of the structural importance of women; without that, the system is unintelligible. [1975, p. 111]

Available statistical data on the types of families found in Thai village households support my contention that the extended-stem family, not the nuclear family, is the dominant form in rural Thai society. The proportion of extended-stem families to nuclear families in all Thai villages for which I have reliable data is set out in table 11.

The data in table 11 (suggested by an earlier, similar table by Evers [1969, p. 122]) show that an average of roughly one-third of the households in the villages on which I have information are extended-stem family households. These data alone raise serious doubts about the loose-structure theorists' contention that the nuclear family is the basic and preferred form in rural Thailand. The most interesting finding in the table is that, except for the case represented by data published recently by Japanese scholars on one small sample of household composition in Bang Khem, a commune southwest of Bangkok (see map 1 for communities mentioned in this chapter), *Bang Chan has the highest percentage of extended family households reported for any village in Thailand on which I have information.* This is a surprising finding, indeed, from the village which gave rise

**Table 11**                     Household Composition
                                  in Thai Villages

| Village (ranked by % of extended-stem families) | Region | Households Nuclear Family | Households Extended-Stem Family | Other | Total No. of Households |
|---|---|---|---|---|---|
| 1. Bang Khem | Central southwest | 53% | 44% | 3% | 45 |
| 2. Bang Chan | Central delta | 59 | 35 | 6 | 298 |
| 3. Ban Pae Lugar | North | 66 | 34 | 0 | 65 |
| 4. Landing | North | 67 | 33 | 0 | 43 |
| 5. Baan Phraan Muan | Northeast | 65 | 31 | 4 | 80 |
| 6. Ban Nong Tuen | Northeast | 70 | 30 | 0 | 119 |
| 7. Don Daeng | Northeast | 68 | 28 | 4 | 80 |
| 8. Chiangmai | North | 62 | 26 | 12 | 206 |
| 9. Bangkhuad | Central delta | a | — | — | — |
| 10. Ban Nai | Central southwest | b | — | — | — |

a"The household . . . members consist of a man, his wife, and their children. Frequently, one of the children will have his wife and children living in the same house or occasionally in an adjacent house in the compound" (Kaufman 1960, p. 21).
b"A household usually consists of three generations living together" (Attagara 1967, p. 18).

SOURCES:
1. Ayabe, ed., 1973, p. 13
2. Janlekha 1955, p. 28.
3. Troger 1960, pp. 192–93 (as quoted in Evers 1969, p. 123).
4. Davis 1973, p. 54.
5. Tambiah 1970, p. 13.
6. Keyes 1975, p. 287.
7. Mizuno 1971, pp. 91–92.
8. Potter, Table 10, above.
9. Kaufman 1960, p. 21 (Kaufman gives no more exact information).
10. Attagara 1967, p. 18 (Attagara gives no more exact information).

to the myth about the loosely structured Thai nuclear family. Bang Chan's percentage of extended-stem family households is much higher than in Chiangmai village or in other villages in the north and northeast recently studied by ethnographers, who all found essentially the same extended-stem family cycle that I described for Chiangmai village. The implication is strong that a similar cycle existed in Bang Chan at the time it was studied but that it was overlooked or misunderstood by Sharp and his colleagues.

The factual material was there (and to their credit, is in their report) but the interpretation was inaccurate. Family life in Bang Chan was not greatly different from family life in other Thai villages, like Chiangmai, except for the greater percentage of patrilocal-stem families.

Census figures on household composition alone, however, do not give an understanding of the family life of a people unless combined with an understanding of the ideal norms governing residence and family life. The contention that the nuclear family and neolocal residence is the ideal in Thailand is erroneous. On the contrary, the extended-stem family, based upon a preferential rule of matrilocal residence, is the basic family form of the rural Thai.

Jeremy Kemp (1970), building upon earlier work by Phya Anuman Rajadhon (1954), showed that almost universally in rural Thailand a young couple are expected to reside initially in the bride's parents' household, and then after a period varying in length, but usually lasting several years, to reside in a house near the bride's family, often in the same courtyard. Kemp cites the works of Charles Madge (1957, p. 42) and Thomas Lux (1966, p. 5) for the northeast; Konrad Kingshill (1965, p. 47), Wijeyewardene (1967, p. 69), and John de Young (1955, pp. 23 and 64–66) for the north; and his own work in Hua Kok village in north central Thailand to support his assertion. Kemp says that reports by Sharp et al. (1953, p. 78), Janlekha (1955, pp. 36–37), and Jane Richardson Hanks (1963, p. 12) seem to indicate that initial matrilocal residence is less common in the lower delta region of central Thailand. However, Kemp incorrectly states that the Bang Chan material contains no evidence of matrilocal bias. Sharp (1963, p. 129), contradicting his statement that "the normal and, with some urban exceptions, ideal family type among the Thai is the nuclear group," says, in the same article, that "the Siamese system is essentially that of the stem family," and that "the youngest daughter, remaining at home to care for her aging parents, may in addition inherit their house and equipment in a kind of feminine junior right." Phillips (1965, p. 24), basing his remarks upon Janlekha's findings (1955, p. 37), notes that of the extended family households in Janlekha's sample of Bang Chan, five out of eight were matrilocal.

Also significant are statements by Lucien Hanks in his recent book, *Rice and Man* (1972), which *imply* a normative preference for matrilocal residence in Bang Chan. When describing the interior partitioning of a Bang Chan house, Hanks writes that "here a newly married daughter and her spouse might live for a year or two," and does not mention the possibility that a son might bring his wife there (Hanks 1972, p. 13). Also, Hanks says that "in the household of a cultivator there is precedent for giving the house to the youngest daughter along with a portion of the cultivated fields, for she with her husband may have cared for the old man or woman through the final years" (p. 81). These recent statements by Hanks indicate a shift in emphasis from the earlier Bang Chan reports.

Like Kemp, I believe that the earlier interpretations of the Bang Chan data need reexamination. Kaufman (1960, p. 29) unequivocally states that in the village of Bangkhuad (only fourteen kilometers from Bang Chan) the prevailing postmarital residence pattern is initially matrilocal, although he mentions exceptions, gives no exact figures, and does not indicate whether he is talking about ideals or statistics. He also states that subsequent residence is patrilocal but does not elaborate and thus further confuses the issue.

Phya Anuman's (1954) and Kemp's (1970) claim (a claim prematurely dismissed by Phillips [1965, p. 27])—that preferential initial postmarital residence with the bride's parents is not only the statistical norm but *also the ideal* for rural Thailand—has been amply confirmed by later ethnographic reports: for the north by Turton (1972), Davis (1973, 1974), Sulamith Heins Potter (1975), and me; for the northeast by Tambiah (1970, p.12), Mizuno (1971, p. 86), and Keyes (1975, pp.282–84).

Of even greater significance are the findings on family life of Steven Piker, because he shows that a strong tradition of matrilocal residence exists in the heart of Thailand's central plain. Marriage in Piker's village, Banoi, a central Thai commercial rice-growing village located five miles from Ayutthaya and about sixty miles north of Bangkok, is village-exogamous and the prevalent rule and practice is matrilocal: the man moves from his village of birth to live with his bride. This rule is enforced by village parents who, Piker says, still arrange most marriages. The bride price (sometimes a buffalo) paid by the groom's parents to the parents of the bride is explicitly recognized as money to pay for the land that the man will eventually inherit from his parents-in-law in their village. After marriage, the man moves to live with, and later near, his wife's family. The young couple often remain in an economically subordinate position until the woman's parents die, when they inherit the house and land. The parental house is inherited preferably by the youngest daughter and her husband (Piker 1964, p. 41). Piker speaks of the isolated social position of the men in his village, who have to leave the village in which their own family and kinsmen live and move to the village of their wives, where all are strangers (Piker 1964, pp. 12–16). Piker's report describes one of the strongest patterns of matrilocality in Thailand; in many areas—such as Chiangmai village, for example—the man's position is stronger because preferential village endogamy allows most men to remain close to their own relatives and friends in their natal village, even though they reside with, and then near, their wife's parents.

Existing evidence on ideal rules governing postmarital residence reinforces the statistical evidence presented in table 11, and allows us to state with some certainty that matrilocal residence, and the matrilocal extended-stem family cycle, is a basic feature of almost all Thai village societies. Even in villages like Bang Chan, where a minority of the extended-stem families are patrilocal, all Thai spend part of their lives in an extended-stem household.

Almost universally throughout Thailand the youngest daughter and her husband remain living with the woman's parents in an extended-stem household throughout their married lives. When the parents die, this couple inherits the house and the farm equipment plus at least an equal share of the farmland, and sometimes an extra share which has been retained by an aged parent (Sharp et al. 1953, pp. 82–83; de Young 1955, p. 23; Kaufman 1960, p. 82; Moerman 1968, p. 94; Mizuno 1971, p. 86; Hanks 1972, p. 81; Turton 1972, p. 221). By the time the wife's parents have died, the couple's own daughters are old enough to bring in sons-in-law to live with them, one after another, making the household a corporate group that exists over generations.

Older daughters who have married and lived with their husbands in the household of the woman's parents for a time, ranging from a few months to several years, and have then settled nearby, still retain social and economic ties with the wife's parental household, achieving final independence only after a long-drawn-out period, sometimes ending only with the death of the woman's parents, when formal title to a share of the land is given over to them.

Any census of household composition of a Thai village (see table 11) will show that the vast majority of households are inhabited by nuclear families. This fact, together with the desire of older siblings' families to achieve independence as soon as possible from the parental household, has led scholars since Sharp et al. (1953, pp. 77–78) to conclude that neolocal residence and the nuclear family pattern is the ideal. It is now clear that this is not the case, and that the nuclear family is only one temporary stage in the structural cycle of the family. For youngest daughters who reside with their parents throughout their lives, even after they marry, the nuclear family is clearly neither the ideal nor the practice. It is equally important to realize that even the older married daughters, who after marriage eventually move out to set up their own independent family and estate, want independence only so that they and their husbands too can have the chance to build up resources; then, when their daughters reach marriageable age, the parents will have the estate to attract sons-in-law to them and thus they will be able to start their own extended family. Previous statements about the nuclear family as the Thai ideal demonstrate a lack of understanding of the family cycle and also of motives of the Thai peasants who act within this social system.

The matrilocal extended-family cycle of the Thai peasants is not so different from the Chinese and Japanese family systems as Embree, Sharp, Janlekha, and others have believed. Charles F. Keyes (1975, p. 296) makes this point in a recent article. He notes that the Thai-Lao family system of the northeast is similar to the Javanese, the Iban, and the Japanese societies, in which domestic groups divide into several "daughter" or "son" groups, with one couple left in possession of the parental household. My own unpublished data from the lineage village of Ping Shan in Hong Kong's New Territories show that extended families with more than one married son are rare in farm families (as they are in all of China) and that the usual practice in Ping Shan is for each son to marry in order of age and set up a separate household near his father's house, dividing the land (sometimes) and the hearth but still maintaining close relationships with his parents and brothers, and leaving the youngest brother and his wife to care for the parents and to inherit the house and sometimes the parents' extra share of land. The contrast between the "loosely structured" Thai peasant family and the tightly structured Chinese family is not as great as some students of Thailand have imagined and is based upon a comparison of imperfectly understood Thai practice with traditional Chinese ideals.

Another structural phase of the matrilocal extended-stem family is the extended family cluster living in a compound. This compound group consists of the cooperating households of the married daughters of a family and their husbands and children, who live near the wife's parents' household, often in the same fenced-in compound area. Mizuno calls these groups "multi-household compounds" (1968, and 1971, pp. 95 and 242); Tambiah calls them "compounds" (1970, pp. 12–14); Keyes (1975, p. 287) calls them "uxori-parentilocal extended families" or "domestic groups"; Moerman (1968, p. 97) calls them a "longhouse"; Hanks (1972, p. 89) terms them a "cluster of households"; Kaufman (1960, p. 21) calls them simply a "household"; Wijeyewardene (1967, p. 66) calls them a "compound group"; and Sharp et al. (1953, p. 79) describes them as "limited families who are closely related—the families of brothers and sisters, for example—[who] may live close to each other, even in the same compound." Although the terms and description differ, all these writers are talking about the same thing: what I shall call the extended family compound. I do not imply that all the members of such units always live within the same fenced-in boundaries; they may live in adjacent court-yards or nearby in the same village. The structural relationship is the important point and not simply the place of residence, although the two often coincide.

As Mizuno, Tambiah, and Keyes have pointed out, the compound is a phase of the extended family cycle which occurs when the dependent families of daughters have moved out of the parental household into separate houses, usually located in the same fenced-in compound as the wife's parents; but, as I pointed out above for Chiangmai village, some-times when land is limited in the parental compound they reside nearby in the same village. Initially at least, they help work the parental rice farm and share rice from the same granary. Over time they gradually obtain their own rice fields and granary. Given the rule of residence within and then near the wife's parents' house, the compound group will eventually include the grandparents, their youngest married daughter and her husband, plus their unmarried grandchildren and their married granddaughters and their husbands.

This group is a matrilocal extended family that includes several house-holds. As Sulamith Heins Potter (1975) points out, the group of cooper-ating men are affines related only through their ties to a line of women. This group operates as a labor team in rice agriculture and cooperates politically, religiously, and in other ways too. It is an important structural unit in the northeast; in the north, where as in Chiangmai village it forms the basis for a matrilineage; and it is also present in the central plains.

## The Bilateral Kindred

For Thai villagers the most important kin group outside the extended family is the bilateral kindred. As I have pointed out above, in Chiangmai village this group is defined as the descendants of one's uncles and aunts and their children (one's first cousins) through both one's father and mother, on both sides of the family. This group is solidary, and obligations between members of the group are considered important. It differs from the compound in that the kindred includes relatives through both one's father and mother, whereas the compound group is usually only part of the matrilateral half of it.

The kindred, an ego-centered, bilateral kin group which is the same only for full siblings, is a universal feature of Thai peasant social structure; it is reported in the ethnographic literature under various names from everywhere in Thailand. In the lower delta region of the central plain around Bangkok, the bilateral kindred is referred to by Sharp et al. as the "cousin group" (a kind of "extended family"), and consists of "the brothers and sisters of an individual's parents, together with the children of these uncles and aunts." In Bang Chan, this kin group is important in ways that are similar to those I have described above for Chiangmai village.

> Brothers and sisters and their children, if they do not live too far apart, are likely to work together in cooperative planting and harvest groups, establishing among themselves rather than with others the reciprocal obligations involved. The extended family contributes richly of its financial and emotional support on ritual occasions such as the ordination or cremation of one of its members. Even when some members of the extended family have migrated to other parts of the realm, contact is usually maintained and occasional visits are exchanged. Members of an extended family will look out for opportunities for economic or other advancement for their relatives. Movements from Bang Chan into Bangkok or from Bangkok back to Bang Chan will frequently be facilitated by members of the extended family. [Sharp et al. 1953, p. 80]

According to Sharp et al. (p. 81), this group is not exogamous: "First cousins may marry."

Kaufman (1960, pp. 23–24) uses the term "spatially extended family" to refer to the bilateral kindred, and he defines the group as "members of a family who shared a common household during their youth and who have now moved away because of marriage or employment and are living in widely separated households, perhaps in different communities." The limits of this group in Bangkhuad, according to Kaufman, extend as far as first cousins. The group is a cohesive unit that helps fellow members in times of crisis. They even share children:

Households with too many children may either promise the next
child to a married sister with no children, or they may ask an unmarried
or widowed sister to come and stay with them . . . or they may let
her adopt the child, at which time she becomes its social mother.
Adoptions are, in almost all cases, made via the female member of
the family.

Kaufman goes on to show how important the kindred is for Bangkhuad
villagers. Kindred members may give economic aid to component members in financial crises. They borrow money from one another or rent
land at a cheaper rate to fellow members than to others. They always
come together at important ritual occasions such as the New Year's festival; they meet to consult about cremations, weddings, and ordinations,
and often share the cost of these expensive rituals. Moreover, as in Bang
Chan, Bangkhuad kindred members furnish contacts in other villages or
in the city and help find jobs or help with the schooling of their kin (Kaufman 1960, pp. 23–25).

The bilateral kindred is a clearly defined structural feature of Piker's
village, Banoi, near Ayutthaya. Piker writes:

> A person's kin will be constituted principally from his parents'
> siblings and their progeny, and his parents' parents. . . . Generally
> those kin whom the villager includes in this category will live in Banoi
> or a neighboring village.
>
> The villager considers himself bound to those he thinks of as close
> relations more or less permanently, and vice versa. In discussing the
> nature of the mutual commitment the villager may or may not include
> an affectional component, he will invariably refer to a range of
> expectations and obligations. In addition to ceremonial assistance,
> the villager feels he can turn to his close relations for assistance,
> economic or otherwise, in difficult situations; and he will do so . . .
> most [villagers give] . . . outright gifts of money in time of need;
> loans without interest; loans of buffaloes . . . ; assistance with farm
> labor . . . and [take] care of the children of one's relations, occasionally
> even for a number of years . . . both parties sporadically extend some
> sort of assistance to each other, and . . . both are satisfied that
> accounts more or less balance over the long haul. [Piker 1964, pp.
> 62–63]

Keyes (1975, p. 289) mentions that marriage between first cousins is
disapproved but possible because marriage is an individual realm. Keyes
discusses at some length what he calls "ego-based descent groups," which

seem to approximate what I call the kindred. According to Keyes, ego-based descent groups attend ceremonies connected with marriage, death, ordination into the monkhood, and sometimes the "soul-tying" ceremony (Keyes 1975, p. 292). He states that "all of these ego-based kin groups are conceived by the villagers as being bilaterally constructed" (p. 294). This would hold true equally for Chiangmai village.

Madge (1957, p. 6) describes the bilateral kindred that is the effective kin group in the villages of the northeast, near Ubon, in the following terms, which are by now familiar:

> Immediate family bonds are strong, between parents and children, between grandparents and grandchildren, between uncles, aunts, nephews and nieces, between brothers and sisters, and between first cousins. Beyond this degree of relationship there is little to distinguish one's behaviour to a relative from one's behaviour to a neighbor, or, indeed, to a stranger.

Mizuno describes a kin group in Don Daeng village in the northeast, which he calls a bilateral kindred and which he says "generally consists of all the descendents of the four grandparents and their siblings" (1971, p. 100). The bilateral kindred is a category of kin who assist in life-cycle rites, exchange of labor, and furnish contacts in traveling. Mizuno discusses two examples of kindreds which do not extend beyond the range of second cousins (p. 104). He adds that "within these limits of kinsmen, the most closely related persons are ego's grandparents, parents, siblings, children, and grandchildren" (p. 102).

Tambiah (1970, pp. 15–18) prefers to discuss kinship, which he says is "bilateral and ego-centered," in terms of *the particularities of ego-oriented reckoning within the generalities of the society or village-wide categorical scheme* [emphasis Tambiah's]" but he also discusses groups smaller than the village as a whole. He describes the increasingly more inclusive kinship groups, including *"luug phuu phii naung"* (the group extending laterally to first cousins, among whom marriage is forbidden), and *"phii-naung"* (the group extending to classificatory siblings/second cousins, between whom marriage is possible but disapproved) (Tambiah 1970, p. 18). Tambiah says that "the wider grouping that assembles at ritual occasions is the bilateral kin, plus affines, the representation . . . being flexible and the factors situational" (1970, p. 17). Although I am not sure that I interpret him correctly, Tambiah appears to define the bilateral kindred as including first cousins which, vertically, would mean the inclusion of the four grandparents of any given person. He says that second cousins (or descendants of grandparents' siblings) form a blurred boundary to this ego-centered group. As in Chiangmai, the kin terms are extended throughout the entire village even to those not recognizably relatives—a fact on which Tambiah rightly places emphasis.

Wijeyewardene, in his attempt to summarize the major features of rural Thai social life, fails to see the significance of the bilateral kindred. He says (1967, p. 66) that "as a general rule for most of Thailand—apart from individual ties maintained between brothers and sisters, children and parents, who are spatially separated—kinship obligation falls off sharply outside the compound group" (1967, p. 66).

Although slightly variable from region to region—the variability in part being real and in part being due to differential perceptions and emphases by the ethnographers—what we have called the bilateral kindred and have described above for Chiangmai village in the north is also found in the lower delta region of the central plain and in the northeast. It appears to be a universal feature of Thai village society and of great importance in villagers' lives.

## Neighbors and Neighborhoods

The importance of neighbors and more formally defined neighborhoods as a feature of rural Thai social structure has not been sufficiently recognized except by Sharp et al. and Lucien Hanks. Neighborhood relations, whether informally or formally defined, have been recognized as important social structural features in other peasant societies (see Potter, Diaz, and Foster 1967, p. 160). An instructive example is from traditional Chinese villages. Martin C. Yang wrote of his pre-revolutionary village, Taitou:

> Close neighborhood associations in many cases supersede the village feeling or the clan consciousness. A family of P'an clan, for example, may have closer relations with some Yang families than with their own clansmen, simply because the Yangs live in the same neighborhood. Frequent contact in daily life brings families together, divided into a number of neighborhoods, or *hu-tung*, which have no reference to the clan. There are nine neighborhoods within the village limits [even though they have no exact delimitations]. [1945, p. 151]

The barrios in Mexican and Phillipine villages, neighborhoods of a more formal sort, are so well-known as to need no further comment. A

particularly perceptive analysis of the role of neighborliness in what other-
wise might be considered a loosely structured village is Stanley Brandes's
recent account of the village of Navanogal in Spain (1973). Brandes
writes that neighborship is a "crucial source of non-kin-based support"
(1973, p. 753). Neighbors help in crisis situations when a family falls ill,
suffers a death, or has a wedding, and they bind their relationship through
reciprocal services and assistance and exchanges of food.

Neighbors and neighborhoods are equally important in Thai villages.
I described for Chiangmai village the formal neighborhood divisions which
are organized to rotate responsibility for sending rice and food to the
temple. This kind of organization is a regional pecularity and is found, to
the best of my knowledge, only in some villages in north Thailand. However, Bang Chan had well defined and named neighborhoods; and there
are in Chiangmai and in other Thai villages more informal neighborhood
groups composed of the four or five households which form a given household's closest neighbors. These are overlapping groups, slightly different
for each household, although they tend to be defined by the lanes which
divide up Thai villages. In Chiangmai and in many other Thai villages
these neighboring households are likely to be related through the matriline,
because of the rule of matrilocal residence; but often neighbors will not
be relatives.

As in the Chinese and Spanish villages described above, relations between neighboring households in Thai villages are extremely close. Men
from neighboring households tend to own adjacent fields (because families
try to live near their fields), and so they often walk to their fields together
in the morning, carrying their plows and other agricultural implements,
and return together in the evening. Since their fields tend to be adjacent,
they cooperate in maintaining the small irrigation canals that water their
fields, and they have to agree on plans to share the water. Neighboring
households tend to belong to the same cooperative labor-exchange group,
and support one another in political matters and in cooperative enter-
prises such as housebuilding. Neighbors are among the first to help in life
crises, such as serious illnesses, births, ordinations, and funerals. They
tend to be (although not always) a close-knit group who frequently visit
each other's courtyards to exchange gossip and information. Neighbors
are so important that they are often treated as kinsmen.

Lucien Hanks describes the formation of a neighborhood in Bang Chan
in the mid-nineteenth century, during the early years of the settlement of
the village. A group of dispossessed people from Bangkok settled along

Kred Canal in Bang Chan. This group consisted of two sets of kinsmen plus some additional households not related to either. Hanks's account is worth quoting:

> The initial distance between nonkinsmen with nearly equal resources was tempered by the need for harvest workers. The exchange of labor among households gracefully allowed each to act as host-for-the-day to all the others. Soon they were greeting each other, out of respect for difference in age, as "older brother" or "mother's younger brother," and gradually trust replaced apprehension. This direction was strengthened on holidays like the New Year festival of spring when young people came respectfully to pour a tiny cup of water on the shoulder of an "older aunt and uncle." [Hanks 1972, p. 98]

Sharp et al. (1953, pp. 30–31) also emphasize the importance of neighborhoods in Bang Chan's social life after the village was established as a community, by showing that this would be one of the most important and essential groups for a hypothetical newcomer to the village to join:

> Bang Chan is divided into three recognized major geographical groups or neighborhoods located in regular succession along both sides of the main canal, their boundaries thus having no correlation with the hamlets or governmental administrative units. A stranger's first social relationships will normally be established with his neighbors in one of these groups on a basis of reciprocal obligations for economic services rendered particularly during planting and harvesting.

Elsewhere in their account, Sharp et al. (p. 126) mention how neighbors cooperate in a house-raising and are, in return, feasted by the owner.

Janlekha (1955, pp. 111–13) elucidates further the nature and operation of Bang Chan neighborhoods in a study published several years after his initial study with Sharp:

> There were three cooperative work groups in Bangchan: (1) *Mu Sapan Yao*, or the Bridge Group, consisting of farm operating families living in the vicinity of the bridge across Bangchan canal; (2) *Mu Na Wat*, or the Near Wat Group, consisting of families living around Wat Bangchan; and (3) *Mu Bon*, or the North Group, consisting of families living in Upcanal Bangchan.

Bang Chan's neighborhoods began to decline in the early 1950s, as the village began to be engulfed in Bangkok's urban sprawl, and a decade later the only vestige of dependence on neighborliness was at temple ordinations (Hanks 1972, p. 124). By the 1970s, Hanks tells us, Bang Chan ceased to exist as a rice-growing community (pp. 148–63), and so, *in their traditional form*, neighborhoods have also ceased to exist in Bang Chan.

Tambiah does not emphasize the neighborhood as a major structural feature of his northeastern village, Baan Phraan Muan. The major settlement is a "dense settlement . . . intersected by narrow lanes" (1970, p. 10). From the map of Baan Phraan Muan, it appears to me that these are the same kinds of lanes which divide Chiangmai village into neighborhoods. In addition, Tambiah not infrequently mentions "the reciprocities of wider kinship, neighbourliness, and village membership" (p. 15). More important, in his chart showing the "religious field" of his village, he indicates that the "Sukhwan" ritual is performed by groups of "household/kin/neighbors" and that the house-blessing rite and the mortuary rites are performed by the same groups.

Another northeastern village, Ban Nong Tuen, described by Keyes, does have five or six neighborhoods called *khum*. Keyes (1975, p. 280) says that "one or more members of every domestic group in a specified khum can, if pressed, trace his genealogy back to a common ancestor who lived only five or six generations in the past." After 1913, when surnames were introduced into Thailand by royal decree, each neighborhood in Keyes's village took the same surname, and so today villagers identify a surname with a particular neighborhood, even though the practice of residence with the wife's family together with the patrilineal inheritance of surnames no longer makes this identification meaningful (Keyes 1975, p. 281). Keyes states flatly that neighborhoods are not important social groups in his village; they are not believed to be kin groups; and they do not regulate marriage, control property, or form a basis for ancestor worship or economic cooperation (1975, pp. 280–81). An exception to this blanket statement is that at least once a year all the households of a neighborhood sponsor a ceremony in which they jointly feed invited monks who perform rituals and bless them. Keyes also says that residential propinquity and the "recognition of consanguineal kin ties among the households of a khum do provide the basis for greater cooperation among kin living within a khum than among those living in different khum" (1975, p. 281), which seems to contradict his earlier denial that these units have any social importance. They seem important to me.

Moerman (1968, p. 9) recognizes in his northern village of Ban Ping the importance of neighbors. He writes of "the security that men feel for

having been born among neighbors with whom they live, worship, and
die." In Ban Ping, as in Chiangmai and many other villages of the north,
neighborhoods are formally defined territorial units for certain purposes.
Moerman writes:

> As in many northern villages (de Young 1955: 115–16) the
> clergy of Ban Ping do not beg for their food. Rather, the village is
> divided into residential sections (*mot*). Every week the households
> of a different section send daily food to the temple. There are as many
> sections as there are holy days in Phansaa and the section whose
> week it is sponsors the holy day services . . . (cf. Moerman 1964:
> 34–35). . . . Although their origin and main task is to provide
> offerings to the temple, the mot are often used as the administrative
> unit for communal labor, school contributions, and other secular
> affairs. [Moerman 1966, p. 142]

Mizuno, writing about the northeastern village of Don Daeng, says that

> the social framework of villagers' daily existence outside the family
> depends on neighbourhood, bilateral kinship ties, intimate small
> group[s] of about [the] same age called *siaw*, and close friendship
> ties called *samakhi* through which people get together at life crises or
> seek connection[s] when they make short trips to other distant
> villages. Within these social networks, the relationship is one of
> mutual-understanding as a local phrase says . . . "to read into other's
> heart to take it into one's own." . . . Proverbs suggest, however, that
> outside this social context people are neither reliable nor trustful.
> [Mizuno 1971, pp. 228–29]

Mizuno also describes the importance of neighbors at funerals: "On the
day when a person has died, relatives, neighbours, and friends gather at
the house to prepare for the funeral . . . [the coffin] is followed by the relatives, neighbours, friends and other villagers" (1971, pp. 183–84). Also
Mizuno mentions that "relatives, neighbours, and friends" attend household blessing rituals (p. 191) and weddings (p. 203).

Like Chiangmai village and Tambiah's village, the compact settlement
of Don Daeng is divided into what Mizuno calls "blocks" (p. 20) and
what I would call neighborhoods, by lanes that divide the village into
eleven sections, but he does not mention the significance of these divisions in the rest of his book; if Tambiah's, Keyes's, and Mizuno's villages
are representative of the northeast, neighborhoods are present, but they
are not as important as in other regions of Thailand.

Kaufman stresses the importance of neighbors in his central delta village, Bangkhuad. He writes:

> The household, although for the most part a self-sufficient economic unit, is not a self-sufficient socio-cultural entity. It constantly requires outside help of various kinds. . . . They sometimes must ask their neighbors for assistance in the fields, and always need their help in constructing a new house. . . . When aid is needed in any phase of the rice cultivation, solicitation of help, whether by means of *khauraeng* [asking people for free labor], *awraeng* [reciprocal labor exchange], or hiring, is first done in the neighborhood of the rice farm irrespective of family ties. As often happens, closely related families occupy contiguous areas and are the first to be asked, not because of family affinity, but merely because of proximity. [1960, pp. 30–31]

**Cooperative
Labor-Exchange
Groups**

In almost all Thai villages cooperative labor-exchange groups, like those described in Chapter 3 for Chiangmai village, are important social structural elements. Even the villagers of Bang Chan, who supposedly lacked organizational ability and cooperative spirit in almost all else, managed to organize such labor-exchange groups (see Phillips 1965, p. 17). Cooperation in rice agriculture by members of the same village is nothing new in Thailand; all indications (see Vella 1955, p. 33) are that it is a traditional feature of Thai village life.

Sharp et al. (1953, p. 30) report many instances in Bang Chan village of what they call "reciprocal obligations for economic services rendered particularly during planting and harvesting," and say that "cooperative harvesting and planting groups" were especially common between "brothers and sisters and their children" (1953, p. 80). Unlike Chiangmai villagers, who use reciprocal labor exchange throughout the cycle of rice-growing, the Bang Chan villagers used it more commonly in harvesting rice than in uprooting and transplanting it. The description that the observers give of reciprocal labor-exchange groups is almost identical to that I have given for Chiangmai village:

> In Bang Chan, as is apparently true elsewhere on the Central Plain, farmers typically take turns helping each other with the harvesting—a cooperative feat made possible because different parcels of land are

planted in such a way as to mature at different times over a harvest period of several weeks. The reciprocal obligations incurred apply not between individuals but between households. Heads of households remember carefully the amount of work owed to and by other households, calculated either on the basis of time worked (so many days and half-days) or on the basis of area worked (so many rai or half-rai). [Sharp et al. 1953, p. 154]

In Bang Chan, as in Chiangmai village, the largest and most active commercial farmers did not bother with reciprocal labor exchange but simply hired laborers for their farms. As reported for many other peasant societies, large-scale commercialized agriculture results in the weakening of traditional forms of cooperative labor exchange. Agriculture becomes a business for profit instead of a way of life; and market advantage becomes more important than social relations with one's fellow villagers. In Bang Chan, as in Chiangmai, it was the middle-sized farmers who utilized reciprocal labor exchange to secure the additional labor needed at transplanting and harvesting, the peak work periods. The small peasants and the landless did not have enough land to engage much in labor exchange, and instead hired themselves out as laborers in the fields of larger village landowners (Sharp et al. 1953, p. 204).

Sharp et al. also report a novel use by Bang Chan farmers of labor exchange to drain their fish ponds and harvest their fish:

When the head of household decides to drain his pool, he will arrange to secure labor and rent an engine. The labor is usually that of relatives, friends, or neighbors; in return for the service of this labor, the host household provides compensation in the form of meals during the day or two required for draining, plus either a predetermined payment in kind or the incurrence of reciprocal obligation. [Sharp et al. 1953, p. 189]

Janlekha, in the account of Bang Chan's economy that he later published, adds more detail about labor exchange. Contradicting the earlier account by Sharp et al., he says that, in addition to cooperative labor exchange at harvesting, Bang Chan villagers also used this institution in other stages of field work: at uprooting, transplanting, and weeding. He also mentions the cooperative pounding of rice (with a large, foot-operated pestle and a mortar), a practice that was disappearing because of the coming of the gasoline-powered rice mills (Janlekha 1955, pp. 111–12). Harvesting "was largely done through a cooperative work group, the proportion of the work done by the family workers themselves and that done through cooperative harvesting being about one to five" (Janlekha 1955, p. 103).

The time spent in the actual performance of labor-exchange work in the fields, from Janlekha's account, was obviously great; even more important socially was the time spent in entertaining and feeding the guest workers. Janlekha stresses that:

> customarily the host provided food to guest workers in cooperative uprooting and cooperative harvesting. To feed some twenty to thirty people was quite a job, thus practically all family workers were occupied in food preparation and serving on these occasions. Our records show that entertaining guest workers started on July 22 and ended on January 24, and that while supervision of cooperative work utilized only 26 man-hours of labor, entertaining the same groups involved as many as 158½ man-hours. [Janlekha 1955, p. 104]

Janlekha (1955, p. 112) says that "cooperative work groups were very informally organized. . . . the work obligation was not collective but was purely bilateral—each farmer receiving help was bound to return the same amount of work to each guest worker individually. There was no such thing as group responsibility." But it is not quite that simple, and Janlekha presents data that do not support his interpretation. In his detailed study of the labor-exchange relationships of the twenty households—not merely twenty individuals—who exchanged labor with a farmer named Chom, Janlekha found that when he listed the labor-exchange partners of these twenty-one households (including Chom's) he came up with the names of only twenty-four households. This means that all but three of the twenty households with whom Chom exchanged labor also exchanged labor only within Chom's group. Thus even though each household's labor-exchange group differed slightly, the exchange network was very "dense" and was restricted almost entirely to one of the three neighborhoods into which Bang Chan was divided, called Mu Sapan Yao (the Bridge Group) (Janlekha 1955, p. 113). Janlekha denies that this is a group at all, but this interpretation is misleading; as in Chiangmai village, so in Bang Chan to an equal extent, reciprocal labor-exchange networks are tightly knit entities (I would call them groups) that structure the social relations of the families involved.

I have already mentioned Lucien Hanks's account of the rise and fall of cooperation in Bang Chan. "Labor exchange between neighbors in Bang

Chan," according to Hanks, "was a symptom of underpopulation, for it disappeared as soon as hired labor became available" (1972, p. 153). This may have been the case in Bang Chan, but it is not the case in Chiangmai village, where labor exchange still exists in an area of extreme population density. The appearance of large commercialized farms and then the eventual disappearance of Bang Chan as a rice-growing community and its incorporation into the suburbs of Bangkok, and the ensuing new employment opportunities, are more likely explanations for the ultimate decline of labor exchange in Bang Chan. As late as 1964, Steven Piker describes cooperative harvest groups in another village, Banoi, in the central plain near Ayutthaya (Piker 1964, p. 53).

Even though de Young noted, in 1955, that labor exchange was dying out in some of the most commercialized rice-growing regions in Thailand (like Bang Chan), he still calls labor exchange "the outstanding form of economic cooperation in village life," which was being used to plant and harvest rice in most rural areas of Thailand. In his northern commune, San Pong, just north of Chiengmai city, this group was called "*mua torb*," "repaying work time." De Young says that there was a tendency for the members of labor-exchange groups to be drawn from neighbors, although, as I have noted for Chiangmai village, the composition of the work groups varied:

> If a farmer has only a few paddy fields, his work group consists of perhaps ten or fifteen persons, mainly his immediate relatives in the village; the reciprocal work group for an average northern farmer, who plants 8 or 10 *rai* of paddy, consists of perhaps thirty-five or forty-five members, representing fifteen or twenty families. [de Young 1955, p. 79]

His findings, except for a slightly higher estimate of the average size of the northern farmer's work group, agree with mine in Chiangmai village.

Again following the theoretical guidelines of Embree and Sharp, under whose guidance his original field work in Thailand began, de Young emphasizes the loosely structured nature of labor-exchange groups in the north. He says (1955, p. 79) that "no record is kept of how many workers or how many hours of work a family contributes. Here as elsewhere in Thai rural social organization the arrangement is loose and informal." De Young's claim that no records are kept is certainly not true for Chiangmai village or for the rest of rural Thailand, and is highly unlikely on the face of it. Reciprocal obligations are not evaded in Chiangmai village because the farmers, many of them illiterate, keep careful records in their heads of how much labor they have given and received. If a household does not fulfill its obligations, it has to hire workers to replace its members or face the sanctions of a public scolding, a performance that I witnessed in Chiangmai village, and one which is not pleasant for the family concerned. De Young must have realized this, because he says in the next sentence that "the principle of exchange is primarily the number of workers: if household A provides two workers for household B at transplanting time, household B in turn sends two workers to A's fields. Reciprocal obligations are seldom if ever evaded" (1955, p. 79). If reciprocal obligations are not evaded, then records must be kept and sanctions exerted; there is nothing loose or informal about this at all.

De Young's claim that the work arrangements are loosely structured is contradicted by Janlekha's account of the labor-exchange activities of the Bang Chan farmer named Chom whom I discussed previously. Chom was away from the village during eight days of the rice-uprooting and transplanting season, when he was supposed to participate in seven cooperative uprootings. This left his family short seven units of labor contribution to the other members of his group. To repay this debt, Chom had to hire a professional piece-worker to do the work. As further evidence of how carefully accounts were kept in these supposedly informal groups, Janlekha notes how units of work were transferred from one member of the group to another in a complex series of transactions:

> Records show that at the end Chom's contribution to each of his twenty fellow members was *individually* equal to the help he received from each of them . . . the exception being the cases with A and B. Chom had contributed three units to A, receiving only two units from the man; but he had received four units from B, giving him only three units of work. This was settled by transferring Chom's credit with A to B which is the general practice. [Janlekha 1955, p. 113]

Labor-exchange relationships of two types are described by Kaufman for his village, Bangkhuad: one type, known as *awraeng*, is the kind of cooperative relationship we have been discussing; the second type, known as *khauraeng*, is one in which landlords or other powerful people demand free help from debtors and tenants, who are obliged to comply.

The *awraeng* relation in Bangkhuad is described by Kaufman (1960: pp. 30–31) as follows: "Awraeng is literally translated *to take one's strength* and means a borrowing or a reciprocal exchange of labor. One goes about soliciting help and promising to return the favor at a future date." He continues:

Farms of 20 or more *raj* are inevitably forced to hire help in addition
to using *awraeng*, for it requires four farmers one half day to harvest
one *raj*. The very large farms have a head coolie to do the soliciting,
and usually employ in addition the method of *khauraeng*. [Kaufman
1960, p. 45]

Kaufman's description of the operating principles of Bangkhuad's labor-
exchange systems is much like those given above for Chiangmai and Bang
Chan, except that Kaufman goes into more detail about how complicated
the transactions can become when a commercialized cash-wage economy
is mixed with a traditional exchange system:

> Use of *khauraeng* and *awraeng* benefits everyone except those with no
> property. These are the methods which are still employed for over 70
> percent of the various cultivation tasks. *Awraeng* is the most widely
> used of the two methods; it guarantees the various individuals who
> participate that they will also get the work done on their own farms.
> *Awraeng* is used for harvesting, transplanting, and pool digging. It
> works in this manner. *A* promises to work 10 *raj* for *B*, if *B* will work
> 10 *raj* for *A* when his fields are ready. If *B* can only work eight *raj*,
> he will send over another person, *C*, who owes *B* two raj, to make up
> *B*'s debt to *A*. If *A* is hiring on a cash basis, then *B* sends *C* and *C* must
> give B the wages for the two *raj*. B, in this case, must return the money
> to *A*. If a farmer shirks his end of the bargain, word gets about and
> next year he will have difficulty getting people to *awraeng* with him.
> [Kaufman 1960, p. 65]

Phillips, again writing about Bang Chan, relegates what he calls "reciprocal work groups" to the minor status of a footnote (1965, p. 22).
Following Janlekha, he describes reciprocal labor-exchange groups as "organized for and limited to rice transplanting and harvesting, membership
in which is completely voluntary and a matter of mutual convenience."
He recognizes that each family carefully counts its labor contribution and
the amount it receives, but he does not make much of this fact.

Further north in the central plain, about sixty miles from Bang Chan
and Bangkhuad, in Piker's village, Banoi, reciprocal labor-exchange groups
are present at harvest time (Piker 1964, p. 53) but not at other times,
indicating that Sharp et al.'s original analysis in Bang Chan was probably
correct and that reciprocal labor-exchange groups continue to be used in
harvesting if not in other farm work.

In the northern village of Ban Ping, Moerman refers to reciprocal labor-
exchange groups simply as "work groups" (1968, p. 39). Work groups

of both sexes help in uprooting, transplanting, and harvesting (1968, pp. 39–41). He distinguishes three types of reward for work (1968, p. 116): fellowship, exchange, and goods (money and rice). Fellowship, according to Moerman, is the motive of kinsmen; goods, either rice or cash, are used by farmers to hire laborers; and exchange—what we have been calling reciprocal labor exchange—is the third mode of labor mobilization.

Moerman's older village informants describe labor exchange in the old days, before the Ban Ping villagers were so deeply involved in commercial rice agriculture:

> the village was the unit for the exchange of transplanting labor. Huge work parties that ensured prompt transplanting were composed of everyone in Ban Ping and everyone in the next village. Each household head would inform the village headman of the days on which he wanted to uproot and plant. The headman would then send a messenger to announce the dates on the main streets of Ban Ping and the neighboring village. Ideally, every household in both villages sent representatives to all transplantings. They were gay occasions for which the farmer would provide good food, drink, and entertainment. [Moerman 1968, p. 136]

The situation described by Moerman's informants represents an extreme example of traditional reciprocal labor-exchange relationships among the Thai-Lue in which an entire village or even larger groups were cemented together by participation in collective agricultural tasks. Moerman's case is not unique in the literature. Lawrence Judd, describing the agricultural activities of dry rice farmers north of Nan, notes that some hamlets worked their swidden jointly, as a large cooperative labor-exchange unit (Judd 1961, p. 138).

By 1968 the situation in Ban Ping village had become less idyllic. By then there were three exchange systems: *lo* (cooperative farming between two or more households); *termkan* (much like George Foster's [1961] dyadic contract), an informal exchange in which return did not have to be immediate; and, most important for our purposes, *aw haeng* (equivalent to our reciprocal labor-exchange groups), in which one had to repay one unit of male labor for each unit of male labor received, the quality of the work also being important (Moerman 1968, p. 117). This is a system of "calculated reciprocity," in which the household replaced the village as the unit of exchange and in which the food offered became more inexpensive and the hospitality less elaborate (1968, pp. 136–37).

In 1968, in spite of commercialization, Moerman still believes that

noncommercial claims on labor are still far more basic to transplanting in Ban Ping than they are in central Thailand. In Ban Ping indirect exchange is used to cement fellowship between close kinsmen. . . . Completely unknown in Ban Ping is the exploitative "*khaurang* system" . . . whereby a wealthy landowner may conscript labor from his tenants, debtors, and other dependents. [Moerman 1968, p. 137]

Moerman's account, together with the evidence from Chiangmai village, from de Young's village, and from Judd's villages near Nan, indicates that labor-exchange systems were just as important in northern Thai villages as they were in central villages like Bang Chan, Bangkhuad, and Banoi. There remains to consider the northeast, as described by Madge, Mizuno, Tambiah, and Keyes.

Madge (1957, pp. 5–6) describes the Thai village social system in the southeast part of northeastern Thailand as

a system well-designed for co-operative social behaviour. Few of its members feel anxiety about their place in it. A reciprocal exchange of services is the unifying factor. . . . Local systems of mutual aid [by which I presume he means cooperative labor-exchange groups, although he is not explicit] are not co-extensive with local kinship systems.

He does not add to this meager account.

Mizuno (1971, p. 58), speaking of his northeastern village, Don Daeng, near Khon Kaen, says that "labour forces are largely provided with the family and kinsmen." There are nineteen cases of what Mizuno (1971, p. 69) calls "joint farming," in which landowners farm with their daughters' husbands' help. From his account, which is usually quite thorough, it appears that cooperative labor-exchange groups are not of great importance in his village.

In Baan Phraan Muan, Tambiah's village in the northeast near Udon, cooperative labor in agriculture is practiced within compound groups, by older couples and the families of their married daughters (Tambiah 1970, pp. 12–13), but Tambiah also speaks of households as independent contracting units "in reciprocal economic services and dyadic contracts," which suggests the presence of larger cooperative labor-exchange groups in the village (Tambiah 1970, p. 14). But since he does not discuss such groups further, I am left in doubt about their status.

Ban Nong Tuen, Keyes's village near Mahasarakham in the northeast, definitely has cooperative labor-exchange groups. Describing rice production, Keyes says that "the main labor source is provided by the constituent kin groups. Only for the harvest, and, for some larger land holders, transplanting, is a larger labor force needed. On these occasions a labor exchange (*waan*) is effected between constituent kin groups" (1967, pp. 16–17). These four accounts suggest that, while present, labor-exchange groups are not as important in the economic and social life of northeastern villages as they are in the north, the central plain, or the lower delta.

## Class Divisions

Socioeconomic classes are defined by their relation to the means of production. In rural Thai villages, as in all peasant societies, the means of production is land. I have pointed out above how economic classes in Chiangmai village society are based upon differential landownership. Although prestige is awarded members of the monkhood, and some prestige is given those with political power not based upon landed wealth, class stratification based upon the ownership of land is one of the principal social structural elements in all Thai villages, as recent political activities by landless and poor Thai peasants indicate clearly.

The persistent stereotype of Thailand as an underpopulated country where land is free for the clearing and the taking is now no more than a myth from the past (see Silcock 1970, p. 40). The Thai population grew from an estimated 5 or 6 million in 1850, 7.3 million in 1900, 17.3 million in 1947 (Ingram 1955, pp. 7–8), to an estimated 43 million in 1975 (Moore 1974, p. 31)—an eightfold increase within a little over a century. The area planted in rice increased from 5.8 million raj in 1850 to 34.6 million raj in 1950—a sixfold increase—but much of this newly reclaimed land, especially in the northeast, is marginal. At present, and for some time past, population has been pressing against resources, creating a situation of scarcity of good agricultural land in many parts of the country. Combined with high interest rates and land tenure institutions which allow the free buying and selling of land, land scarcity has led to the emergence of new-style landed and landless classes in the villages (see also Sharp 1963). Although in premodern days class stratification certainly existed in Thailand, landlessness and tenancy have increased in modern times— especially in places like the central plain and in Chiengmai, where the land is rich and productive.

Increased class differentiation of a modern kind among the peasantry was first noticed in central Thailand early in the twentieth century and was caused by the commercialization of rice agriculture, the reclaiming of land,

and the purchase of landed estates by wealthy Bangkok residents, both Chinese merchants and Thai aristocrats who obtained land through government connections. When the first systematic surveys of land ownership were taken in the 1930s, by Carle C. Zimmerman (1931) and James M. Andrews (1935), they found a large landless class in the villages of the central plains. Between 1930 and 1950, according to James C. Ingram's account (1955, p. 57), regions outside the central plain continued to practice what he calls the old subsistence agriculture, based upon communal cooperative labor exchange.

Zimmerman's 1930 survey found that the percentage of landless villagers in Thailand ranged from a high of 36 percent in the central plain to 27 percent in the north, 18 percent in the northeast, and a low of 14 percent in the south (Zimmerman 1931, p. 18). The rate of tenancy and landlessness was correlated with the degree of commercialization of agriculture: in the south and the northeast less than 20 percent of the rice produced was sold (and this mainly locally), in the north 40 percent was sold, and in the central plain approximately 60 percent was sold (mainly on the international market) (Zimmerman 1931, p. 19). Zimmerman (1931, p. 48) found that the overall cash income of the peasants at that time was dependent upon the degree of commercialization of agriculture: in the central plain the peasants were best-off, in the south and north fairly well-off, and in the northeast the poorest. This does not mean that in the areas of high tenancy there were no poor people; especially in the lower delta region of the central plain, many of the tenants did not do well and their relations with absentee landlords were not good. Zimmerman points to the lower delta near Bangkok as a trouble point:

> The chief tenant problem is in Dhanyaburi and the eastern irrigation district [an area in the lower delta north of Bangkok]. Here nearly all the families are tenants. Relationships between some of the landlords and tenants were not particularly good. . . . Tenure contracts are generally for one year. Consequently neither the landlord, who oftentimes lives in Bangkok, nor the tenant will improve the farms or the homesteads. [Zimmerman 1931, p. 19]

On the basis of his survey of representative Thai villages in different parts of the country five years later, Andrews (1935) presents a picture of the Thai agricultural economy and land situation similar to Zimmerman's. Tenancy and landlessness were lower in the north, south and northeast; and in these regions landlords and tenants were usually neighbors, living side by side. In central Thailand, however, the rates of landlessness and tenancy were higher, and much of the best land near Bangkok was owned by absentee landlords. Even in this area of high tenancy, however, Andrews does not consider rents exorbitant, except in bad years when crops failed and the landlord was not close enough to the situation to reduce the rent proportionately (Andrews 1935, p. 109).

From both Zimmerman's and Andrews's findings, it appears that in the period between 1930 and 1935 the central Thai peasants, many of whom were tenants, had a much higher level of living than peasants in other regions of the country. However, this must be balanced off against the insecurity of the tenants' tenure, which was renewed only from year to year, the presence of a landless laboring class, their heavy dependence upon international markets, and the fact that a large share of the produce went to people who were not producers of the rice.

The situation did not change much over the following two decades. Writing in 1955, de Young describes the rural economic situation in terms not very different from those of Zimmerman and Andrews. He says that "except in the area around Bangkok and Rangsit [north of Bangkok], most Thai peasants are independent farmers living in a subsistence economy. It is estimated [by the FAO Committee of Thailand (1949, p. 30)] that 80 percent of the farmland of Thailand is owned by small, independent farmers" (de Young 1955, p. 75). De Young (1955, p. 76) is skeptical about the FAO estimate, and so am I. He warns that "even though most Thai farmers own at least part of the land they cultivate, tenant farmers are also common throughout the kingdom," especially in parts of the central plain. By 1955, I suspect that internal developments in the country-side—population increase especially—were already beginning to create a situation that was soon to make many rural Thai villagers desperate enough to threaten the established order of Thai society.

Wijeyewardene concludes, from his attempt to analyze the findings of the *Census of Agriculture 1963*, published by the National Statistical Office in 1965, that even though everyone recognizes that the incidence of land-lessness and tenancy is greatest in the central plain, he suspects that it is "greater than reported" for other areas as well, one reason being that many farmers are counted as landowners rather than landless only because of their ownership of a fragment of house plot. Wijeyewardene concludes that "it is not easy to determine how widespread are landlessness and the lack of agricultural opportunities . . . throughout Thailand" (1967, p. 80). Given statistical difficulties like this (and others, such as a change in the

definitions of what is to be considered north, south, central, and northeast
Thailand), Wijeyewardene was prevented from making definitive conclusions. Let us leave aside these gross governmental statistics, useful as they
are, and focus upon the land ownership and social stratification patterns
revealed in the anthropological village studies; and let us begin, as usual,
at the beginning, with Bang Chan.

Sharp et al. (1953, p. 28) tell us first off that in a social system like
Bang Chan's, characterized by "vagueness," "there is no clear class structure which would require alignment with one stratum rather than another."
Later, they qualify this statement by remarking that "in these distinctions
between the 'big man' and the 'little man' there is a clear indication of a
tendency towards social stratification along class lines within a peasantry
which traditionally was rather undifferentiated and immobile" (1953, p.
31).

Later in their account of Bang Chan society and economy, Sharp et al.
reveal that there was indeed class stratification in the community based
upon the differential ownership of land, and that there was a large class of
tenants and landless laborers: of the farm operators, 23 percent owned all
their land, 33 percent owned part of their farms and rented the rest (part-
tenants), and 44 percent rented all their land (full tenants). Class differentiation *within the farming population* of Bang Chan was further indicated by the fact that farms ranged in size from 4 to 110 raj. Of the land
farmed by Bang Chan farmers, almost 60 percent was rented from landlords on one-year verbal contracts (Sharp et al. 1953, pp. 147–48). Even
though the average 20 percent share of the crop paid by Bang Chan tenants was not exorbitant compared to the share paid in other countries in
Asia (and elsewhere in Thailand, where it approaches 50 percent), the
fact that many farmers rented most of their farms and had no security of
tenure and that they had to pay out 20 percent of their produce to landlords can certainly be described as a class-exploitative situation.

At the bottom of the class structure of Bang Chan, below the landowners, the part-tenants, the tenants, and the long-term laborers who work
for fixed wages, were the "perhaps fifty to 100 persons [out of a population of about 1,600] who receive wages on a piece-work basis for such
short-term tasks as uprooting the seedlings, transplanting, and harvesting. . . . All able-bodied and relatively poor local people are at least potential piece workers in these two processes; this includes less affluent
children of school age (eight to fourteen years), who work before and
after school hours" (Sharp et al. 1953, p. 154). The farm laborers (to be

distinguished from those who participate as partners in labor exchange) were hired mainly by the busier and larger farmers who did not have time to participate in labor exchange. Finally, Sharp describes a dynamic situation in which Bang Chan villagers tried to improve their class situations through economic advancement:

> Particularly since the war, the small farm operator in Bang Chan . . . seek[s] to improve his economic position so that he moves upward in the local scale or, if more successful, outward and still further upward towards an urban center. . . . Indeed, one of them distinguished two classes into which most of the Bang Chan population fits. The majority are "chickens" or progressive farmers who actively seek to improve their economic status; the others are "ducks" or laggards satisfied with traditional or "poor" standards. . . . It is clear that the former group, which includes local leaders and persons with high prestige, is on the increase. [Sharp et al. 1953, p. 31]

Sharp et al. describe the same kind of motives and values for social mobility within the village class structure that I have described for Chiangmai village.

In his later study of the Bang Chan farm economy, Janlekha found that the land situation had worsened since the previous study a few years earlier by Sharp et al. Farm operators had decreased from 80 to 72 percent, while farm laborers had increased from 9 to 13 percent and petty traders from 2 to 7 percent (1955, p. 43).

Janlekha emphasizes the stratification of the Bang Chan community in 1953, especially the difference between the small landowners and the large landlords who worked a part of their farms and rented out the rest to poorer families in the village. He says that "in the relatively high population pressure areas such as Bangchan . . . , the difference between farmers owning a small area of land and a large area is so great from the standpoint of economic and social position as to warrant having two subdivisions of the conventional "owner-operators" (p. 56). Using Janlekha's suggested class breakdown and combining it with other information he gives about landless laborers and peddlers, we find that the class stratification of Bang Chan is as follows: 4 percent of the households were landlord-operators, 29 percent were owner-operators, 8 percent were part owner-operators, 37 percent were tenants, and 22 percent were farm laborers and petty peddlers. This means that about 60 percent of the households of Bang Chan (the tenants and the laborers and peddlers) were landless. The five leading landlord-operators, according to Janlekha (p.

46), owned a total of 693 raj, averaging 139 raj per operator, whereas the average farm contained only about 22 raj.

I cite all these figures to show that the community of Bang Chan was not loosely structured or amorphous. Class stratification based upon differential land ownership was an essential feature of the village's social structure. There was more than a "tendency" toward stratification in Bang Chan. Also, the heavy dependence upon landlords (many of them absentee landlords) indicates how clearly Bang Chan fits into the overall class structure of Thailand. Near Bangkok much of the land was owned by members of the city elite.

The meaning of such a rate of tenancy is not difficult to predict and is not as sanguine as Andrews would have it. Sharp et al. (1953, p. 202) remark: "In the bumper season of 1948–49, by a realistic standard which is commonly and widely used for the measurement of farm profitability, more than four out of every ten farmers in the sample were operating at a loss. We consider this finding one of the most significant facts emerging from our year's study of Bang Chan."

The landed class of Bang Chan must have dominated the community as it does in Chiangmai village. There was and is nothing at all loosely structured about Bang Chan or other Thai villages from this point of view: the landed classes in a village run that village pretty much as they see fit. When Phillips (1958) speaks of the *leaders* of Bang Chan village making decisions about an election campaign, there is little doubt in my mind as to which class in the village these leaders came from (more of this below).

Kaufman, in his description of the village of Bangkuad, clearly recognizes the class structuring of its social life. He says that although there are no beggars in Bangkhuad, there are great differences in wealth: "some households have no land to cultivate while others have 200 *raj* or more . . . [and] 22 percent of all households plow no land while 18.5 percent plow over fifty *raj*." (1960, p. 55).

The class breakdown of Bangkhuad's agricultural population (135 out of 147 families in the village work in agriculture) is as follows (Kaufman 1960, p. 66): 12.5 percent of the village agricultural households own and rent out land (landlords); 18.5 percent own all their land and do not rent-in any (rich and middle peasants); 10.3 percent own part of their land but have to rent-in the rest (lower middle and poor peasants); 34 percent rent-in all their land (poor peasants); and 23.7 percent of the village agricultural households neither own nor rent land—they are landless laborers (the designations "landlords," etc., are mine, the figures are Kaufman's).

Kaufman is also cognizant of the social and political importance of wealth in village society. He mentions that village headmen are usually from the wealthy class of the village (1960, p. 56). He also confirms my analysis of the importance of wealth in the social life of Chiangmai village:

> Wealth plays an important, though at times, subtle role in the community. A farmer with money is in a position to exert pressure on many other farmers. . . .
>
> At the other extreme are the landless farmers. These individuals feel constantly the economic pressure of being landless and at the mercy, each year, of large land owners. . . . The feeling of insecurity and inferiority which they exhibit is only partially due to the attitude of others, and is primarily based on their feelings of guilt for not being able to contribute to the temple. Many of them do not attend *wat* services because they cannot afford a *baht* for the collection bowl. [Kaufman 1960, pp. 35–36]

Moreover, Kaufman (1960, p. 64) says that each year the differences between the wealthier and poorer village households increase, establishing beyond doubt what might be expected from our earlier discussion of the high tenancy rates in the central plains region of Thailand—a classical Marxist type of class differentiation in the countryside resulting from a capitalist form of economic development. (For a discussion of Marx's theory and a critical assessment of it as it applies to modern Chinese rural social and economic history, see Potter [1968].)

In Piker's village, Banoi, five miles from Ayutthaya in the heart of the central plain, the land situation is even worse. Piker speaks of the rise of a landless class of villagers as a chronic problem in his area (1964, p. 17). He says that "in Banoi sixty percent of the families . . . are either landless or own so little land (5 rai or less) that they must subsist largely on the basis of wage labor . . . performed during the plowing and harvest periods; [however] . . . these labor periods combined . . . do not provide sufficient yearly income" (Piker 1964, pp. 21, 35).

Piker shows how land shortage is affecting the social patterns in his village; because of the land shortage, the old social pattern whereby a man moves to his wife's village and inherits land there from her parents is being disrupted because there is no land to inherit and other alternative arrangements have to be made (1964, p. 15).

Piker recognizes the social importance of stratification in village life: the big difference, he says, is between the 40 percent of the village households who have land to farm and support themselves, and the 60 percent who do not. The main problem in Banoi is absentee landlordism. Piker notes that "at present, two thirds of the land [in the commune in which his village is located] . . . is owned by people who don't live in the district. . . . It is no exaggeration to point out that . . . a genuine rural proletariat has grown up—a class of people with virtually no property, who support . . . themselves . . . on their own labor" (Piker 1964, p. 36). Piker says that the problem is becoming worse: in the 1930s "almost every family owned sufficient land to support themselves as the fortunate forty percent now do" (1964, p. 35).

Landlessness has led to attitudes of resignation and dependency among Piker's villagers. There is a belief (similar to George M. Foster's "image of limited good" [1965]) that one cannot get ahead in Thai society on one's own efforts, but must depend upon pleasing some powerful patron who holds the key to advancement (Piker 1964, p. 113). Given such inequality in the distribution of land in the area studied by Piker, this is a fairly realistic attitude, for there is little hope for advancement by one's own efforts. I am not one who swallows the myth about great social mobility in Thai society; I have seen and read little about peasant villagers significantly improving their class situation.

The northeastern villages, located in the poorest part of Thailand, show internal class differentiation, but it is less marked than in other regions of Thailand. In the northeastern villages around Ubon, where Madge studied, he found some differentiation in land ownership within each village, but all the farmers owned at least some land (Madge 1957, pp. 12–13, 22–23). Of Pa-ao, a village he studied, Madge says the following:

> One does not find the extremes of poverty and affluence that appear in peasant societies where there are a few landowners and many landless labourers. Except in the disintegrating villages near Ubon itself, nearly every household owns land, though in some cases the holding is so small or unproductive as to be of little use. There is at Pa-ao, for example, an even gradation of wealth, with about 10 percent of households conspicuously prosperous, about 20 percent in real hardship, and the remaining 70 percent somewhere in between. [Madge 1957, p. 47]

Although the class differences Madge describes are not as striking as those described by Piker, there are definitely classes present; they seem significant to me, and undoubtedly more so to the villagers who live in Pa-ao. The differences in farm income in Pa-ao were marked: of the 69 households whose income Madge describes 13 have a yearly income of about 2,800 kilograms of rice; 25 have 1,800; 17 have 1,500; and 14 households have 840 (Madge 1957, p. 50). There were definitely differential wealth and levels of living in the village although, according to Madge, even the wealthier households were not particularly well off. In Pa-ao, as in many areas of the northeast, the total landholdings of a family do not give an accurate indication of the family's wealth because much of the land newly reclaimed is marginal and is not farmed every year. The best land is that near the ponds and streams where an assured water supply is available, and the ownership of this land means wealth for a farm family (Madge 1957, p. 51).

The class stratification of Pa-ao was evident in the ownership of water buffaloes and cattle, which are a means of investing savings and a measure of prestige. In 1953 the wealthier class (22 percent of the households) owned 59 percent of the animals, in addition to harvesting 36 percent of the land harvested (Madge 1957, p. 55).

Mizuno's more recent description of Don Daeng, the village he studied near Khon Kaen in the central northeastern part of Thailand, is similar to that given by Madge. There are no really large landlords within or near the village, and the villagers own most of the land they farm (Mizuno 1971, p. 62). Still, land is not equally distributed among the villagers, and ownership of land divides the village into different strata: 14 percent of the richest households of Don Daeng own 38 percent of the land in the village; whereas 60 percent of the households own only 23 percent of the land, and the middle 26 percent of the households own the remaining 39 percent of the land (Mizuno 1971, p. 63). It may be true, as Mizuno says, that there are only three landlords and one tenant in the village; but there are certainly a few very rich farmers, some middle farmers, and a sizable number of marginal families at the bottom of the class scale who own almost no land at all, even though some of these (as in Chiangmai village) are dependent families of landowning fathers-in-law and will eventually inherit land.

In his chapter on social stratification, Mizuno summarizes findings based upon a survey in which he asked his villagers to rate their fellows on the basis of prestige. Aside from the special prestige given to the abbott, monks, and schoolteachers, Mizuno concludes that "in the final analysis, . . . when villagers evaluate the status position of household heads in terms of prestige, they . . . consider family background . . . best recognized in terms of the developmental stages of [the] family cycle; and . . . land relation and land size" (Mizuno 1971, p. 118). Mizuno's analysis is somewhat difficult to understand because he confuses the family cycle with class stratification, as if land were in unlimited supply and, automatically, the older one became the more land he controlled. However, when he finally divides the village into six strata (from upper-upper to lower-lower), he does it on the basis of the amount of land owned. In my opinion, and in Mizuno's as well (see 1971, p. 119), land ownership is the basic determinant of class standing and prestige in Don Daeng. The wealthier villagers own, as in Madge's region, large numbers of cattle and horses, which are prestige symbols (Mizuno 1971, pp. 121–22).

Furthermore, Mizuno stresses the desire for social mobility within the village as one of the most powerful life-goals of his villagers. A young man starts off in life dependent upon his father-in-law. At middle age he reaches a plateau from which, through hard work, he may come to own as many as fifty raj of farm land:

> Farmers may dream to own as much as 50 *rai* of farm land in their life time. When they will get [old enough to] control some of their filial [daughters'] families through joint farming, some of them can . . . nearly attain the goal, while others remain far below it. [Mizuno 1971, p. 127]

Baan Phraan Muan, Tambiah's village, between Udon Thani and Nong Khai, across from Vientiane (again, see map 1 for village locations), does not show the marked economic differentiation found in Bang Chan. According to Tambiah (1970, p. 23), there are differences in amount of land owned by village households, but they are not great. He says (1970, p. 24) that "there is very little renting in or renting out of land, and landlord-tenant categories are not important in village economy. . . . The hierarchy in the village is primarily of a generational nature rather than a creature of economic maldistribution." Like Mizuno, Tambiah warns against interpreting as landlessness the status of dependent young couples who stand to inherit land from their parents.

Nevertheless, while economic differentiation is not sharp here, compared with Bang Chan or other villages like Bangkhuad or Banoi in the central plain, it is by no means absent; I think it still important, in spite of Tambiah's protestations to the contrary. The importance of class differentiation based upon differential land ownership and wealth is suggested early (1970, p. 8) in Tambiah's general introductory description of his village, when he mentions that some of the houses of his village have wooden walls and some have bamboo walls. This shows wealth differences, just as it does in Chiangmai village, and brings to mind the old Chinese proverb about the importance of matching families of appropriate classes in marriages: "Wooden doors should face wooden doors, and bamboo doors should face bamboo doors."

Moreover, Tambiah's data on land ownership do not support his conclusions that his community is egalitarian. Of the 129 village households on which he had rice land ownership data from the government (the reliability of which is questionable), 10.8 percent owned more than 40 raj; the median was 13.5 raj; and 10.8 percent were landless (Tambiah 1970, p. 24). The data on land ownership given by Tambiah are too meager to permit a conclusive analysis, but they do show differential ownership of land; and I strongly suspect that this is translated into differential power and prestige in village society, although Tambiah does not agree with this interpretation.

Furthermore (and this would hold true for all Thai village communities on which I have information), the *relative* lack of class differentiation in Baan Phraan Muan is not normative; it is not valued. Even in this village, the whole tenor of the Buddhist religion's merit-making, in Tambiah's words, has "empirical objectives—that is, . . . seeking a prosperous rebirth" (p. 54). Again, "merit-making is, in part, expressly directed to hastening rebirth and also to securing a better rebirth than the existing one" (p. 55). If Tambiah's villagers are egalitarian in fact (compared to central plain villages), they are not in ideology; they exhibit the same achievement motivation as other Thai villagers.

The village of Ban Nong Tuen, Keyes's northeastern community near Mahasarakham, in the center of northeastern Thailand, which Keyes describes as "culturally a typical . . . Thai-Lao village" (Keyes 1967*b*, p. 1), is important because it shows that not all northeastern villages have impressed anthropologists as being egalitarian.

Ban Nong Tuen is clearly differentiated by classes based upon land ownership. Keyes tells us that of the ninety-nine kin groups (roughly equivalent to families) in his village, 18 percent lack sufficient land to grow rice for the family to eat and have to engage in handicrafts, grow upland crops, fish more intensively, or engage in some other marginal economic enterprise to make ends meet. Even then, five out of these eighteen poor households had to depend upon relatives' charity in order to maintain a bare existence (Keyes 1967*b*, p. 17).

This situation is not new. Because of a shortage of good agricultural land, Keyes (1967*b*, p. 15) says that between 1935 and 1963 at least seventy-five family groups emigrated from the village to seek a better living. Keyes also implies that some families in the village are quite well-off. They have corrugated iron roofing, radios, store-bought clothing, bicycles, and sewing machines; and they are able to sponsor more elaborate merit-making ceremonies. Keyes mentions that the ownership of land is essential for men if they are to take part in decisions which affect the entire village (Keyes 1975, p. 290).

Millard F. Long, citing figures from a Thai government survey of household expenditures (Thailand 1964, p. 19), emphasizes the stratification in terms of income of northeastern villagers. He says that "income among farmers is not, as has sometimes been claimed, equally distributed; the upper 2% of villagers in the Northeast received 10 times as much cash income per capita as the lowest 78%, and also consumer [sic] in kind five times as much" (Millard F. Long 1966, p. 355).

Another study in the province of Khon Kaen, made in 1962 by Janis F. Long, showed that 4 percent of the village farmers had more than three times the incomes of the other farmers in their village; 4 percent received less than one-fifth the mean income of their village; and median income was 20 percent below the mean income (Janis F. Long et al. 1963, pp. 64–65).

From Moerman's somewhat confusing account it is difficult to abstract a coherent picture of stratification in his northern Thai-Lue village, Ban Ping, and to assess the relation between stratification and landownership. Moerman (1968, p. 104) claims that land shortage is no problem in Ban Ping: "Since there is land for all, no one is forced to leave the village. Ban Ping thus presents a sharp contrast to land-hungry central Thailand, where many families are disintegrated by poverty . . . and their members forced to find urban employment." Moreover there "is the relative absence of economic stratification. Compared with central Thai villages, Ban Ping suffers no conflict between landlord and tenant, no feeling of economic subjugation, little conspicuous difference among levels of living" (1968, pp. 104–5).

These statements by Moerman represent the situation after 1953 when the availability of distant new lands and their exploitation by tractors had significantly modified an earlier situation of land scarcity. Although land could be freely cleared and claimed long after the settlement of Ban Ping, Moerman tells us (1968, pp. 91–92) that "by about 1935 the quest for land had become fairly pressing." In 1965, Moerman (1968, pp. 185–86) went back to find that the villagers who had remained in Ban Ping had reverted to the more traditional kind of agriculture. By that time the situation may have started to return to the conditions of land scarcity reached in 1935. But on this I have no information.

Moerman's account is also internally inconsistent. Although he makes statements about the relative absence of economic stratification in Ban Ping, he elsewhere says things that indicate definite economic stratification in his community. For example, he says (1966b, p. 151) that one of the most important consequences of differential wealth is the ability to serve as a sponsor for ceremonies initiating village young men into the temple as novices or monks: a sponsor "validates his status as a devout and substantial elder," while "the costs of the reception and ceremonies . . . preclude a poor man from being asked to become a sponsor" (Moerman 1966b, p. 153). These statements certainly indicate some degree of class differentiation in the village.

Since, to the best of my knowledge, nowhere does Moerman give a breakdown of the distribution of landownership in Ban Ping, it is difficult to resolve the inconsistencies in his account. It is possible to say only that economic stratification is certainly present in Ban Ping but that according to Moerman it is less than that found in the central plains villages. Moerman (1968, pp. 84, 114) is, however, too sanguine about the land situation in northern Thailand.

In other northern Thai villages, in the commune of San Pong, near Chiengmai city, de Young found marked class differentiation. In 1949, 27.7 percent of the farmers of the region he studied were tenants (de Young 1955, pp. 76–77), a situation similar to the one I found in Chiangmai village and close to the average figure for tenancy in the north reported by Zimmerman (1931) earlier.

Given all the evidence that we have amassed about the universal presence of economic class differentiation in Thai villages, Wijeyewardene's statement (based partly upon a paper by Keyes [1964]) is incredible:

> We are on surer ground in discussing internal stratification. Clearly this is universally low in Thai villages. Respect and status accrue to individuals on the basis of wealth [sic], age, education, piety, and occupation, but there is no report of anything like the stratification of

Indian villages, nor even China's former differentiation between land-owning gentry and peasantry. The traditional ranking system does not appear to have created status differences *within* villages, and though there are now signs of the emergence of a wealth-based *élite*, particularly on the Central Plain, Thai villages must be characterized as equalitarian. [Wijeyewardene 1967, p. 74]

I doubt that such a description of Thai villages was true even in pre-modern times when land was much more plentiful than at present; even then there was a difference between freemen and slaves. It certainly is not true in modern times. Although, as we have seen, it varies in degree in different regions of the country depending upon the population density, the fertility of the soil, the availability of irrigation facilities, the nearness to towns and cities, and the commercialization of agriculture, class stratification based upon differential ownership of land is a universally present structural feature of all Thai villages. Furthermore, contrary to Wijeyewardene's statement (1967, p. 74), in Thai villages it is the landed class which has dominant political power, and village leaders are almost always drawn from this class. Finally, the desire to improve one's class status within the village community and rise from landless laborer to tenant and then, one hopes, to landlord is one of the most powerful motivating forces for Thai peasants. The scarcity of land resulting from population growth in Thailand and its unequal distribution is bound to create acute social and political tensions in the future.

## The Junior-Senior Relationship

If social structure is defined broadly, to include the crucial social relationships in a society, in addition to the socioeconomic class structure and the enduring groups and institutions which give a particular society its characteristic form, then the junior-senior relationship must be seen as one of the basic structural features of rural Thai society. As I define this principle, it refers to differences in social status as well as differences in age.

The attitudes, sentiments, and gestures of respect associated with the relations between persons of different status are instilled early in the socialization of Thai children, one of whose earliest social acts is to make the waj gesture of respect with clasped hands raised to show respect and deference to a social superior.

The Swiss psychologist E. E. Boesch stresses how conformity to hierarchical patterns of social relations is instilled in the child early during his socialization: "The Siamese child experiences much discipline; in the course of his childhood he has to sacrifice much of his natural inquisitiveness, his spontaneous initiatives and impulses . . . the hierarchic order of relationships diminishes the impulses for creativity, discussion and experiment" (Boesch 1962, pp. 39, 43; translated and quoted by Mulder in Evers 1969, p. 21).

Within the contexts of family and kin there are definite patterns of respect between ego and his parents, parents' siblings, siblings, and cousins. Status and relative generation and age are all expressed in the kinship terms used between relatives.

Sharp et al. describe best the importance of seniority in the Thai kinship system:

> Symbolic behavior which probably carries the most real connotations of respect for seniority is that found in the kinship system. Many kin can not be thought of except in terms of being older or younger than the speaker or other social referent point. All brothers and sisters are "elder brother," "elder sister," or "younger sibling." . . . Similar outward forms of respect [the waj gesture] are owed to the honored guest, to the teacher, . . . and to higher officials. . . . [Sharp et al. 1953, p. 84]

Sharp et al. emphasize the importance of the junior-senior relationship in Bang Chan society:

> Before appropriate interaction can occur, a person must be defined as being male or female; child, adult, or aged; more or less affluent; priest or layman; official or non-official. These definitions are made necessary because each of these statuses requires a recognition of superiority or inferiority; the woman is subordinate to the man, the young to the old, the layman to the priest. [1953, p. 28]

Phillips, in his book *Thai Peasant Personality* (1965), also places special emphasis on this aspect of Thai social relations:

> . . . the attitudes of respect that one sees are perhaps distinctively Thai. Almost all the literature on Thailand refers, at one point or another, to the patterns of respect . . . existing between people, both within and without the family. These patterns are based, in the first instance, on the status inequalities that exist in almost all social

relationships: within the family, usually in terms of the relative ages of people; elsewhere, in terms of age, wealth, power, knowledge, religious or governmental role. [Phillips 1965, pp. 32–33]

Lucien Hanks sees the junior-senior relationship mainly in terms of reciprocity and mutual benefit:

A rich man cannot help a rich man, but he can help a poor man; so a landed man can help a landless man, but not another landed man. The image of the good household reveals parents caring for their obedient children, older siblings tending their less competent juniors, and the able providing for the weak. To these various benefactors is assigned the authority to initiate action, while the recipient dutifully returns appropriate services within the limits of his resources. [Hanks 1972, pp. 84–85]

Hanks is describing the ideal. In reality, junior-senior relationships are not always or even for the most part based upon mutual benefit and reciprocity. Often, as in the cases described by Janlekha (1955, p. 67) for Bang Chan and by Kaufman (1960, pp. 30, 36), in which landlords make demands for free labor from their tenants, who dare not refuse for fear of losing the right to rent their land, the relationship is frankly exploitative and the tenant is not free to simply break the contract.

In Kaufman's account of Bankhuad village social structure, he describes the older-younger relationship (*phi-naung*) as "the most important determinant of social behavior in the community" (Kaufman 1960, p. 31). Younger people extend kin terms such as grandfather and grandmother, uncle and aunt, to older people throughout the community who behave with sobriety and rectitude (p. 32). Kaufman refers to junior-senior relationships other than those based on age, as "status-respect" relationships. These are abbot-monk, monk-layman, monk-laywoman, village headman-farmer, district officer-villager, district officer-village headman, commune headman-village headman, teacher-pupil, teacher-villager, head schoolteacher-teacher, storekeeper-customer, temple boy (who serves the monks and novices)-lay children, doctor-laymen (p. 33). The same senior-junior relations Kaufman found in Bangkhaud would be found in most Thai villages.

In his excellent examination of character and socialization in the village of Banoi near Ayutthaya, Piker (1964) places the junior-senior relationship in its social context. Thai villagers, he says, seek dependency relationships, but they are ambivalent about establishing them because they distrust and suspect the motives of others (p. 45). This distrust extends to the parent-child relationship. As I described above for Chiangmai village, parents hope their children will repay their kindness and the trouble they took to raise them by caring for them in their old age, but they cannot rely on their children, and thus the parents retain the formal title to their property as long as they can to protect themselves (pp. 66–68, 110–11). Piker also describes the dominant-subordinate relationships between landlords and tenants, and between farmers and landless laborers in Banoi, where landownership is concentrated and only 40 percent of the village families have enough land (owned or rented) to subsist on (pp. 19–21).

Madge and Keyes place emphasis on the importance of junior-senior relations in their northeastern villages. Madge (1957, p. 25) stresses the honor and respect owed the abbot and monks, the head teacher of the school, and the village headmen in the villages he studied near Ubon. Keyes stresses the responsibility young people feel to repay the debt they owe their parents for bringing them up. To repay this debt, they are expected to help work the family farm from their teens until they reach adulthood and marry. Sons have a special obligation to enter the monkhood for a year or two to make merit for their parents. Daughters repay their parents by residing with or near them, caring for them until they die, and worshiping them after their death (Keyes 1967, pp. 10, 13, 19).

Also, in his paper "Local Leaders in Rural Thailand" (1970), Keyes distinguishes several types of leaders who are considered "big men" and fill respected roles in village society: headmen; some permanent monks and abbots; village elders (wealthy men of a religious background who may head village factions); entrepreneurs who have established ties with merchants outside the village; town-based middlemen; and district office functionaries. Keyes sees junior-senior relationships as existing both within the village and also between the villagers and people outside.

In his discussion of religion and ritual in the northeastern village of Baan Phraan Muan, Tambiah brings out an important new aspect of the relations between juniors and seniors in rural Thai society; he describes the village as a social universe, with a scheme of social categorization which divides the village into two strata, seniors and juniors, defined on the basis of age and kinship, and maintaining relations of respect and authority. All the elders in the village are referred to collectively as *phau mae-phuu thaw*: persons of father and mother status. These *phuu thaw* (as they are called) expect respect from the *luug laan*, child-grandchild-

nephew—a category which includes all members of the junior generation
(Tambiah 1970, pp. 15–17).

Reciprocity between the phuu thaw and the luug laan takes place
asymmetrically, in ritual as well as in socioeconomic terms. One manifestation is that a young man who becomes a novice or monk makes merit
for his parents or a recently deceased grandparent as an act of filial piety
(Tambiah 1970, pp. 102–3). Tambiah remarks that "ordination is an
event in which merit is transferred by the monk who is of a filial generation to his elders, who in fact install him in this office. . . . We thus begin
to see, in the institution of monkhood, a pattern of reciprocity and exchange of values between the parental and filial generations in the village"
(1970, p. 107).

In his discussion of *sukhwan* rites, which bind the spiritual essence of
a person to his body and bring him luck and prosperity, Tambiah again
sees ritual as expressing reciprocity between the senior and junior generations. But in the sukhwan rites the participants "stand in a relationship
of reciprocity that is a reversed image of that between monk and layman,
youth and elder, as signified in the village institution of monkhood" (Tambiah 1970, p. 223). In the sukhwan rite of marriage (which Tambiah sees
as crucial for understanding the place of elders in the village community),
the couple pay their respect to the elders who bless the union:

> It is a married elderly woman who leads the couple to the chamber,
> and it is elders who take precedence in the binding of the wrists of
> the couple and in turn receive respects [sic] and gifts from the couple—
> all of which signifies that it is the elders who are establishing the
> marriage and who are appropriate for transferring blessings.
> [Tambiah 1970, p. 234]

The ritual reciprocity between senior and junior generations in Baan
Phraan Muan, emphasized by Tambiah, is probably universal in Thai
villages—it is certainly found in Chiangmai—and it matches the asymmetrical economic reciprocity between generations stressed by Mizuno, by
Piker, and by many other writers on Thai village life. The young couple
depend upon the parental generation for their land; in return they help
with the farm work and submit to the authority of the senior family members. Later, in old age, the senior family members are dependent upon
their children for support, burial, and worship after death.

Lucien Hanks believes that important and effective relations in Thailand always involve status inequality, so that one member always has

authority over another: "In the West we consider a reciprocal exchange possible only between cooperating equals; inequality of station seems to constrain us. The Thai, however, because they assume symbiosis to form the basis of reciprocity, deem an inequality to be essential" (Hanks 1972, p. 84).

Without accepting Hanks's characterization of "the West," I do accept his emphasis on the importance of relations between unequals—what I have called junior-senior relationships—to the structure of Thai society. I would, however, add two reservations: one is that this relationship is often exploitative and, following Piker (1964), filled with ambivalence, distrust, and uncertainty; and the second is that this does not mean that relations between status equals are of no importance in Thai society. The relations between classmates of the same university, students of the same technical schools, members of the same village or ethnic group, members of the same sibling and cousin group, and members of the same social class are of crucial importance in Thailand too.

### The Entourage

Relations between juniors and seniors form the building blocks for the entourage, a higher-level social structure which Lucien Hanks has described in a series of seminal essays (1962, 1966, 1972, 1975). An entourage (commonly referred to as patron-client relations in other societies) is a hierarchically organized group in which a number of subordinates support a leader who holds their allegiance by successfully advancing their interests. Entourages and similar structures are a basic feature of Thai society at all levels. Wilson (1962, pp. 116–17) calls entourages "cliques" and sees them as "the foundation of political life in Thailand" at the national level, where they combine to form structures similar to political parties, coup groups, and so on, which Wilson (1962, pp. 246–52) calls *khana.*

In his book *Rice and Man* (1972), Lucien Hanks is most successful in his use of the concept of entourage to elucidate the dynamics of Thai peasant social structure. Hanks believes that entourages begin in the family, where parents have authority over children, and elder siblings have authority over their juniors. He sees the household itself as a kind of entourage (Hanks 1966, p. 59), whose strength depends upon the ability of the family head to hold retainers. Hanks states three important principles governing the household and kin entourage:

(1) The greater the resources that a man has at his disposal, the greater the number of reciprocities that he can form. . . . (2) The greater the resources, the more enduring are the reciprocities that are established, assuming good stewardship. Poor households tend to lose members easily. . . . Wealthy households need have little fear of competition. . . . (3) Household heads seek to gain and hold the maximum numbers of reciprocities possible within the limits of their circumstances. The system gives its greatest plaudits to those with the largest following. [Lucien Hanks 1972, p. 86]

I feel these principles to be important in the understanding of Thai peasant family and village social life. Furthermore, they rest on basic Thai values. As Piker (1964, p. 120) points out, Thai value nothing more than to achieve the status of a "big man"—a commander of men who can attract followers whom he can dominate, direct their lives and activities, dispense or withhold rewards from them, and demand their subservience and loyalty. Associated with this dominant value orientation (the obverse side of the same coin) is the pattern of dependency. In Piker's village, and generally throughout Thai society, personal advancement or success is believed to be dependent on finding an effective patron or entourage leader who can further one's case. According to Piker, this leads to "an assessment (fairly realistic and accurate) which minimizes achievement values, which identifies paternalistic favoritism as the most likely avenue to spectacular personal advancement, and which accords intrinsic individual worth little practical value unless it is abetted by useful personal connections" (1964, p. 114).

In his book-length social and economic history of Bang Chan (1972), Lucien Hanks describes the significance of entourages and their changing nature within this one village community. He also describes how important the relations between villagers and outsiders were to the members of the community. Since Hanks develops this idea in such detail, the reader is referred to his book for the full account.

In addition to Lucien Hanks's account, Sharp et al. mention that a person moving into Bang Chan village might eventually build up relationships on a variety of grounds which "may in time lead into group membership relations . . . with admission into a vaguely defined clique of shifting membership" (Sharp et al. 1953, p. 32).

Sharp et al. clearly describe entourages in Bang Chan which connected village people with more powerful outsiders:

A person may more readily win friends locally, or keep them loyal and interested, if he is able to establish a kind of client-patron relationship with people in the district seat, the capital, or some high ranking temple who have political, economic, or religious power or influence which may be called upon to affect the interest of residents of Bang Chan. [Sharp et al. 1953, p. 33]

Along the same lines, Sharp et al. (1953, pp. 34–35) state that "the lack of formal organization or structure in Bang Chan society creates problems for any outsider who wishes to deal with the community" . . . because "the important influence of any headman may run through lines of friendship or kinship which extend outside rather than within the hamlet over which he supposedly has authority."

As mentioned already, Piker (1964, pp. 111–12) also stresses the importance of hierarchically organized groups and implicitly gives evidence for the presence of entourages in Banoi.

Although Kaufman does not go into great detail about cliques or entourages in his village, Bangkhuad, he does indicate that they are present and gives some hints on how they function. He speaks of the power that a respected farmer with money has over many other farmers and landless villagers who are dependent upon him (1960, p. 36). He says that village headmen are elected because of their wealth and their willingness to help other farmers, which makes it likely that they are entourage leaders (1960, p. 56). Kaufman also describes "groups which resemble cliques, insofar as they include the same members more often than not, possess a definite *esprit de corps*, and meet casually with only occasional prearrangement. There are four kinds of cliques: the drinking companions, the card gambling companions, the *wat* discussion groups, and the *dekwat* [temple boys]" (1960, pp. 37–38). In addition, Kaufman (1960, p. 38) tells of "two groups of middle-aged farmers (four or five in each group) who gather informally from time to time."

Aside from the card-playing and drinking groups which are hierarchically organized, most of these cliques are not entourages as we have defined them; they are not hierarchically organized and not very important. Entourages in Bangkhuad are made up of the wealthy farmers and their retainers, connected by the institution of khauraeng, a forced mobilization of labor. Kaufman indicates that some measure of political stability is maintained in Bangkhuad because the wealthy farmers who are probably leaders of entourages balance one another in power (1960, p. 69). That there is some division in the community is indicated by the fact that in an election for headman in one of the three administrative villages making up Bangkhuad, the votes were split among four candidates: 47, 17, 11, and 4 (p. 77).

For the northeast, there is little or no information on entourages from Tambiah or Madge. Mizuno's conception of multihousehold compounds composed of a parental family ("core operators" in his terminology) plus dependent families (mainly of married daughters) fits very well Hanks's model of a family and kinship group held together by asymmetrical reciprocal relationships, which I have called a family entourage (see Mizuno 1971, chaps. 2, 3, and 4). In the following statement Mizuno indicates that he considers the family and kin entourage the basic structural feature of his northeastern Thai village. He says:

> the total structure of the village is analytically viewed as the interrelation of the various elements of the three structural phases which are all linked to the multihousehold compounds. Therefore the present author would like to characterize the total social structure of Don Daeng village by the name of "compounds-type of social structure." [Mizuno 1971, p. 245]

Keyes (1970), in a general article in which he reviews an enormous amount of data on local leadership in Thailand, remarks—correctly, I believe—that in rural Thai villages, abbots, village headmen, commune headmen, schoolteachers, and entrepreneurial middlemen may or may not be important leaders. Elders, whose power comes from within the village, are the other important leaders Keyes discusses (1970, p. 94). "In any village," he says, "only a small number of middle-aged men will become important village leaders whether they be 'elders' or 'synaptic leaders' " (leaders connecting the village to the outside). Each of these kinds of leaders, Keyes implies, has an entourage, the members of which advise and assist them (1970, pp. 114–15). According to Keyes, there are also three kinds of leaders from outside the village—district bureaucratic officials, middlemen who buy and sell village produce, and politicians—who often have villagers as members of their entourages. Keyes says that "being a member of the entourage of a powerful official, or more recently, politician, may appeal to some villagers far more than aspiring to a power position within the village" (1970, p. 116).

In northern Thailand, I have found Hanks's conception of the entourage useful in analyzing the social structure of Chiangmai village. Within the village I showed how couples (and not simply men, as Hanks and others would have it from a rather male-centered viewpoint) try to accumulate property and establish an estate which will be large enough to provide an inheritance sufficient to keep their sons in the village and attract good sons-in-law to marry their daughters and establish dependent satellite families. I called this a family entourage and recognized it as an important aspect of Chiangmai village family life.

Also, in my analysis of Chiangmai village I showed how leading land-owning families form entourages by attracting not only dependent daughters' families but also poor landless laborer families. All these dependents can be mobilized to aid their entourage leader (the patron) when necessary—in agricultural labor, housebuilding, or at ceremonial events. In addition, I said that one of the village headmen is a member of the entourage of a rich Chinese merchant from Chiengmai city. Membership in this entourage gives the headman business and political connections outside the village community.

Edward Van Roy, in a series of works (1966, 1967, 1969, and 1971), has developed Hanks's notion of the entourage as the key principle of Thai peasant social structure. He describes the entourages which connect villagers with important persons in the outside society, especially with patron-middlemen who deal in the miang (fermented tea) trade between upland Thai villagers north of Chiengmai city and the lowlanders (Van Roy 1971, pp. 113–24).

Van Roy claims that there is much evidence of the presence of entourages in central Thailand, where Hanks developed the concept, and that entourages are well-documented in the north by Wijeyewardene (1967, pp. 82–83) and Moerman (1964, 1966a, and 1968). Wijeyewardene mentions that "in the South Village area [north of Chiengmai city] important contacts with the administration appear to be largely channeled through 'patrons' of one sort or another. These patrons could be government servants, landowners, traders, or merely wealthy kinsmen. Such relationships seem to be particularly important when illicit activities are involved." Here Wijeyewardene is referring mainly to extra-village relationships.

Wijeyewardene also believes that patron-client relations (based upon traditional forms) are still widespread in Thai rural areas in a modified form. He refers to the khauraeng system in Bangkhuad, which we discussed above, as an example. He also believes that "in rural areas the clustering of clients around a patron [what Van Roy and I would call an entourage] does not perhaps create a large or formally organized association, but it has to be considered an organization of a type, and is, moreover, essential to the social system as a whole" (1967, p. 83).

Van Roy (1971, pp. 116–19) tries to demonstrate, using Moerman's data on Ban Ping, that the entourage form of organization is the structural key to Ban Ping society, particularly the ties that Moerman's villagers had with outside tractor drivers from the town. What bothers Van Roy is that Moerman does not recognize this. In his article, "Kinship and Commerce in a Thai-Lue Village," Moerman insists that the relations between his villagers and outsiders like the tractor owners were simple economic ones which did not involve the multiple ties and reciprocities that Van Roy found between his upland miang-growing villagers and their patrons.

I believe that entourages are probably present in Ban Ping but that they are not as important elements in that village's social structure as they are in Van Roy's area. Van Roy is trying to make more of the entourage as a structural principle of rural Thailand than is warranted. Nor are entourages as important in the lowland village of Chiangmai as they are in Van Roy's upland villages, though to a certain extent (the case of the village headman) they do link Chiangmai villagers to the outside world. In Chiangmai, the villagers sell their garlic, peanuts, and lamjaj to many different brokers, and often switch from year to year; although some long-term relations are established, they do not approach the strength of the ties that Van Roy describes.

## Factions

A faction, according to Ralph Nicholas's definition (1965, pp. 44–46), is a political conflict group of nonpermanent and noncorporate nature, which is activated in disputes over the control of resources and men and is recruited according to diverse principles. These principles of recruitment, as Sir Raymond Firth writes, are

> usually structurally diverse—they may rest upon kin ties, patron-client relations, religious or politico-economic ties or any combination of these; they are mobilized and made effective through an authority structure of leader and henchman, whose roles are broadly defined and whose rewards in many cases depend upon the leader's discretion. [Firth 1957, p. 292]

As defined here, the faction is very similar to the entourage, the structural element I have just discussed, and it is admittedly somewhat arbitrary to separate them. I chose to do so on the basis of size, stability, and function. Thai village factions are often composed of two or more leaders and their entourages; and whereas entourages are multifunctional, factions are activated mainly in the political arena. I have to make this distinction in Chiangmai village, where there are many entourages attached to wealthy villagers, and wealthy villagers who are leaders; but frequently the entourages divide into two major factions when disputes arise over major political issues which concern the village as a whole. As I shall show below, in some Thai villages factions are centered around only two leaders or leading families; in such circumstances, entourages and factions may be identical. There are also cases where no factions are reported in the village, either because one group dominates the village completely or because the ethnographer did not notice or report them.

Kirsch (1967, pp. 70–77) and Keyes (1970, pp. 114–17) are the only two writers who to my knowledge have discussed Thai village factionalism in detail, although Keyes cites literature which shows that factionalism in rural northeastern Thailand, at least, is widespread (1970, p. 116).

One reason why little attention has been given to factionalism and conflicts within Thai villages is that it has been assumed that Thai rural communities are so amorphous that there are no factions. Phillips (1965, p. 30), discussing the nature of Bang Chan village society, calls the community "placid" and writes of Bang Chan that:

> In this type of cultural situation, one does *not* find arising the type of community power struggles or schisms apparently characteristic of many peasant communities (see Foster 1960–61). Bang Chan is indeed a placid community because no family has the organizational means or the quality of familial cohesiveness necessary to assume a dominant social, political, or economic position. Individuals assume important positions and individuals disagree and squabble, but rarely families. [Phillips 1965, p. 38]

Kirsch suggests that factions may have been found in Bang Chan but were simply overlooked (1967, p. 75). Keyes (1970, p. 115) believes that factions are absent in what he calls the "Central Thai" type of rural social system but are present in what he calls the "Northeastern" type (see Keyes 1970, p. 94, for an explanation of these types).

Keyes believes that factional disputes rarely lead to the division or breakup of a Thai village.

> because village factions, like national factions in Thailand, are never fixed groupings since individuals often shift their allegiances when they

perceive that their personal interests will be better served by doing so. Moreover, the cultural value on maintaining harmony serves to prevent public confrontations. . . . Although factionalism never reaches major proportions in rural Thailand, it remains important in considerations of village leadership. [Keyes 1970, p. 116]

I disagree with Phillips and Keyes and believe that factionalism is important and widespread in rural Thailand. I would go further and consider factions a principle element in Thai peasant social structure.

My experience in Chiangmai village, where factions were manifest and distinct, and where a factional dispute ended with the abbot of Chiangmai denouncing the village headman of Chiangmai Two over the temple loudspeaker, suggests to me that factions are an integral part in the political life of Thai villages. Signs of factionalism in neighboring villages were evident and factional conflict not infrequently (contrary to Keyes's findings) resulted in the fission of one village into two communities. From this limited evidence, plus additional material garnered from the literature, I infer that factionalism is an integral part of most if not all Thai villages; and in this they would be similar to most peasant villages throughout the world (see Foster 1960–61 and 1965).

Keyes is incorrect in his assertion that factionalism is restricted to his northeastern-type villages and is not found in the central Thai type. There is palpable evidence (as Kirsch surmised) of the existence of factions within the community of Bang Chan. The most obvious source of factionalism in Bang Chan was between the Buddhist majority and the Moslem minority. As Sharp et al. (1953, p. 29) tell us, "in Bang Chan a person's religious status must also be defined: he is either Moslem or Buddhist. In the former case he joins a small formal corporate congregation with its own religious officials which forms a tightly integrated group centering about a mosque. His religious role includes a number of Malayan and Middle and Near Eastern behavior patterns peculiar to his group." These religious and cultural differences among the 10 percent of Bang Chan's population who are Moslems indicates religious factions. This is confirmed by evidence Kaufman (1960, p. 18) gives about attitudes toward Moslems in the nearby village of Bangkhuad. He says that "though villagers maintain that no prejudice exists between Thai-Buddhist and Thai-Islamic peoples, there appears to be mutual suspicion and a lack of intimacy between the two as well as certain misunderstandings based on religious and cultural differences." Again, Kaufman (1960, p. 75) points to evidence of conflict between the two religious groups: he says that "the *kamnan* [commune headman] . . . is not highly respected by the other hamlet headmen because 'he can neither read nor write,' although the actual resentment may well derive from the fact that he is a Moslem. . . . In matters of great urgency, the *kamnan* may be circumvented. In practice, . . . he is always by-passed."

However, there is no need to depend completely on indirect evidence or supposition to establish that there were factions in Bang Chan. Sharp et al. tell us about Bang Chan factions in straightforward and unequivocal terms:

> one of the factions in Bang Chan centers about the family of the head teacher and his wife, who have thus become subject to criticism by adherents of another faction. Thus some people claim that the head teacher received his appointment as the result of an understanding between government officials and his aunt, who contributed the land adjacent to the wat on which the school building was constructed in 1935. . . . Such critiques of the formal staff organization of the school help keep alive *an undertone of factional rivalry which appears in a number of different aspects of the Bang Chan community culture* [emphasis mine]. [1953, pp. 69–70]

Later Sharp et al. (1953, p. 75) tell us about another faction in Bang Chan: "The family of the head priest is associated with a faction opposed to the one which is led by the family of the head school teacher, and factionalism has been known to enter judgments of the head priest, however much he is supposed to stand above the secular rivalries of the community centering about his wat."

Another probable source of factionalism in Bang Chan were the three recognized residential neighborhoods into which Bang Chan was divided (and which the reader will recall were bound together by labor exchange and neighborly ties). Sharp et al. give no evidence that these neighborhoods acted as political factions, but I would be surprised if they did not. I also suspect that the headmen of the seven administrative villages among which part of the Bang Chan population was distributed, and the two communes into which they were divided, may have been the founders of factions; but again I am arguing on the basis of my experience in Chiangmai village and my general familiarity with other peasant village communities around the world, and not on the basis of evidence that these political divisions actually were the basis for factionalism in Bang Chan.

It is difficult to conceive how the "big men," "village headmen," and other important "leaders" of Bang Chan, described by Sharp et al. and by

Phillips, would have failed to combine into factional alliances to dispute important issues on the rural community level at least. It is also difficult to understand why Lucien Hanks, who has done so much to develop the concept of entourage, has failed to make more of the role of leaders in factions and in conflict within Bang Chan. Contrary to Keyes, factionalism does assume major proportions in rural Thailand (see Keyes 1970, p. 116). Keyes's own village divided in 1968 (Keyes 1975, p. 277).

In his northeastern village of Ban Non Tuen, Keyes (1967, p. 8) says that men who marry into the village are treated somewhat separately, to the extent that they cannot be the village headman or keeper of the village shrine. A similar situation exists in Chiangmai, where the headman of Two, an outsider, is the subject of disapproval because other members of the village do not believe that it is right for an outsider to be headman. In Chiangmai, and probably in other villages too, groups of such disaffected men can be the basis for the formation of political factions.

Another basis for political factionalism is geographical place of origin of groups within a village. As I related above, the Fang village to which many Chiangmai villagers have emigrated over the past few decades is divided into two factions based upon province of origin; emigrants from Lamphun Province have settled the southern half of the village, while emigrants from Chiangmai village and Saraphi (in Chiengmai Province) have settled north of the village temple, dividing the village into two factions based upon geographical place of origin and associated cultural differences.

In northeastern villages, Keyes (1970, p. 115) claims that factionalism is rife (although to the best of my knowledge he has not described factions in his village of Ban Nong Tuen). This finding is reinforced by Kirsch (1967, pp. 70–77) for his northeastern Phu Thai village. Mizuno (1971, chap. 6), however, does not report factionalism within his village, apparently because of the strength of the current village headman and his council of three powerful leaders, who happen to be the headman's brothers-in-law. Tambiah (1970, p. 10) mentions that his village, Baan Phraan Muan, is divided from a nearby "small hamlet," which is populated by an overflow of young settlers from the parent village. This geographical division may become the basis for factional divisions within the community, but we are told little about this possibility, since Tambiah is mainly interested in ritual and religion.

For northern Thailand, neither Wijeyewardene (1967) nor de Young (1955) reports factions, Wijeyewardene because he has no evidence of them, and de Young because he does not discuss the subject. However,

Moerman (1966b, p. 159) mentions in passing several cliques or factions in Ban Ping, some of which are formed by men who served together in the temple as novices or monks.

From the limited evidence available on factionalism in rural Thai communities, one can only agree with Wijeyewardene (1967, p. 74) that "it is surprising at first sight that the literature . . . is so devoid of references to factionalism." He notes the evidence for factionalism in Bang Chan but says that "unless there has been widespread sociological myopia, the only conclusion one can draw is that Thai villages do not present the conditions for factions to form."

Unlike Wijeyewardene, and following the lead of Keyes and Kirsch, I do believe that there has been the same kind of "sociological myopia" in regard to social conflict and factionalism that there has been in regard to socioeconomic classes. I believe factions are an integral part of rural Thai social structure and that future research will find them based upon the following: (1) alliances between leaders in culturally and politically homogeneous villages, who are struggling to gain power in their community; (2) administrative village divisions of natural communities; (3) conflict between different ethnic groups and religious groups living in the same community; (4) conflict between groups originally from different geographical places of origin; (5) conflict between groups in a single community belonging to the entourages of patrons outside the community; and (6) conflicts between groups belonging to different political parties.

## The "Natural" Village Community

The spatially defined rural village, which receives the allegiance of its members, furnishes an important part of their social identity, manages its own affairs and its common property, and has its own temple and school, is present in all parts of Thailand as an ideal cultural model, although in many areas the actual form of communal life only approximates it. As I pointed out above, the extent to which this principle is realized varies from place to place because of different ecological, economic, and demographic circumstances, and the nature of rural administration (see below). In the northeast the nucleated village is the predominant form; in the north and in central Thailand both nucleated and nonnucleated villages are found; little is known about the south, but I suspect that nucleated villages are more common than nonnucleated. Although different types of villages are found in all regions, it is mainly in parts of the lower delta region of the central plain and in densely settled areas like parts of the Chiengmai Valley that rural communities like Bang Chan appear to be least like the model of the nucleated village, spatially separate from surrounding communities.

That rural Thai communities vary from the less nucleated communities like Bang Chan in the lower delta region to the more nucleated settlements of the northeast and much of the rest of Thailand has long been recognized by students of rural Thailand (e.g., see Phillips 1965, p. 17); but the image of rural Thai communities projected to the scholarly world outside the ranks of Thai specialists through the books of Sharp et al., Phillips, Wilson, and Lucien Hanks is misleading because these writers have not clearly pointed out how different in some ways Bang Chan is when compared with other Thai villages. The image of the loosely structured rural Thai village which has weak patterns of village allegiance, lacks feelings of cooperation and solidarity, has no corporate identity, owns no collective property, and has no means of governing its internal affairs (see chapter 1 of this book) is the image that is widely held in the scholarly world. Hanks (1972, p. 15) says that "Bang Chan with its school, temple, and stores, rather than a discrete segment of society, becomes a center of orientation for the rice growers in its vicinity." It is only in this way, says Hanks, that Bang Chan is more than "an arbitrary slice of a countryside."

Although in discussing the earlier history of Bang Chan he describes the formation of nucleated and solidary hamlets, Hanks does not make it clear enough to his reader that Bang Chan, as he and Sharp et al. first described it around 1950, was not representative of most Thai farming communities. Furthermore, it is evident from the data given by those who studied Bang Chan that their description of the community as it existed around 1950 greatly overemphasized its loose structure and overlooked basic features of social structure that Bang Chan shared with all other Thai villages at that time.

Although no one would deny that Bang Chan in the 1950s was not as nucleated and spatially isolated as are present-day Chiangmai and many other Thai villages that we have discussed in this book, internal evidence from the accounts of Bang Chan by Sharp et al., Janlekha, and Hanks indicates that there was more structure to Bang Chan society than they would have us believe and that Bang Chan around 1950 was a fairly distinct community.

Bang Chan village was an important part of the identity of the people who lived there; the community was socially distinct in that it was endogamous and kin terms were extended widely throughout the village; it owned common property; it had leaders who arranged its affairs and made decisions for the community as a whole; and it was symbolized by the temple, which was the social, political, and recreational center of village life. Bang Chan itself, in 1950, did not correspond to the loose-structure model of Thai society formulated by those who studied the village.

The way that Bang Chan was defined—"as composed of all hamlets whose headmen and the majority of whose population patronized this wat" (Janlekha 1955, p. 24)—made the boundaries of the community seem more blurred than they really were. If the community of Bang Chan had been demarcated simply as those people who attended the temple and the school and patronized the stores, a more clearly bounded community would probably have been discernible. By confusing the community with administrative units, all was mixed at the beginning, even though this defi-nition may have seemed useful at the time. Also, symbol should not be confused with reality. There was a functioning community in Bang Chan composed of six or eight little hamlets existing before the temple was built in the 1890s (Hanks 1972, pp. 105, 112). The community of Bang Chan existed before the building of the temple and not vice versa, although the temple may have cemented existing ties. All Thai villages build a temple to symbolize their existence once they reach a size sufficient to support one; and Bang Chan was no exception to this rule.

The Bang Chan school, as in other Thai villages, was another unifying force in the community. In the public school, according to Sharp et al. (1953, p. 30), children "get to know children from all over the village with whom they will associate as adult members of the Bang Chan com-munity." The notion that the community held no property in common is shown to be erroneous by Janlekha's own statement that, in addition to the temple and the school, the community owned as "public land" an esti-mated 100 raj of canals (1955, p. 48).

The natural community of Bang Chan, as Sharp et al. and Janlekha call it to distinguish it from the government administrative divisions, also clearly had leaders who possessed the authority to act on behalf of the community as a whole. The presence of village leadership was obscured by the in-sistence of those who wrote of Bang Chan on distinguishing between formal and informal leaders and institutions, and their tendency to ignore what they called the informal. Only by doing this were they able to depict Bang Chan as a loosely structured, amorphous community incapable of sus-tained community action.

The leaders of Bang Chan—what Sharp et al. in an unguarded moment call "the effective social structure of Bang Chan"—were, as they recognize, the "priests and lay committee" associated with the wat (1953, p. 36). As in most Thai villages, the head priest and the lay committee associated with the temple were greatly concerned with all community affairs, and the priest is described as "a mainspring of social activity" (Sharp et al. 1953, p. 59). Life in Bang Chan is described by Sharp et al. as "rich in organized social activity," and the temple as the focus of "religion, recreation and social cohesion" (1953, p. 67).

The actual leaders of Bang Chan appeared when their presence was required, for example, to meet with outside dignitaries or to organize important cooperative undertakings for the good of the community as a whole. Sharp et al. relate an incident that occurred in 1949 when the head of the Food and Agricultural Organization, accompanied by the princely chairman of Thailand's FAO Committee and other officials visited Bang Chan. They were greeted by an "informal committee which included not only the seven headmen and three government school teachers, but also the head priest of the temple and half a dozen other 'big men' of the community" (Sharp et al. 1953, p. 35). These "big men" of Bang Chan correspond to the wealthy and respected community leaders of Chiangmai and other Thai villages; they were undoubtedly from the rich landed sector which dominated the social and economic life of the village.

Bang Chan not only had leaders, but these leaders and the community as a whole were not lacking in cooperative spirit, and they were capable of carrying out a joint undertaking when they wanted to (contrary to the claims of Phillips [1965, p. 17]). One example related by Sharp et al. is the story of an attempt by local people to organize a credit cooperative before the war.

> The co-operative was wanted and requested by the local people. But in setting it up, the central government agency worked only through the official administrative hierarchy, [who] were not in a structural position to carry out [the plan]. . . . A brief investigation of the actual functioning of both the formal and informal social structures of Bang Chan would have indicated that the co-operative, organized as it was, was doomed to failure, and that an alternative organization through the temple or through an informal group of leading men who work together would have been more likely to succeed. [Sharp et al. 1953, pp. 36–37]

A dramatic example of village cooperative action under the direction of community leaders is the case related by Sharp et al. of the campaign to build a new Bang Chan school to replace the old one, which had been declared unsafe. The temple and the school cooperated in raising money for the new school. Sharp et al. (1953, p. 74) describe

> a purely ad hoc organization, essentially an informal committee, consisting of about eight villagers, some of whom were not parents of school children, together with five headmen, the four men teachers, and the priest. A majority were on the lay committee which managed the secular affairs of the wat.

The eight leaders who happened to help organize the campaign to raise money for the new school, as Sharp et al. describe them (1953, p. 48), were those "few who most nearly approach a middle-class status, who are accorded prestige for their relative wealth and learning, and who are in a position to lead—the storekeeper, the educated and better-off farmers, the school teachers, the head priest, the petty district functionary," all of whom were relatively prosperous and vocal.

Howard K. Kaufman's 1953–54 study of the village of Bangkhuad, in the lower delta region twenty-five miles from the center of Bangkok and only fourteen kilometers from Bang Chan (see map 1), shows the importance of the structural element of the village as a whole even more clearly than Bang Chan (Kaufman 1960). Like Bang Chan, Bangkhuad is a frontier settlement dating from the late nineteenth century. In 1905, when the village became populous enough, the villagers built a temple to serve as a religious and social center (Kaufman 1960, p. 15).

Bangkhuad is a linear, ribbon-type village, settled along both banks of a canal. It is clearly separated from neighboring villages, which means that the alleged lack of clearcut boundaries characteristic of Bang Chan is not typical of all the lower delta villages near Bangkok. The nearest settlements are one kilometer to the north and several hundred yards to the south. Internally, Bangkhuad village is divided into three administrative hamlets, in an arbitrary fashion (1960, p. 17).

Kaufman adds that, "in contrast to Bangchan, where the community can be defined by *wat* attendance, Bangkhuad is in part an isolate within which the members feel and act as a unit, predominantly through family ties and extensions, and secondarily through *wat* affiliations" (1960, p. 18). Still, the wat is important as a symbol and a focal point of community life. In addition to its religious activities, it is a community center where entertainments are given and dances are performed; a counseling center where villagers come to inquire about auspicious days for important undertakings; a place to be cured of certain illnesses by the application of holy water; a community storehouse where musical instruments, lamps, and kitchenware may be rented for home celebrations; a news agency; a bank where the poor may borrow money; a landlord which rents houses to six villagers; and a house where the aged can seek refuge (1960, p. 113). As in most delta villages, says Kaufman, village and temple affiliations in Bangkhuad are usually one and the same (1960, p. 70).

Kaufman describes the village of Bangkhuad as important in the self-identification of the people who live there (1960, p. 18). The villagers have a strong in-group feeling which, as in Chiangmai, occasionally manifests itself in fights between young men from Bangkhuad with men from other villages over real or imagined insults and over courting young women (1960, p. 79), and in a generalized hostility between Bangkhuad people and members of other villages (1960, p. 80).

Bangkhuad has leaders who give advice on important affairs and in effect govern the village. The abbot of the temple is one of the most respected members of the community (but not the most powerful) (1960, pp. 68–69, 118). The temple committee and the village headmen, wealthy and respected, together with the abbot establish policy for the temple and the village as a whole (1960, pp. 56, 83, 112).

If, as Kaufman claims, Bangkhuad is typical of the lower delta villages of the central plain, then most lower delta villages (the region where many scholars have assumed loose-structured villages were characteristic) are not loosely structured or amorphous. This does not mean that there are *no* areas in the lower delta where genuinely amorphous settlements are found; Attagara (1967) describes the commune of Napa in Chonburi south of Bangkok, which *appears to be* quite amorphous, but Attagara, whose book is on folklore, does not give us enough information on Napa's social structure to make a firm judgment.

Piker's village of Banoi, in the heart of the central plain near Ayutthaya, north of the lower delta region, is another example which shows that the village community as a whole is an important structural element, even in the central-plain villages of Thailand. In my opinion, the ethnographic data that Piker gives us for Banoi do not support his general theoretical pronouncements about the loosely structured nature of Thai rural communities (see Chapter 1 of this book for a summary of Piker's views).

In spite of the fact that, like Chiangmai, Banoi is divided into two administrative hamlets, Banoi village as a whole is the effective village unit. Piker (1964, p. 3) writes that "all villagers consider themselves residents of Banoi, not of one or the other numerically delineated hamlets." Again: "The village of Banoi is compact. The houses are grouped in compounds, varying from two to five houses in number" (1964, pp. 3–4). Neighboring villages are clearly separated geographically from Banoi, some close and some more distant.

Nevertheless, Piker claims that Banoi is not socially or psychologically important to its residents:

> The Thai peasant lives in a village that is loosely organized in the extreme. He allows himself to become involved in few binding interpersonal commitments; and those he does establish are, in many cases, as likely to be with individuals in a neighboring village as with fellow villagers. The community is in a real sense, atomistic or individualistic. [Piker 1964, p. 8]

There is, or so it seems to me, a possible explanation for this discrepancy between Piker's views and mine. As I pointed out above, Banoi is the most extreme example of matrilocal residence reported in Thailand because it is coupled with village exogamy, where most men marry outside the village and a man moves to live in his wife's village. In most Thai villages there is preferential village endogamy, and most male villagers marry within their village (as in Chiangmai). If most men in Banoi have moved in from nearby villages to live with their wives, they will still retain strong ties with their parental village and their natal family. This basic social fact explains another feature which Piker claims characterizes Banoi society: the lack of interpersonal commitments and binding ties. Would not this be the expectable outcome of a social structure which has the "majority of adult males reside in a location other than that of their close friends and most immediate kin, that is, the kin to which they feel the strongest commitment," and wouldn't this "contribute to the sense of personal isolation" (Piker 1964, p. 15)?

Another reason why Banoi does not exhibit the kind of solidarity that I would expect from such a compact and nucleated village, based on the evidence from the rest of Thailand, is that the process of land concentration has proceeded furthest in Banoi and a large proportion of the villagers are now a landless proletariat of farm laborers, whereas in 1940 they all were landowners. As I pointed out above, most of this land is in the hands of absentee landlords who cannot fulfill their traditional role as village leaders. Social and economic change, which has created an alienated, landless, rural proletariat; matrilocal residence coupled with village exogamy;

and the blinders effect of the loose-structure paradigm all combine, in my opinion, to explain Piker's interpretation of his nucleated village of Banoi.

Evidence for the importance of the village as a whole as a fundamental principle of Thai peasant social structure is even more clear and unequivocal in the northeast. Charles Madge (1957), in his description of the rural villages he surveyed near the city of Ubon in northeastern Thailand, portrays them as mostly "compact clusters of houses," although there are some ribbon settlements along the roads near newly developing towns like Ubon. Madge describes the social organization of the villages he studied as follows:

> Each village has a common interest in its Wat, in its schools, in its nongs [lakes or ponds], in its wells, in its cart-tracks and in its bridges. Farmers help each other in tasks which are more than a single household can tackle on its own. Neighbours help each other in the building and repair of houses. All the villagers are used to following the lead of their elected headman and he can get voluntary labour for work which needs doing in the common interest. . . . the Headman, the Abbot and the Headmaster, are the three accepted leaders of the community; . . . they all work together on problems of community interest. [Madge 1957, p. 22]

Baan Phraan Muan, Tambiah's village near Udon and the Mekong River, in the northern part of northeastern Thailand, which he studied in 1961–62, is clustered, a distinct ecological unit, and is clearly separated from other villages by three or four kilometers (Tambiah 1970, pp. 10–11). The natural village settlement is also a *muban*, an administrative village, with one headman. Tambiah describes his village as "inward looking" and as "a sharply perceived social universe" (1970, p. 25).

Since marriage is primarily endogamous, most people have many cognatic and affinal kinsmen in the village. Kinship terminology is extended throughout the entire village in "village-wide status categories which divide the village into hierarchical segments" (1970, pp. 15–16).

The village as a whole is also an important entity for merit-making, in spite of the fact that "from the doctrinal point of view the quest for salvation is a strictly individualistic pursuit" (1970, p. 54). Tambiah places special emphasis on this point, which I also think important:

> the merit-making occasions *par excellence* are the collective calendrical rites held at the temple. That is to say, merit-making, although particularistic in intent, is usually done in a collective context. Such

occasions are by far the most conspicuous religious activity in the village. In this sense merit-making as a collective ethic directed to a community institution—the *wat* and its monks—provides occasions for residents of a village to assemble periodically. The village as a territorial community is clearly manifest on these occasions. [Tambiah 1970, p. 57]

In the same vein, Tambiah stresses that the sponsoring of an ordination rite as well as of a mortuary rite is a matter "of collective interest to the village" (1970, p. 107). Like other villages throughout Thailand, Baan Phraan Muan has a wat committee composed of the abbot and secular lay leaders of the community. Tambiah sees the wat committee as formally linking and facilitating the interaction between the temple and the village households.

As a dramatic example showing that his village is a corporate and cooperative unit capable of organized, long-term, structured action, Tambiah describes the beginnings of a ten- to fifteen-year cooperative project to build a bood, or temple, undertaken by his villagers under the central direction of the wat committee, and with collective contributions of funds, material, loans, and labor by all the villagers. The kind of well-organized activity he delineates for Baan Phraan Muan is the same kind of activity that Chiangmai villagers carried out when building their new school and in maintaining their irrigation system.

Mizuno's northeastern village, Don Daeng, is located just south of the town of Khon Kaen, roughly halfway between Tambiah's village to the north and Madge's villages in the south. The villages of this area are nucleated and separated from neighboring villages by distances averaging one to three kilometers (Mizuno 1971, p. 16). The village of Don Daeng was not founded until about 1900, and is thus later than many of the lower delta villages like Bang Chan and Bangkhuad, indicating that the differences between the lower delta and the rest of the country are not mainly due to age of the villages (a hypothesis I considered at an earlier stage of my thinking but later rejected). The unity of Don Daeng is symbolized by the enshrined village guardian spirits (one call *pu ta* and the other *lag ban*), and by the village wat, built by the Don Daeng villagers soon after their settlement had become stabilized. Thirty years after settlement, some Don Daeng villagers founded a new village, Don Noi ("little Don"), about a hundred meters away. This branch village has its own guardian spirits, but its residents still attend Don Daeng temple (Mizuno 1971, p. 19), a situation I termed fission and also described as part of the structural cycle of Thai village communities when they reach a certain size.

Other village institutions are the primary school and a public hall where village meetings are held (1971, p. 21). Mizuno summarizes the importance of Don Daeng village as a unit:

> Don Daeng village is ecologically distinct from other villages and, at the same time, coincides with [the] administrative unit at the lowest level. The nucleated village has a short history, but it has been settled long enough to develop a common life around the *pu ta, lag ban, wat* and village hall. The inhabitants possess a feeling of living together, and identify themselves through its name or such stereotyped image as "our village is peaceful and cooperative, having seldom *nag len* or gangsters, but many in other villages." In spite of the fact that the temple and school are shared with other neighboring villages, there is a sense that they both are their own. [1971, p. 27]

The village headman, together with what Mizuno calls an advisory council of village leaders, calls meetings and asks villagers to contribute money or labor to communal undertakings (Mizuno 1971, p. 145). Villagers cooperate in repairing breaks in the embankment of their lake (p. 146); they also take turns serving as night watchmen to protect against thieves and robbers. Headmen and villagers catch rapists, chase buffalo thieves, and adjudicate many disputes at the village or commune level (pp. 148–50).

Under the leadership of the headman and the by now familiar temple committee, temple ceremonies are arranged for the villagers. Also, Don Daeng village and its offshoot Don Noi cooperated in the construction and repairing of their common temple. Mizuno relates how special committees were appointed to raise money from the households of the two villages to construct a new preaching hall, an enterprise which took four years to complete (1971, p. 152).

Mizuno also discusses how the headman, village leaders, and villagers contributed their labor to build a road, a health center, school buildings, and wells in the government-sponsored Community Development Program (1971, p. 162).

Finally, Mizuno stresses the effective leadership in his village. The most prominent leaders, men from the wealthiest strata of the village, form an informal advisory council to help the headman manage temple and village affairs with what Mizuno terms "the voluntary cooperation of their fellows" (1971, p. 165).

Charles F. Keyes's village of Ban Nong Tuen, located fifteen kilometers east and south of the town of Mahasarakham, completes my discussion of how the village-as-a-whole element is manifested in the structure of northeastern Thai villages. Like most of the other villages discussed, Ban Nong Tuen is a nucleated settlement surrounded by rice fields (Keyes 1967, p. 4). Keyes tells us that the village is an important element of a person's social identity: "Northeastern Thai villagers identify with the village in which they live in much the same way as people in some other societies identify with descent groups to which they belong" (1967, p. 4). Marriage is mainly endogamous.

Collective community action is organized by village leaders—the headman and his assistant plus an informal group of mature male "elders"—who, in Keyes's words, possess "one or more of the traits of wealth, experience in the Buddhist monkhood, skill in one of the traditional arts, or ability to intimidate other villagers." These men form the membership of the temple committee, the school committee, and the community development committee (1967, p. 9). This was in the early 1960s, at the time of Keyes's original study. In 1968, Keyes tells us, Nong Tuen was split into two administrative villages (an example of initial village fission), but the community was still operating as a single unit in contexts other than rural administration (1975, p. 277).

Michael Moerman's paper, "Ban Ping's Temple: The Center of a 'Loosely Structured' Society" (the first important attempt to deal critically with the loose-structure model by presenting empirical data) brings us to northern Thailand. Moerman tells us that, as in much of northern Thailand, "the village of Ban Ping is a physically and administratively demarcated named community of kinsmen whose children attend the same school. . . ." The village is unified not only by the temple but also by the village spirit cult (1966, p. 138).

Ban Ping, according to Moerman, is more highly organized than the villages of central Thailand. Like Chiangmai, the village is divided into residential neighborhood sections called *mot* which rotate sending food to the temple (1966, p. 142). Ban Ping village's solidary organization is also indicated by the fact that the temple committee can summon a meeting of all male villagers and assess all adults an agreed-upon sum of money so that the village as a whole can finance the ordination of novices and priests (1966, p. 150).

Like almost all the other Thai villages I have discussed, but to a greater extent, Ban Ping is an endogamous community. Also, almost everyone has the same surname and can trace descent back to fourteen ancestral couples (1966, p. 151) .

The temple is important in village society because community property (mats, dishes, plates, and so on, which can be borrowed by villagers as in Chiangmai) and the temple's money are under the care of the lay temple committee. The village committee and the temple committee of Ban Ping are formal organizations run by the prominent men and elders of the community (Moerman 1966, pp. 161, 163).

Moerman summarizes his argument by pointing out that

> the temple acts to equalize private wealth, to structure voluntary kinship, and to provide an enduring corporate organization which trains and certifies village leaders and holds village property. The temple, although a focus of village loyalty and a repository of Lue traditions, also binds the local community to the nation. In its ritual and rationale, the temple dramatizes reciprocity, the basic principle of Ban Ping's social life. [1966b, p. 167]

Moerman adds that he is not convinced that the concept of loose structure has much value for depicting Thai society (1966, p. 167).

## The Administrative
## Apparatus of the State

Thai peasant social structure cannot be understood without taking into account the wider world within which Thai peasants live. This wider social universe includes the Thai nation, dominated by the upper classes in Bangkok, and the wider world, whose economic and political currents increasingly have affected the lives of the villagers. The opening of Thailand to international trade in the nineteenth century and the subsequent commercialization of agriculture—particularly the growth of Thailand's international rice trade—have created economic pressures, reinforced by the population explosion over the last century, which threaten to burst apart the village societies described in this book (see Piker 1975). New international political pressures resulting from the outcome of the Vietnam War, coupled with the land shortage in the countryside and the rise of a landless proletariat, threaten civil war between Chinese- and Vietnamese-style peasant revolutionary armies and the urban elite. Others have and will discuss these wider national and international events; here I will simply acknowledge their importance and concentrate on the administrative structures at the local level within Thailand, which was that part of the wider world most immediately relevant to understanding present village social structure when we were in Chiangmai.

The Thai state and the upper classes which control it are interested in maintaining control of the countryside so that they can continue to dominate the nation, collect taxes, conscript soldiers, and modernize the countryside in their own way through community development programs, cooperatives, and a controlled land reform. All of these measures so far have been half-hearted and relatively unsuccessful.

State policy is implemented through the government's rural administrative apparatus (see Potter, Diaz, and Foster 1967, p. 167). As in most peasant societies, state bureaucrats drew uniform grids across the countryside, paying little attention to how the resulting administrative units corresponded to preexisting social, economic, and religious networks of the peasantry, about which the state functionaries usually knew little and cared less. Consequently, administrative villages and communes often are different from nonadministrative residential communities, temple affiliations, market ties, and irrigation system memberships, creating a rural society of great complexity.

Thailand's modern rural administrative structure, based upon a combination of traditional Thai village practice (which included a village headman) and British rural administration in Burma and Malaysia (which included district officers and village leaders) was instituted at the end of the nineteenth and the beginning of the twentieth century (Siffin 1966, pp. 72–73).

In 1970 (see Neher 1970, p. 1) the country's administrative structure consisted of 71 provinces, divided into 530 districts, subdivided into 4,926 communes (subdistricts called "tambon," consisting of an average of ten administrative villages) and some 50,000 administrative villages ("muban") like Chiangmai One and Two. State administration is hierarchical, with orders coming from the top down and with little feedback from the villagers, who would in most cases prefer to be let alone.

Key administrative personnel are the provincial governors and the district officers, who are appointed by the central government in Bangkok. District officers are the key figures in local administration. They look after constituencies of 5,000 to 150,000 persons and govern 86 percent of the total Thai population. As far as most village people are concerned, the district officer is the government. He is a distant figure whom few see, and he usually serves in one district for only a short time before being transferred elsewhere, so that he seldom becomes acquainted with the local people.

The district officer supervises a staff of twenty to fifty members, including representatives of the central ministries, such as health, irrigation, and community development (Neher 1970, p. 5). District officers have a wide spectrum of duties and responsibilities, ranging from officiating at ceremonial occasions, like the opening of a new road, to submitting reports on the district to provincial and central government officials. The district officers are usually so inundated with a sea of paperwork that they would have little time to visit the countryside even if they had the inclination to do so.

The district officer and his staff, the lowest levels of state officialdom, are buffered from the villagers by a group of local representatives, a hinge group in rural Thai society, connecting the peasants with the government. These intermediaries are the village headmen and the commune headmen, Janus-like functionaries who represent the government to the people and the people to the government.

Village and commune headmen are elected by the adult members of each administrative village (such as Chiangmai One and Two). Often the election for village headman is *pro forma*, and the villagers choose an assistant headman or someone else whom the outgoing headman has groomed as his successor; sometimes, however, lively rivalry exists and elections are contested (see Kaufman 1960, pp. 75–78; and Moerman 1969, pp. 537–38, for a description of the election of village headmen). In most cases headmen serve for long periods until they die or until they retire, around the age of sixty (but see the different situation described by Moerman [1969], where headmen served for an average of only three years). The administrative village headmen elect the commune headman (the kamnan) with the approval of the district officer; he has higher status and is a higher-level intermediary between the village headmen and the district officer. Both commune and village headmen receive small salaries and have the right to withold 3 percent of the taxes they collect for the government; they also are paid informal fees by villagers for helping them with government business such as recording the inheritance or sale of property, freeing people from jail, and so on; and they have the added privilege of wearing a quasi-military brown uniform on ceremonial occasions. Village headmen receive enough perquisites and formal deference and prestige (see Moerman 1969, pp. 543–45) to make the office sought after throughout most of Thailand, as it certainly is in Chiangmai village; but in some places (see the situation described by Moerman for Ban Ping [1969, p. 538]), men do not wish to serve as headmen.

The main duties of the Thai village headman are well known: he attends monthly meetings at the district office where the district officer passes down policy decisions from the central government, which the headmen pass on to their fellow villagers in informal meetings or by word of mouth upon their return home. The headman and the commune headman maintain law and order in their bailiwicks; that is, they maintain the customary law of the village, ignoring minor violations such as the illegal making and selling of rice wine and gambling. In the case of a robbery or theft, where village and national law coincide, they organize posses to apprehend the criminals and deliver them to the police, who have headquarters at or near the district office. Minor disputes are often settled within the village, with the headman serving as mediator. Headmen also have the authority to mobilize men in their administrative village to maintain and repair the roads, the school, and the temple, and, in areas such as Chiangmai village, they often serve as foremen in the irrigation systems. In recent years they have been active in community development. The headmen are the instrumental leaders of their administrative villages; they are responsible for seeing that things the villagers and the government wish done are done.

As Moerman (1969) points out, the headmen are in a difficult situation, especially in solidary communities where the natural community and the administrative village coincide, because they are caught in a double bind: On the one hand they are expected to represent and be loyal to their village constituencies, on the other, they are expected to carry out the policies of the central government. Opinion differs as to whether the major loyalty of the headmen and kamnan lie with the district office and the central government or with their local communities. Moerman describes one extreme in Ban Ping, a corporate northern community, where the primary loyalty of the headman is to the village and his major role is to protect his village from the demands of the central government (1969, pp. 546–47). An opposite situation is described by Sharp et al. (1953, pp. 41–51) in Bang Chan, where administrative villages and the "natural community" do not coincide as they do in Ban Ping. Sharp et al. see Bang Chan headmen as creatures of the government, subservient and loyal to the district officer rather than to their fellow villagers.

Keyes (1970), building upon Moerman's discussion, but using confusing terminology, formulates two types of rural systems on the basis of how closely the formal administrative apparatus corresponds to the local peasant society: the "Central Thai type" is a local system where the natural peasant village and the administrative village are not isomorphic; and the "Northeastern type" is a local system where the peasant village and the administrative village are one and the same (for example, Moerman's village of Ban Ping). Keyes believes that headmen in the Central Thai systems are not very powerful because they do not have the support of a unified nuclear village, whereas headmen in the Northeastern Thai system have the strength and prestige given by both the formal government and the peasant village combined. Contrary to Moerman, Keyes cites evidence from his own village (actually in the northeast) and from many other studies of Northeastern-type villages which indicate that the headmanship is much sought after and that Ban Ping is either unusual or else Moerman misinterpreted polite modesty for real reluctance to assume the role of headman (see the literature cited by Keyes [1970, p. 105]).

The power of the administrative village headman varies in different Thai local communities. His position is most influential where he is a wealthy man who has served as a monk or novice and who has strength of character, ambition, and leadership qualities. Such a forceful man, in a situation where natural village and administrative village coincide, is in a pivotal position to affect the lives and fortunes of his fellow villagers. Poorer headmen, with less force of character and less ambition, who serve in a rural administrative village made up of chunks carved from several natural village communities, would be much less important and the administrative village would be less important in the lives of the people there.

We must recognize that everywhere in rural Thailand there are definite limits to the power of the village headman because he is subject to the advice and support of powerful men in his village—wealthy landlords, influential teachers and priests, and entrepreneurs (see Keyes 1970)—whose approval he needs before he can implement government policies or start any important undertaking. Usually the headmen of rural Thai administrative villages are themselves from the rural upper class to begin with, or are the pawns of wealthy and powerful men. Local leaders, formal and informal, comprise a buffer group that has been fairly successful in carrying out only those few central government programs which they perceive to be in their interest, negating the rest. Even with the great emphasis upon community development and rural security by the Thai government in recent years, the local villages still retain a measure of local autonomy.

It is time, I think, to cease talking of Thai rural administrative villages as if they were simply a formal but unimportant part of the social life of the Thai peasant. Thai villagers have lived under this administrative system for almost a century. They have elected leaders within it, organized group community projects within it, paid taxes within it, and participated in community development projects within it. It is no longer to be dismissed as something artificial and not of importance in rural Thai social structure. It is almost as important as the so-called "natural village community" in the many areas where the two do not coincide. The administrative village is also a part of the self-identity of Thai villagers. Even Chiangmai village children were aware of their membership in Chiangmai One or Two. The administrative village and its leader, in some areas at least, rivals the natural village community as the most important communal structure in rural Thailand, and it must be given more weight by social scientists than it has been given in the past.

The importance of the administrative village and its frequent lack of congruity with the natural compact residential community (where it exists), together with the fact that networks of school attendance and temple attendance sometimes do not correspond to either, makes rural Thailand a place of great complexity. There is a great variety of local social systems, no two of which are exactly the same; here one structural principle is dominant, and there another. Rural Thai society also includes economic and social relations (such as marketing networks and larger temple cults) about which so little is known that I have not included them here. These crosscut both the natural residential communities and the larger administrative units.

The villages I have examined in this chapter show different combinations of natural village, administrative village, temple allegiance, and school attendance. These should suffice as samples of the possible combinations of these structural elements. These different types are set out in diagrammatic form in figure 6.

Type A is the simplest and most common arrangement in rural Thailand, and approximates the ideal village in the Thai villagers' minds as well as the stereotyped "village" in most social scientists' minds. Type A is a local system in which the natural village community is nucleated and clearly separated spatially from surrounding communities. It consists of one administrative village with one headman. And it has one school and one temple attended solely by those who live in the village. Ban Nong Tuen in the early 1960s (Keyes 1967b, p. 3) (it split into two administrative villages in 1968 [see Keyes 1975, p. 377]), South Village (Wijeyewardene 1967, p. 70), and Ban Ping (Moerman 1968, 1969) are examples. Al-

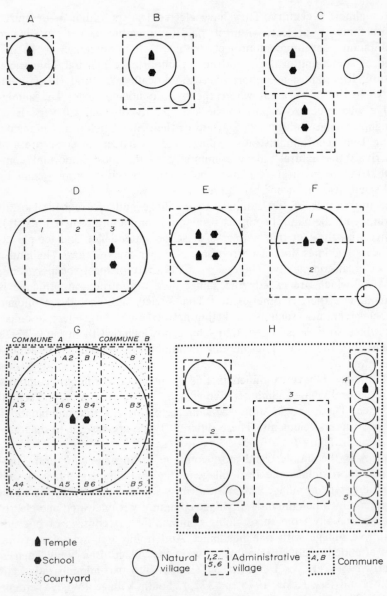

**Fig. 6**                        Types of Thai rural
                                  systems

though all types of local systems are probably found in all parts of Thailand, Type A is probably most characteristic of the northeast, the north, the south, and most of the central plain outside of the lower delta region.

Type B is Type A in a process of growth, after a smaller satellite community has split off and formed an independent residential community but continues to use the temple and school of the parent community; the smaller community, in areas where village guardian spirits exist, may have its own separate spirit. Examples of Type B are Baan Phraan Muan (Tambiah 1970, p. 10) and Don Daeng (Mizuno 1971, p. 27).

Type C is one large natural village which has split in two (or, alternatively, it is two once separate villages which have almost grown together). Each is a separate administrative village, with its own school and temple, but, in addition, there is a smaller satellite community (separately established or spun off from the other two), some of whose residents attend the temple and school in one of the larger villages, and some of whose residents attend those of the other large village. In Type C, the smaller satellite community has already achieved the status of an individual administrative village and elects its own headman. This arrangement is found in part of Bang Khem commune (Ayabe 1973, p. xv) but is undoubtedly found elsewhere.

Type D is a large nucleated, natural village community which is divided into three or more administrative villages but which has only one temple and one school. Bangkhuad (Kaufman 1960, p. 17) approximates this model, although it is a linear village, strung along a canal and not tightly nucleated; also, some Bangkhuad villagers at the extreme edge of the community may attend a neighboring temple or school.

Type E is a large nucleated village which has split in two, or, alternatively, two once separate natural villages which are growing together into one residential community. In any case, each of the separate halves is an administrative village with its own school and its own temple, and villagers who live in one administrative village attend only their temple and school. This type is exemplified by two villages in Bang Khem commune (Ayabe 1973, p. xv).

Type F is a large nucleated village divided into two administrative villages like Type E. The large village, although divided administratively, has only one temple and one school to which all villagers go. Ban Nong Tuen, Keyes's village, changed from Type A to this type in 1968 (Keyes 1975, p. 277).

The variant of Type F shown in figure 6 is more complicated because it also includes a bit of a neighboring natural village in one of its administrative villages. The members of the edge of the adjoining village may go to the school or the temple in their administrative village, but usually they do not; instead, they attend the school and wad of their natural village. The example which suggested this model is, of course, Chiangmai village.

Type G was suggested by Bang Chan (Sharp et al. 1953, air photo; Janlekha 1955, map 1; and L. Hanks 1972, p. 8) and by Ban Nai (Attagara 1967, pp. 14–15). Both villages are in the lower delta region around Bangkok. Here the nucleated village community is at its weakest. This local community is divided into a number of different administrative villages which may or may not correspond to hamlet clusterings along separate canals. If we follow the definition of Sharp et al., the local system centering on the temple and school includes only those administrative villages in which most of the people attend the temple and school. I chose not to define the community in this way, and define it instead as all those people who actually attend the temple and the school. This would include some people in the local community who live in administrative villages a majority of whose residents may attend school or temple elsewhere.

Finally, I have included a model of one sample commune (map of San Pong commune given by de Young [1955, pp. 15, 19–20]). At the commune level, the possible combinations of administrative village, natural village, temple, schools are, of course, much greater. De Young does not indicate schools on his map, but if they were shown the system would be even more complex. It is possible to have a large number of different arrangements of this kind in the various communes of rural Thailand with each local system having its own structural characteristics and problems. A problem that should receive more study than it has so far is to describe the market networks, the religious networks, and the kinship networks of large scope and to see how these fit or fail to conform to the larger administrative units.

## The Wad

The Buddhist temple and monastery is the final important element in rural Thai society. It became clear to me in the discussion of variations in local systems in the previous section that the wad, with its temple committee and other important social and political functions, is often an independent structural element and not merely an expression of an existing village community. Since I have written at such length about the role of the wad in Chiangmai village and (in this final chapter) in other Thai villages, and since from the beginning all anthropologists who have studied rural Thailand (see especially Moerman 1966*b* and Tambiah 1970) have stressed the social importance of the wad, there is no need here for me to do more than acknowledge the crucial importance of the wad as one of the eleven structural elements that in various combinations give Thai peasant social structure its characteristic form.

# Notes

## Preface

1. For my wife's account, see "A Northern Thai Village Family," by Sulamith Heins Potter, Ph. D. dissertation, University of California, Berkeley, 1975. Most of the data presented in my book are our joint property, although I am solely responsible for the interpretation presented here.

## Chapter One

1. The nature of theoretical systems, and the effect of crucial scientific facts on the structure of these systems, were discussed earlier by Talcott Parsons in his book *The Structure of Social Action* (1949, pp. 6–11).
2. There are many other examples of ethnographic paradigms. Two from the field of Chinese studies spring to mind: Maurice Freedman's (1958) paradigm of the asymmetrically segmented Chinese lineage, which he substituted for the prevailing vague notion of "clan" and stimulated research by a generation of anthropologists; and G. William Skinner's paradigm of rural marketing and social systems in China, which many scholars have employed with profit (Skinner 1964).
3. In addition, Embree (1950) said that personal property is unsafe in Thailand; that poem exchanges are less formalized than in Japan; that cabaret girls are given more freedom to come and go as they please; that the Thai school system is less formal than Japan's; and that Thai houses are less tidy.
4. I think it likely that some of the unusual features of villages like Bang Chan and Bangkhuad in the lower delta suburbs of Bangkok—such as patrilocal residence, patrilocal extended families, a high bride price, and so on—may be due to the influence of early part-Chinese settlers whose ethnic origin (after several generations of marriage to Thai women) was forgotten. There is also the possibility of acculturative influence from Bangkok, a heavily Chinese city. Furthermore, the Saen Saab Canal, the main canal from Bangkok to the northeast, which made it possible to settle Bang Chan, was dug by Chinese, some of whom may have settled in the area.

225

5. By singling out these scholars as the most important theorists in the loose-structure tradition, I do not mean to imply that their writing on loose structure represents all they had to say about Thailand. The work of Sharp et al. was the pioneering study of rural Thailand. Wilson has made important contributions to the understanding of Thai politics, and Phillips's work on Thai personality has been pathbreaking, as has Lucien Hanks's concept of entourage (see Lucien Hanks 1962, 1966, 1972, 1975). Piker's recent work (1975) on changes in rural Thailand, particularly his recognition of the emergence of a rural proletariat, is a real contribution to Thai studies.

6. Sharp denied, at one point, that Bang Chan was representative of all Thai rural communities (Sharp et. al. 1953, p. 7) and in a later paper (1963) modified somewhat his characterization of Thai society; Phillips has repeatedly shown an awareness of variation in rural Thailand and has denied that loose structure as a blanket term can be used to describe Thai Society as a whole, or even Bang Chan village society as a whole (1969, p. 28); Piker restricts his statements to the Central Plain (1969, p. 75); and Lucien Hanks, equally aware of variations in rural Thailand (see Hanks and Hanks 1964), has not only described the social history of Bang Chan in terms of kin groups, extended families, and solidary settlements (1972), but has also been one of the few scholars to attempt to describe the concrete way in which Thai society *is* structured (see Lucien Hanks 1966).

## Chapter Two

1. The title of this chapter is borrowed from Reginald LeMay's book *An Asian Arcady: Land and Peoples of Northern Siam*, Cambridge: W. Heffer, 1926.

2. Family planning services for Chiengmai city and the surrounding countryside began in 1963 at McCormick Hospital in the city with the introducton of the Margulies coil IUCD, later changed to the Lippes loop. In 1965, McCormick added the use of depot medroxyprogesterone acetate (DMPA, Depo Provera), a contraceptive injected every three months. Later, six-month injections and oral contraceptive pills were used. The program has been remarkably successful. In 1972, about 80,000 women received contraceptives at the hospital or through its extension services. The Thai government has an effective family planning program based upon the dispensing of oral contraceptives by trained nurses and midwives at village health stations. For further descriptions of these programs see McDaniel (1973) and the articles by McDaniel and Pardthaisong cited in the bibliography.

   Results similar to those we found in Chiangmai village (see below) were also found in the village of Ban Pong, where McCormick Hospital did a two-year study of the effectiveness of their program (see McDaniel and Pardthaisong 1973*b*).

3. The Northern Thai are often referred to as Thai Yuan, and sometimes as Lao. Seidenfaden (1958, pp. 100–101), a student of Tai peoples (including those outside of Thailand), describes them as follows:

   *The Thai Yuan* of North Thailand, numbering more than two millions, people the former monthons or circles of Phayap and Maharastra; i.e. the now abolished vassal states of Chiengmai, Lamphun, Lampang, Nān and Phrae. The Thai Yuan resemble their southern brethren but are generally a little taller and of a fairer complexion. The women are known for their

good looks, and many are very pretty, being lithe and graceful creatures. . . .
The men used to dress in short trousers or pha nung and a short sleeved
shirt. The women mostly still wear the horizontally striped skirt or phā
sin with a long sleeved blouse. . . . The Thai or Laos Yuan were formerly
named *Laos phung dam* or the Black bellied Laos, alluding to their
custom of tattooing their bellies, contrary to the Laos of Northeastern
Thailand and the Mekhong valley, who were called *Laos phung khao* or
the white-bellied Laos because of their thighs being tattooed, *not* their
stomachs. According to another line of division the Eastern Thai, i.e.
those of Thailand and Laos are *Thai Noi*, the lesser Thai while the Western,
the Shans, represent the Greater Thai or *Thai Yai*. The Thai Yuan speak
a Thai dialect which is somewhat different from that spoken in the
northeast and also from "the King's Siamese," containing fewer Khmer
and Pali loan words. Formerly they used the Burmese, or rather Mon,
alphabet now substituted by the Thai, which is taught in the schools.
With regard to the style of architecture this is, in case of the temples,
somewhat influenced by the Burmese due to the latter's more than 200
years' occupation of the country.

Kunstadter (1967, p. 397) refers to them as the Northern Thai, Khon
Muang, and Yuan. Further information on the classification of the various Tai
(Tai, as distinguished from Thai, is a general term which includes members
of this ethnic group outside of Thailand) groups can be found in LeBar,
Hickey, and Musgrave (1964). Davis (1974, pp. 1–3) also gives a useful
summary of Northern Thai social structural features.

## Chapter Three

1.   The recent merging of Chiangmai and a neighboring village along a road
     to the northwest is an exception to this statement. Not all villages, or even
     most villages in the Chiengmai Valley, are spatially separated from neighboring
     villages (see de Young 1955, pp. 8–12, and Hanks and Hanks 1964, p. 199,
     for a discussion of settlement patterns).
2.   For a description of the role of Buddhist priests and novices who live in Thai
     village temples, see Kingshill (1965), Pfanner and Ingersoll (1962),
     Ingersoll (1966), Moerman (1966*b*), Tambiah (1968, 1970), and Bunnag
     (1973).

## Chapter Five

1.   A Thai government irrigation official told me that there are hundreds of these
     local irrigation systems in the Chiengmai Valley watershed today.
2.   Translated from Northern Thai into Central Thai by Monk Mahakamon
     Chootikmanto. Published by the Department of Irrigation, Bangkok, 1967.
     The work was translated into English for me by Professor Narujohn
     Iddhichirachiras of Chiengmai University. See, also, Nimmanahaeminda (1965).
3.   I should caution the reader that I by no means carried out an exhaustive study
     of all aspects of irrigation system Y; that would have taken more time than
     I had available. For example, a farmer's cooperative group was organized
     on the basis of this organization. There is room for much more research on
     traditional Thai irrigation systems.

## Chapter Six

1. See also Wijeyewardene (1968) for a discussion of Chiengmai courtship.

## Chapter Seven

1. Mizuno (1971, p. 92) cites data that also belie the oft-repeated statement that family and kin roles in rural Thailand are not well defined. In my opinion, Mizuno's study of his northeastern village produces findings that challenge the loose-structure notion just as effectively as our work in Chiangmai, although he does not draw this conclusion.

2. Kemp (1970) cites data, including his own from north central Thailand, that show matrilocal residence to be widespread in the country.

3. Wijeyewardene's statement that "the norm for the Thai peasant household in all parts of the country is that the elementary family is the residential unit" (1967, p. 65) is simply not accurate; his statement ignores the structural cycle of the Thai domestic group.

4. Compare Keyes's (1975) similar description of the domestic cycle in his northeastern village.

5. Compare the inheritance cases cited by Mizuno (1971, pp. 88–91). According to Mizuno, although some men may inherit land from their parents, in practice it is usually women who inherit the rice fields. In Mizuno's village the daughter who lives with her parents and cares for them in their old age inherits their retained share of the property as well as her own share. There are comparable tendencies in Chiangmai village, but this is not normative.

6. Chiangmai terms of reference are quite different from the Central Thai kinship terminology given by Jane Bunnag (1973, p. 12), who erroneously describes her system as the Thai kinship terminology, thus continuing the practice of generalizing about all of Thailand from the central plain region. The Chiangmai terms of reference for the grandparents are not the same as those used by the Central Thai as described by Bunnag, and they do not distinguish between maternal and paternal grandparents. Also, Chiangmai villagers have different terms for father's and mother's siblings than do the Central Thai; the Chiangmai terminology of reference is more bilateral. The Chiangmai terms also differ from those reported by Mizuno for his northeastern Thai village (1971, pp. 109–10).
   Finally, the terms of reference reported here differ slightly from those which Kingshill (1965, appendix D, pp. 235–37) calls "Lanathai terms." According to our informants, the villagers refer to ego's father's younger brother as ʔAaw, instead of Aa; and mother's younger brother is referred to as ʔAaw, also, instead of Naa. Also, ego's older brother is referred to as ʔAaj, instead of Pii Aaj, as reported by Kingshill.

7. Like Andrew Turton (1972, p. 218), we were surprised to find matrilineal descent groups in Chiangmai. I am grateful for Turton's article and for the article by Richard Davis (1974) relating their prior and independent discovery of these kin groups. That all of us, working independently, should have come to the conclusion that there are matrilineal descent groups among the Northern Thai should perhaps dispel some of the doubts and polite disbelief expressed by Thai and American colleagues to whom I have related our

findings. William Klausner's description of matrilineal clans in the northeast is significant also ((1972, pp. 57–58).

I should add that, although I recognized the existence and the importance of matrilineal kin groups soon after we arrived in Chiangmai village, the people of Chiangmai were not anxious to tell about this aspect of their lives. One of the families with whom we stayed in the village scheduled, apparently by design, their annual sacrifice to their lineage spirits on a day that they knew we would be away from the village. Fortunately, we found out about the event and my wife was able to witness it. (See also, the experience of Turton, who apparently had similar difficulties [1972, p. 227].)

Because of such difficulties in researching this topic, I did not find out as much about Chiangmai matrilineal descent groups as I should have liked; and I am still more cautious than either Turton or Davis and less willing at this point to go beyond what Turton (1972, p. 217) calls "a low level of interpretation." Much more work needs to be done on Thai kinship and kinship groups now that we have moved beyond the point of simply dismissing them as loosely structured.

8.   Like Turton's (1972, pp. 219–20), my data indicate that Chiangmai matrilineages trace their descent from a group of sisters, rather than from one apical ancestress.

Turton (1972, p. 219) found that none of the descent groups in his village were more than six generations deep, with most of them falling into the three- to four-generation range. This is similar to Chiangmai village, although some of the larger Chiangmai groups are eight generations deep. This fact is not evident on the two lineage genealogies diagrammed here (figure 5) which are in fact eight generations deep; the two most junior generations were omitted by my informants (elderly women) when they told me the names of lineage members. These two junior generations do exist and do belong to the lineages.

9.   Turton (1972, p. 219) found that his population of 180 households consisted of members of 67 separate descent groups. I have not chosen to call groups which consist of only one or a few households matrilineages, even though they may formally fit that definition. Descent groups in Turton's village ranged from 1 to 24 households in size, with a median size of 4 households.

As in Chiangmai village, Turton found that a large portion of the population of his village was included in only a few of the larger lineages. Unlike in Chiangmai, only two of the descent groups in Turton's village had more than 10 locally clustered households. The kin groups in Chiangmai village are larger. Turton's guess that the matrilineages have a critical mass of 10 households before they split is clearly not the case in Chiangmai village.

# Bibliography

Amyot, Jacques

1964. "Intensive Village Study Project, April–May, 1964: Ban Nonlan, Amphur Uthumphonphisai, Sisaket: Preliminary Report." Bangkok: Chulalongkorn University, Faculty of Political Science.

1965. *Provisional Paper on Changing Patterns of Social Structure in Thailand, 1851–1965.* Delhi, India: UNESCO Research Center.

Andrews, James M.

1935. *Siam: Second Rural Economic Survey, 1934–35.* Bangkok: Bangkok Times Press.

Attagara, Kingkeo

1967. "The Folk Religion of Ban Nai, A Hamlet in Central Thailand." Ph.D. dissertation, Indiana University.

Ayabe, Tsuneo, ed.

1973. *Education and Culture in a Thai Rural Community: A Report of the Field Research in Tambon Bang Khem, Thailand (1970–71).* Fukuoka, Japan: Kyushu University, Faculty of Education, Research Institute of Comparative Education and Culture.

Barnes, J. A.

1972. *Social Networks.* Reading, Mass.: Addison-Wesley.

Benedict, Paul K.

1943. "Studies in Thai Kinship Terminology." *Journal of the American Oriental Society* 63: 168–75.

Blanchard, Wendell, et al.
1958. *Thailand: Its People, Its Society, Its Culture.* New Haven: Human Relations Area Files Press. Reprinted in 1968 as *Area Handbook for Thailand.* 3d ed. Co-authors: Harvey M. Smith, Donald W. Bernier, Frederica M. Bunge, Frances Chadwick Rintz, Rinn-Sup Shinn, and Suzanne Telleki. Washington, D.C.: Foreign Area Studies, The American University.

Boesch, E. E.
1962. "Autoritaet und Leistungsverhalten in Thailand." In *Thailand Studien.* Schriften des Instituts fuer Asienkunde in Hamburg, 15. Frankfurt: Alfred Metzner Verlag.

Bott, Elizabeth
1971. *Family and Social Network.* 2d ed. London: Tavistock Publications.

Brandes, Stanley H.
1973. "Social Structure and Interpersonal Relations in Navanogal (Spain)." *American Anthropologist* 75: 750–65.

Bunnag, Jane
1973. *Buddhist Monk, Buddhist Layman: A Study of Urban Monastic Organization in Central Thailand.* Cambridge: Cambridge University Press.

Caldwell, J. C.
1967. "The Demographic Structure." In *Thailand: Social and Economic Studies in Development,* edited by T. H. Silcock. Canberra: Australian National University Press.

Chootikmanto, Mahakamon, trans.
1967. *The Laws of King Mengrai, King of Lannathai.* Bangkok: Department of Irrigation.

Curtis, Lilian Johnson
1903. *The Laos of North Siam.* Philadelphia: Westminister Press.

Davis, Richard
1973. "Muang Matrifocality." *Journal of the Siam Society* 61: 53–62.

1974. "Tolerance and Intolerance of Ambiguity in Northern Thai Myth and Ritual." *Ethnology* 13: 1–24.

de Young, John E.
1955. *Village Life in Modern Thailand.* Berkeley and Los Angeles: University of California Press.

233	Bibliography

Embree, John F.	1950. "Thailand, a Loosely Structured Social System." *American Anthropologist* 52: 181–93.

Evans-Pritchard, E. E.	1940. *The Nuer.* Oxford: Oxford University Press.

Evers, Hans-Dieter	1969. "Models of Social Systems: Loosely and Tightly Structured." In *Loosely Structured Social Systems: Thailand in Comparative Perspective,* edited by Hans-Dieter Evers. New Haven: Yale University, Southeast Asia Studies, Cultural Report Series 17.

Evers, Hans-Dieter, ed.	1969. *Loosely Structured Social Systems: Thailand In Comparative Perspective.* New Haven: Yale University, Southeast Asia Studies, Cultural Report Series 17.

Firth, Sir Raymond	1957. "Introduction to Factions in Indian and Overseas Indian Societies." *British Journal of Sociology* 8: 291–95.

Foster, George M.	1960–61. "Interpersonal Relations in Peasant Society." *Human Organization* 19: 174–78.

1965. "Peasant Society and the Image of Limited Good." *American Anthropologist* 67: 293–315.

Fraser, Thomas S.	1966. *Fishermen of South Thailand: The Malay Villagers.* New York: Holt, Rinehart and Winston.

Freedman, Maurice	1958. *Lineage Organization in Southeastern China.* London School of Economics Monographs on Social Anthropology 18. London: Athlone Press.

Geertz, Clifford	1959. "Form and Variation in Balinese Village Structure." *American Anthropologist* 61: 991–1012.

1973. *The Interpretation of Cultures: Selected Essays by Clifford Geertz.* New York: Basic Books.

Geertz, Hildred, and Geertz, Clifford	1975. *Kinship in Bali.* Chicago: University of Chicago Press.

Goody, Jack, ed.            1962. *The Developmental Cycle in Domestic Groups*. Cambridge: Cambridge University Press.

Haas, Mary R.             1964. *Thai-English Student's Dictionary*. Stanford: Stanford University Press.

Hanks, Jane              1963. *Maternity and Its Rituals in Bangchan*.
Richardson                Ithaca: Cornell University, Department of Asian Studies, Southeast Asia Program, Data Paper 51.

Hanks, Lucien M.          1962. "Merit and Power in the Thai Social
[Jr.]                     Order." *American Anthropologist* 64: 1247–61.

                          1966. "The Corporation and the Entourage: A Comparison of Thai and American Social Organization." *Catalyst* 2: 55–63.

                          1972. *Rice and Man*. Chicago: Aldine.

                          1975. "The Thai Social Order as Entourage and Circle." In *Change and Persistence in Thai Society: Essays in Honor of Lauriston Sharp*, edited by G. William Skinner and A. Thomas Kirsch. Ithaca: Cornell University Press.

Hanks, Lucien, M.,        1964. "Siamese Tai." In *Ethnic Groups of
Jr., and Hanks,           Mainland Southeast Asia*, edited by Frank M.
Jane R.                   LeBar, Gerald C. Hickey, and John K. Musgrave. New Haven: Human Relations Area Files Press.

Hanks, Lucien M.,         1965. *Ethnographic Notes on Northern
Jr.; Hanks, Jane R.;      Thailand*. Ithaca: Cornell University, Depart-
and Sharp, Lauriston,     ment of Asian Studies, Southeast Asia Program,
eds.                      Data Paper 58.

Ingersoll, Jasper         1966. "The Priest Role in Central Village Thailand." In *Anthropological Studies in Theravada Buddhism*, edited by Manning Nash. New Haven: Yale University, Southeast Asia Studies, Cultural Report Series 13.

Ingram, James C.          1955. *Economic Change in Thailand Since 1850*. Stanford: Stanford University Press.

Janlekha, Kamol Odd       1955. "A Study of the Economy of a Rice Growing Village in Central Thailand." Ph.D. dissertation, Cornell University. Published by Ministry of Agriculture, Bangkok, n.d.

| | |
|---|---|
| Jones, Delmos | 1969. "The Multivillage Community: Village Segmentation and Coalescence in Northern Thailand." *Behavior Science Notes* 3: 149–74. |
| Judd, Laurence C. | 1961. "Chao Rai: Dry Rice Farmers in Northern Thailand." Ph.D. dissertation, Cornell University. |
| Jumsai, M. L. Manich | 1967. *History of Laos, Including the History of Lannathai, Chiengmai.* Bangkok: Chalermnit. |
| Kaufman, Howard Keva | 1960. *Bangkhuad: A Community Study in Thailand.* Locust Valley, N.Y.: J. J. Augustin. |
| Kemp, Jeremy H. | 1970. "Initial Marriage Residence in Rural Thailand." *In Memoriam, Phya Anuman Rajadhon*, edited by Tej Bunnag and Michael Smithies. Bangkok: Siam Society. |
| Keyes, Charles F. | 1964. "Status and Rank in a Thai-Lao Village." Mimeographed. |
| | 1966. Review of *Thai Peasant Personality*, by Herbert P. Phillips. *American Anthropologist* 68: 793–94. |
| | 1967*a*. *Isan: Regionalism in Northeastern Thailand.* Ithaca: Cornell University, Department of Asian Studies, Southeast Asia Program, Data Paper 65. |
| | 1967*b*. "Baan Noong Tyyn: A Central Isan Village." Mimeographed. To appear in *Thai Villages*, edited by Clark Cunningham. |
| | 1970. "Local Leadership in Rural Thailand." In *Local Authority and Administration in Thailand*, edited by Fred R. von der Mehden and David A. Wilson. Los Angeles: University of California, Academic Advisory Council for Thailand. |
| | 1975. "Kin Groups in a Thai-Lao Community." In *Change and Persistence in Thai Society: Essays in Honor of Lauriston Sharp*, edited by G. William Skinner and A. Thomas Kirsch. Ithaca: Cornell University Press. |
| Kingshill, Konrad | 1965. *Ku Daeng, The Red Tomb: A Village Study in Northern Thailand.* 2d ed., rev. Bangkok: Bangkok Christian College. |

236     Bibliography

| Kirsch, A. Thomas | 1966. "Development and Mobility Among the Phu Thai of Northeast Thailand." *Asian Survey* 7: 370–78. |
| | 1967. "Phu Thai Religious Syncretism." Ph.D. dissertation, Harvard University. |
| | 1969. "Loose Structure: Theory or Description." In *Loosely Structured Social Systems: Thailand in Comparative Perspective*, edited by Hans-Dieter Evers. New Haven: Yale University, Southeast Asia Studies, Cultural Report Series 17. |
| | 1973. "The Thai Buddhist Quest for Merit." In *Southeast Asia: The Politics of National Integration*, edited by John T. McAlister, Jr. New York: Random House. |
| Klausner, William J. | 1972. *Reflections In A Log Pond: Collected Writings*, Bangkok: Suksit Siam. |
| Kuhn, Thomas S. | 1970. *The Structure of Scientific Revolutions.* 2d ed., enlarged. Chicago: University of Chicago Press. |
| Kunstadter, Peter, ed. | 1967. *Southeast Asian Tribes, Minorities, and Nations.* Princeton: Princeton University Press. |
| Lebar, Frank M.; Hickey, Gerald C.; and Musgrave, John K., eds. | 1964. *Ethnic Groups of Mainland Southeast Asia.* New Haven: Human Relations Area Files Press. |
| Le May, Reginald | 1926. *An Asian Arcady: Land and Peoples of Northern Siam.* Cambridge, England: W. Heffer and Sons. |
| Long, Janis F., et al. | 1963. *Economic and Social Conditions Among Farmers in Changwad Khonkaen.* Bangkok: Kasetsart University. |
| Long, Millard F. | 1966. "Economic Development in Northeast Thailand: Problems and Prospects." *Asian Survey* 6: 355–61. |
| Lux, Thomas | 1962. "Mango Village: Northeastern Thai Social Organization." M.A. thesis, University of Chicago. |

1966. "The Internal Structure and External Relations of a Northeastern Village." Final Report to the National Research Council of Thailand, Bangkok. Mimeographed.

Madge, Charles    1957. *Survey Before Development in Thai Villages.* New York: UN Secretariat (United Nations Series on Community Organization and Development, D/25).

Marx, Karl    1965. *Karl Marx: Pre-Capitalist Economic Formations*, edited by E. J. Hobsbawm. New York: International Publishers.

1969. "The British Rule in India." In *Karl Marx and Frederick Engels: Selected Works in Three Volumes.* Moscow: Progress Publishers. [Originally published in the *New York Daily Tribune*, June 25, 1853.]

McDaniel, Edwin B.    1973. "McCormick Hospital, Chiang Mai, Thailand, Family Planning Program, Historical Background." Mimeographed. Chiengmai, Thailand: McCormick Hospital, OB-GYN-Family Planning Department.

McDaniel, Edwin B., and Pardthaisong, Tieng    1973*a*. "Depot-Medroxyprogesterone Acetate as a Contraceptive Agent: Return of Fertility After Discontinuation of Use." *Contraception* 8: 407–14.

1973*b*. "Evaluating the Effectiveness of a Two-Year Family-Planning Action Program at Ban Pong Village, in Northern Thailand." Bangkok, Thailand: Chulalongkorn University, Institute of Population Studies, Paper 5.

McGilvary, Daniel    1912. *A Half-Century Among the Siamese and Lao.* London: Fleming H. Revell Co.

Mizuno, Koishi    1968. "Multihousehold Compounds in Northeast Thailand." *Asian Survey* 8: 842–52.

1971. *Social System of Don Daeng Village: A Community Study in Northeast Thailand.* Kyoto, Japan: Kyoto University, Center for Southeast Asian Studies, Discussion Papers 12–22.

1973. "Japanese Scholarship on Southeast Asian Villages—A Socio-Anthropological View." In *Foreign Values and Southeast Asian Scholarship*, edited by Joseph Fischer. Berkeley: University of California Center for South and Southeast Asian Studies, Research Monograph No. 11.

1975. "Thai Pattern of Social Organization: Note on a Comparative Study." *Journal of Southeast Asian Studies* 6: 127–34.

Moerman, Michael      1964. "Western Culture and the Thai Way of Life." *Asia* 1: 31–50.

1965. "Ethnic Identification in a Complex Civilization: Who Are the Lue?" *American Anthropologist* 67: 1215–30.

1966*a*. "Kinship and Commerce in a Thai-Lue Village." *Ethnology* 5: 360–64.

1966*b*. "Ban Ping's Temple: The Center of a 'Loosely Structured' Society." In *Anthropological Studies in Theravada Buddhism*, edited by Manning Nash. New Haven: Yale University, Southeast Asia Studies, Cultural Report Series 13.

1967. "Thai-Lue," In *Southeast Asian Tribes, Minorities, and Nations*, edited by Peter Kunstadter. 2 vols. Princeton: Princeton University Press.

1968. *Agricultural Change and Peasant Choice in a Thai Village*. Berkeley and Los Angeles: University of California Press.

1969. "A Thai Village Headman as a Synaptic Leader." *Journal of Asian Studies* 28: 535–49.

1975. "Chiangkham's Trade in the 'Old Days.' " In *Change and Persistence in Thai Society*, edited by G. William Skinner and A. Thomas Kirsch. Ithaca: Cornell University Press.

Moore, Frank J.      1974. *Thailand: Its People, Its Society, Its Culture*. New Haven: Human Relations Area Files Press.

Mulder, J. A. Niels       1967. "On the Structural Analysis of Thai
                          Peasant Village." *Journal of the Siam Society*
                          55: 273–77.

                          1969. "Origin, Development, and Use of the
                          Concept of 'Loose Structure' in the Literature
                          about Thailand: An Evaluation." In *Loosely
                          Structured Social Systems: Thailand in
                          Comparative Perspective*, edited by Hans-Dieter
                          Evers. New Haven: Yale University, Southeast
                          Asia Studies, Cultural Report Series 17.

Nash, Manning             1965. *The Golden Road to Modernity: Village
                          Life in Contemporary Burma.* New York: John
                          Wiley and Sons.

Nash, Manning, ed.        1966. *Anthropological Studies in Theravada
                          Buddhism.* New Haven: Yale University,
                          Southeast Asia Studies, Cultural Report
                          Series 13.

Neher, Clark D.           1970. *Rural Thai Government: The Politics of
                          the Budgetary Process.* DeKalb, Ill.: Northern
                          Illinois University, Center for Southeast
                          Asian Studies.

Nicholas, Ralph W.        1965. "Factions: A Comparative Analysis." In
                          *Political Systems and the Distribution of Power.*
                          Association of Social Anthropologists of the
                          Commonwealth, 2. London: Tavistock
                          Publications.

Nimmanahaeminda,          1965. "The Irrigation Laws of King Mengrai."
Kraisri                   In *Ethnographic Notes on Northern Thailand,*
                          edited by Lucien M. Hanks, Jane R. Hanks, and
                          Lauriston Sharp. Ithaca: Cornell University,
                          Department of Asian Studies, Southeast Asia
                          Program, Data Paper 58.

Parsons, Talcott          1949. *The Structure of Social Action.* 2d ed.
                          Glencoe, Ill.: The Free Press.

Pfanner, David E., and    1962. "Theravada Buddhism and Village
Ingersoll, Jasper         Economic Behavior: A Burmese and Thai
                          Comparison." *Journal of Asian Studies*
                          21: 341–66.

Phillips, Herbert P.

1958. "The Election Ritual in a Thai Village."
*Journal of Social Issues* 14: 36–50.

1965. *Thai Peasant Personality: The Patterning
of Interpersonal Behavior in the Village of Bang
Chan.* Berkeley and Los Angeles: University
of California Press.

1967. "Social Contact vs. Social Promise in a
Siamese Village." In *Peasant Society: A Reader*,
edited by Jack M. Potter, May N. Diaz, and
George M. Foster. Boston: Little, Brown.

1969. "The Scope and Limits of the 'Loose
Structure' Concept." In *Loosely Structured
Social Systems: Thailand in Comparative
Perspective*, edited by Hans-Dieter Evers. New
Haven: Yale University, Southeast Asia Studies,
Cultural Report Series 17.

Piker, Steven

1964. "An Examination of Character and
Socialization in a Thai Peasant Community."
Ph.D. dissertation, University of Washington.

1968a. "The Relationship of Belief Systems to
Behavior in Rural Thai Society." *Asian Survey*
8: 384–99.

1968b. "Sources of Stability and Instability in
Rural Thai Society." *Journal of Asian Studies*
27: 777–90.

1969. " 'Loose Structure' and the Analysis of
Thai Social Organization." In *Loosely
Structured Social Systems: Thailand in
Comparative Perspective*, edited by Hans-Dieter
Evers, New Haven: Yale University, Southeast
Asia Studies, Cultural Report Series 17.

1975. "The Post-Peasant Village in Central
Plain Thai Society." In *Change and Persistence
in Thai Society: Essays in Honor of Lauriston
Sharp*, edited by G. William Skinner and
A. Thomas Kirsch. Ithaca: Cornell University
Press.

Potter, Jack M.

1968. *Capitalism and the Chinese Peasant:
Social and Economic Change in a Hong Kong
Village.* Berkeley and Los Angeles: University
of California Press.

1970. "Land and Lineage in Traditional China." In *Family and Kinship in Chinese Society*, edited by Maurice Freedman. Stanford: Stanford University Press.

Potter, Jack M.; Diaz, May N.; and Foster, George M.; eds.
1967. *Peasant Society: A Reader*. Boston: Little, Brown.

Potter, Sulamith Heins
1975. "Family Life in a Northern Thai Village." Ph.D. dissertation, University of California, Berkeley.

Punyodyana, Boonsanong
1969. "Social Structure, Social System, and Two Levels of Analysis: A Thai View." In *Loosely Structured Social Systems: Thailand in Comparative Perspective*, edited by Hans-Dieter Evers. New Haven: Yale University, Southeast Asia Studies, Cultural Report Series 17.

Rajadhon, Phya Anuman
1954. *The Story of Thai Marriage Custom*. Bangkok: National Institute of Culture, Culture Series 13. Reprinted in 1956 as *Thailand Culture Series* 13. 3d ed. Bangkok: National Institute of Culture.

1958. *Five Papers on Thai Custom*. Ithaca: Cornell University, Department of Asian Studies, Southeast Asia Program, Data Paper 28.

Seidenfaden, Erik
1958. *The Thai Peoples: The Origins and Habitats*. Bangkok: Siam Society.

Sharp, Lauriston
1963. "Thai (Siamese) Social Structure." *Proceedings of the Ninth Pacific Science Congress on Anthropology and Social Sciences, Bangkok, November, 1957* 3: 120–30. Bangkok.

Sharp, Lauriston; Hauck, Hazel M.; Janlekha, Kamol; and Textor, Robert B.
1953. *Siamese Rice Village: A Preliminary Study of Bang Chan, 1948–1949*. Bangkok: Cornell Research Center.

Siffin, William J.
1966. *The Thai Bureaucracy: Institutional Change and Development*. Honolulu: East-West Center Press.

Silcock, T. H.
1970. *The Economic Development of Thai Agriculture*. Ithaca: Cornell University Press.

| | |
|---|---|
| Silcock, T. H., ed. | 1967. *Thailand: Social and Economic Studies in Development.* Canberra: Australian National University Press. |
| Skinner, G. William | 1957. *Chinese Society in Thailand: An Analytical History.* Ithaca: Cornell University Press. |
| | 1964. "Marketing and Social Structure in Rural China, Part I." *Journal of Asian Studies* 24: 3–43. |
| Skinner, G. Willian, and Kirsch, A. Thomas, eds. | 1975. *Change and Persistence in Thai Society: Essays in Honor of Lauriston Sharp.* Ithaca: Cornell University Press. |
| Soontornpasuch, Suthep | 1963. "The Thai Family: A Study of Kinship and Marriage Among the Central Thailand Peasantry." Master's thesis, London University. |
| Steward, Julian H. | 1955. *Theory of Culture Change: The Methodology of Multilinear Evolution.* Urbana: University of Illinois Press. |
| Tambiah, S. J. | 1966. Review of *Thai Peasant Personality*, by Herbert P. Phillips. *Man* 6: 424. |
| | 1968. "The Ideology of Merit and the Social Correlates of Buddhism in a Thai Village." In *Dialectic in Practical Religion*, edited by E. R. Leach. Cambridge: Cambridge University Press. |
| | 1970. *Buddhism and the Spirit Cults in North-east Thailand.* Cambridge: Cambridge University Press. |
| Textor, Robert B. | 1967. *From Peasant to Pedicab Driver.* New Haven: Yale University Southeast Asia Studies, Cultural Report Series 9. |
| Thailand. National FAO Committee | 1949. *Thailand and Her Agricultural Problems.* Bangkok: Ministry of Agriculture. |
| Thailand. National Statistical Office. Office of the Prime Minister. | 1964. *Advance Report, Household Expenditure Survey B. E. 2505.* Bangkok. |
| Thailand. National Statistical Office | 1965. *Census of Agriculture, 1963.* Bangkok. |

Thompson, Virginia | 1941. *Thailand: The New Siam.* New York: Macmillan.

Troger, Ernst | 1960. "Ban-Pae-Lungar: Studie zur Siedlungs-, Wirtschafts-und Bevoelkerungsgeographie eines Dorfes in Nordthailand." *Mitteilungen der Oesterreichischen Geographischen Gesellschaft* 102: 165–90.

Turton, Andrew | 1972. "Matrilineal Descent Groups and Spirit Cults of the Thai-Yuan in Northern Thailand." *Journal of the Siam Society* 60: 217–56.

Van Roy, Edward | 1966. "Economic Dualism and Economic Change among the Hill Tribes of Thailand." *Pacific Viewpoint* 7: 151–68.

1967. "An Interpretation of Northern Thai Peasant Economy." *Journal of Asian Studies* 26: 421–32.

1971. *Economic Systems of Northern Thailand: Structure and Change.* Ithaca: Cornell University Press.

Van Roy, Edward, and Cornehls, James V. | 1969. "Economic Development in Mexico and Thailand: An Institutional Analysis, Part Two." *Journal of Economic Issues* 3: 21–38.

Vella, Walter F. | 1955. *The Impact of the West on Government in Thailand.* University of California Publications in Political Science, 4. Berkeley and Los Angeles: University of California Press.

Wijeyewardene, Gehan | 1965. "A Note on Irrigation and Agriculture in a North Thai Village." In *Felicitation Volumes of Southeast-Asian Studies Presented to His Highness Phince Dhaninivat.* Bangkok: Siam Society.

1967. "Some Aspects of Rural Life in Thailand." In *Thailand: Social and Economic Studies in Development*, edited by T. H. Silcock. Canberra: Australian National University Press.

Wilson, David A. | 1959. "Thailand and Marxism." In *Marxism in Southeast Asia: A Study of Four Countries*, edited by Frank N. Trager. Stanford: Stanford University Press.

|  | 1962. *Politics in Thailand*. Ithaca: Cornell University Press. |
| Wittfogel, Karl A. | 1957 *Oriental Despotism: A Comparative Study of Total Power*. New Haven: Yale University Press. |
| Wolf, Eric R. | 1966. *Peasants*. Englewood Cliffs, N. J.: Prentice-Hall. |
| Yang, Martin C. | 1945. *A Chinese Village: Taitou, Shantung Province*. New York: Columbia University Press. |
| Zimmerman, Carle C. | 1931. *Siam Rural Economic Survey, 1930–31*. Bangkok: Bangkok Times Press. |

# Index